One Classroom, Many Worlds

TEACHING AND LEARNING IN THE CROSS-CULTURAL CLASSROOM

JACKLYN BLAKE CLAYTON

HEINEMANN
PORTSMOUTH, NH

Heinemann
A division of Reed Elsevier Inc.
361 Hanover Street
Portsmouth, NH 03801–3912
www.heinemann.com

Offices and agents throughout the world

The author and publisher wish to thank those who have generously given permission to reprint borrowed material:

Figure 2–1 is used by permission of Jaime S. Wurzel, Boston University, School of Education.

Figures 4–1, 4–2, and 4–3 are excerpted from "Bicognitive Process in Multicultural Education" by A. Castañeda and T. Gary in *Educational Leadership,* December 1974, 32:3. Reprinted with permission from ASCD. All rights reserved.

Figures 4–4 and 4–5 are excerpted from *Multiple Intelligences in the Classroom, Second Edition* by Thomas Armstrong. Copyright © 2000 by Thomas Armstrong. Reprinted by permission from ASCD. All rights reserved.

Figure 7–1 is reprinted from "Psychological Acculturation of Immigrants" by J. Berry, U. Kim, and P. Boski in *Cross-Cultural Adaptations* edited by Y. Y. Kim and W. B. Gudykunst. Copyright © 1988 by Sage Publications, Inc. Reprinted by permission of Sage Publications, Inc.

Library of Congress Cataloging-in-Publication Data
Clayton, Jacklyn Blake.
 One classroom, many worlds: Teaching and learning in the cross-cultural classroom / Jacklyn Blake Clayton.
  p. cm.
Includes bibliographical references.
 ISBN 0-325-00548-6 (alk. paper)
 1. Multicultural education—United States. I. Title.
 LC1099.3.C53 2003
 370.117—dc22
                     2003016439

Editor: Danny Miller
Production coordinator: Sonja S. Chapman
Production service: John Probst, The GTS Companies/York, PA Campus
Cover design: Jenny Jensen Greenleaf
Compositor: The GTS Companies/York, PA Campus
Manufacturing: Steve Bernier

Printed in the United States of America on acid-free paper

07 06 05   DA   2 3 4 5

Contents

111456

Acknowledgments

COUNTLESS PEOPLE HAVE HELPED ME WITH THIS BOOK. SOME OF them are aware of it and many are not. My students, from elementary through university, have taught me much over the years, have supplied examples, have helped me define and refine my ideas. To them all go special thanks.

Danny Miller, my editor at Heinemann, provided encouragement, editorial help, and advice all along the way. His support warmed my heart. Marilyn Crocker of Crocker Associates and Anita Danker of Assumption College read earlier drafts despite their own pressures and schedules. Their comments resulted in greater clarity. I am very grateful to them all.

Our children, John and Cathryn, offered invaluable help. They read earlier drafts and made suggestions; they responded to requests for all manner of technological, editorial, and professional assistance. My husband, Paul, may have gotten himself in for more than he bargained when he initially made the suggestion, many years before I finally took it, to write this book. His patience, support, guidance, and help have been unending, as is his love. I am forever and deeply grateful to my family.

West Hyannisport, MA
February 2003

Introduction

Do not judge your neighbor until you have walked for two moons in his moccasins.

—Cheyenne (American Indian) proverb

*I*n late spring of my freshman year in college in Ohio, the after-class appointment with my "Freshman Comp" professor was not going well; my confidence was draining quickly. Rubbing his forehead with his hand accentuated the despair in his eyes; he finally looked at me and, with a semester's worth of frustration said, "You just don't know how to write idiomatic English." He closed his grade book and left the classroom.

I was dumbfounded, crushed, crestfallen. I had arrived the previous fall upon graduating with honors from a prestigious high school for girls in New England. My two years there had been to ease the transition from the land of my birth to the rigors of college in the United States. Born in Turkey, where my Anglo-American parents were missionary educators for more than four decades, I had been very much a part of the Turkish community as I was growing up. My playmates were Turkish; I attended a Turkish elementary school. I was also surrounded by English at home and in much of our social life. Furthermore, one-year sabbaticals for my parents had meant first and eighth grades in the United States for me, without any major adjustment issues. Back in Turkey, as part of my preparation for high school in the United States, I had attended a high school for

1

*dependents of U.S. military personnel for two years. And so with con-
fidence I had come to college. I was proud to be bilingual and bicultural; the professor's comments shredded my self-image.*

THE ISSUE IN COLLEGE WAS NOT LEARNING ENGLISH; I GREW UP
with English at home. I had had a lot of practice in both oral and written
forms not only in the States but also in Turkey, through constant contact
with teachers from the United States in my parents' school and through my
correspondence courses. A doctoral seminar I took thirty years later finally
clarified that fateful meeting with my "Freshman Comp" professor: I had
been writing in English, but using some lingering Turkish rhetorical structures. The tragedy of that professor's comment was the impact it had on my
life for those intervening thirty years. He had convinced me that I couldn't
write and that nothing could be done to correct my deficiency.

The United States in the Twentyfirst Century

Classrooms across the United States are becoming rainbows of race and culture. Urban, suburban, and rural settings; cities, towns, and villages all have
increasing numbers of students whose native language is not English and
whose cultural background is not the dominant Anglo-American culture of
this country. By 1910, the end of the first decade of the twentieth century,
13.5 million immigrants were living in this country. Of those, 11.8 million
were from Europe, that is, 87.4 percent of the total number of immigrants
(U.S. Census Bureau 2001). While that majority endured prejudice once they
arrived, much of their basic cultural orientation was not significantly different from the dominant Anglo culture of the United States. By 1998, almost
the end of the twentieth century, more than 26.3 million immigrants were
living in the United States, with people from Asia, Latin America, and the
Caribbean (not Europe) comprising 77.5 percent of the total foreign-born
population (Camarota 1999). While the percentage of immigrants relative to
our total population has gone down (14.7 percent in 1910 to 9.8 percent in
1998), the variety and number have increased. In other words, more people
from backgrounds very different from the dominant culture live within our
borders these days than ever before.

Though the diversity of our nation's classrooms is increasing dramati-
cally, mainstream teachers are often not adequately prepared for these cross-
cultural students. While Bilingual Education (BE) teachers or Teachers of
English to Speakers of Other Languages (TESOL) may study some cultural

topics in addition to their linguistic emphases, mainstream teachers often do not have that opportunity. As a result, they are frequently perplexed or intimidated in their relationships with the recently arrived English Language Learners (ELLs) in their classrooms. Many mainstream teachers feel abandoned, without instruction or even tips on how to approach or teach these students. As immersion efforts (giving ELLs one year to grasp social and academic English) increase across the United States, these mainstream teachers will face more and more students who have not yet fully acculturated to a bilingual or bicultural life. Also, cultural issues extend far beyond the "newly arrived immigrant" phase; immigrant students who have become fluent in English and second-generation students are often caught in a tug between the culture of home and that of the school. In the classroom, teachers wonder why Fatma can't seem to join in group activities or why Tomo is so gloomy or why Mariane always likes to work with someone. Teachers search for ways out of the fog of discomfort and confusion brought on by the lack of preparation for diversity.

One strategy involves becoming acquainted with the customs and traditions of one or two particular cultures. However, for us to be cognizant that differences exist among cultures or to make a laundry list of those differences is not sufficient. It carries risks of stereotyping. Furthermore, a student from a culture that has not yet been "listed" becomes a puzzle. Instead, I believe that understanding some of the building blocks of *all* cultures is the keystone that holds together the variety of world views and creates a more solid structure for meaningful interactions between the teacher and the students and among students themselves.

As immigrants have become more numerous throughout the country in the past two decades, many mainstream teachers have become familiar with what to expect linguistically from their ELLs. Most teachers assume that learning English is the primary task of linguistic-minority students; indeed, the students think so as well (Clayton 1996). However, learning a language involves more than just linguistics; it involves culture. We learned a folk dance in elementary school Spanish class; we tasted not only *brie* and *petits fours* in high school French class but also practiced ordering from a French menu; we sang German *lieder* not just to improve our vocabulary. But, of course, culture is deeper than those overt forms studied in foreign language classes. The covert aspect runs very deep. Everyone in the world experiences cultural conditioning from birth. The family is the primary socializer for a child. Culture is our first language. Even before we learn words, we understand the verbal and the non-verbal give-and-take within our families. Over the years of our childhood, we learn how to gain praise; we see or feel the disappointment in faces and actions of others when we do not fulfill expectations. As we begin to utter sounds in our earliest days, we learn not only the words of language that has meaning for the family and community but also the tune that weaves the words together. We learn the rhythm, the tone of the language, the rests and measures which translate linguistically into the meaning of a nod or shake of the head, how or whether to verbalize doubts, how to greet people, which pauses mean an interruption is permissible, and much more.

As an important aspect of identity, language marks only one part of our cultural conditioning. Other forces fashion us in the ways considered important and valuable in our family and community. From the beginning, we learn what is important and what is not, who belongs in our in-group and who in the out-group, what constitutes our self-worth, what makes us laugh or cry, and the like. This complicated but assumed process starts as soon as we are born and happens so unconsciously that we are not at all aware of its occurrence. The conditioning shapes not only our language in childhood but also our very soul, and how we perceive the world. Though the process is universal, what is taught and absorbed is not; it varies from culture to culture, even from family to family.

Cultural conditioning continues in school, the secondary socializer. The verbal and non-verbal messages sent by the teacher, the administrators, peers, and textbooks all extend their influence to shape the student to the values considered important by the dominant culture of the community. For example, learning to line up to go to lunch subtly teaches how the dominant culture feels about orderliness and taking turns; textbooks convey what the dominant culture considers important enough to warrant attention; peers communicate acceptable behavior, clothing, snacks. When this conditioning matches what the student has brought from home, as it usually does with dominant-culture students, the compatibility between home and school is hardly noted. However, for the spectrum of linguistic, racial, ethnic, or socioeconomic minorities, the absence of that compatibility leads to upheaval or discord for the students and, thereby, for the teacher.

The Background of this Book

This book is an outgrowth of two strands: one personal and the other professional. As mentioned in the opening vignette, I grew up in Turkey, with Anglo-American parents and Turkish friends. As a bicultural, bilingual child growing up overseas, I absorbed both Turkish and Anglo-American ways and attitudes, which, of course, I assumed to be normal. I visited the United States with my parents during year-long sabbaticals when I was six and when I was thirteen and then came alone when I was sixteen to complete high school. My stateside family consisted of my two older brothers who had preceded me to the United States along with my extended family of grandparents, aunts, uncles, and cousins. As I reflect on it now, even in those years, I started dealing with many issues that did not seem to be common to my new friends. In my last two years of high school and then college, I did not need to learn English, but I did need to learn how to fulfill different classroom expectations. Recitation, parroting back what the teacher expounded had been my experience in elementary school, not critical thinking or independent research. Other, non-academic attitudes played at the edges of consciousness throughout my life. Even after living more of my life in the United States than in Turkey, I found my instincts different from my husband's (a bonafide Anglo-American) when, for example, hospitality to friends of friends or "duty" to fulfill some far-flung requests spoke more urgently to me than to him. I puzzled as to where all this was coming from.

Professionally, my interest in the topic grew as, in my capacity as an ESOL (English to Speakers of Other Languages) teacher, I talked with mainstream teachers about the linguistically diverse students we shared. I felt that the teachers' questions seemed to have more to do with culture than with language acquisition. Subsequently, working on my doctorate as well as teaching graduate students helped define more clearly the domains that I felt were reflected in the classroom.

The Content of this Book

Some of the building blocks that shape cultural conditioning, of not only long-term immigrant and short-term sojourner students but also our own, form the structure of this book. In separate chapters, it seeks to look at aspects of culture that are essential for a classroom teacher to understand.

- *Chapter One* delves a little into the concept of culture, points out the universality of ethnocentrism, and explores the ease and disservice of stereotyping.
- *Chapter Two* looks at the basic, fundamental differences between cultures in the socialization of children. Using the collectivistic/individualistic paradigm, I examine a variety of continua describing family orientations. "Color blindness" (feeling that white/black/tan, we are all the same) ranks as an important issue here as well.
- *Chapter Three* explores the ways in which values can differ from culture to culture, using Kluckhohn's framework that organizes the general attitudes of a culture toward five specific domains (e.g.,

relationships between people, orientation toward activity). Naturally, variations occur within a culture, as well as between cultures.

- *Chapter Four* investigates the impact of culture on the way we perceive, think, and learn. Of course, diversity exists within a culture, but so do some general tendencies. All students bring with them a learning style shaped by home, community, and school. The question lies in how much of a match exists between teacher and student.

- *Chapter Five* points out how oral and written communication can differ across cultures, how rules of communication or self-presentation can dictate interactions between children and superiors, and why using the family language at home is a supportive measure for ELLs.

- *Chapter Six* looks at three areas of non-verbal communication: body language, vocal cues, and some cultural assumptions about time and space.

- *Chapter Seven* discusses newcomers' experience of acculturation. Ethnic urban enclaves and melded suburban dreams show different responses to immigration. Teachers encounter the throes of their immigrant students' lives and, in turn, can play a role in shaping students' responses.

- *Chapter Eight* addresses many teachers' discovery that their own culture plays a major role in their classrooms. Schools around the world reflect the larger society and hence education is not culture-free. In the United States, a distinct Anglo-American slant shapes the classroom culture of dominant-culture educational systems. Additionally, the chapter explores cultural expectations of parental involvement in the classroom.

- Finally, *Chapter Nine* presents my view of multicultural education. Our shrinking global community necessitates multicultural education for all, not just for those who have linguistic, racial, or ethnic diversity in their classrooms. ELLs are gifts that deepen our understanding of other cultures as well as our own.

This book also pursues discernment of our own cultural footing. Noted anthropologist Edward T. Hall has said: "The best reason for exposing oneself to foreign ways is to generate a sense of vitality and awareness—an interest in life which can come only when one lives through the shock of contrast and difference" (Hall 1973, 30). Many teachers of the dominant Anglo-American culture are at a loss to describe outstanding cultural characteristics of *their* culture or to explain how some of the basic beliefs of this country pervade their classroom. If they have not had to face a difference between their way of life and the school's, in the way that linguistic- or cultural-minority families do each day, the task is difficult. Learning how these building blocks of culture shape others' behaviors and attitudes includes a better understanding of the dominant Anglo-American culture of the United States. My goal is to help teachers celebrate the invisible riches in their own briefcase as well as those in the students' backpacks, both of which carry much more than lesson plans, books, and lunches.

In each chapter, in addition to general suggestions that apply to the classroom, I have also included in separate textboxes a few specific questions or prompts to consider. The material becomes more relevant when pushed out of the cerebral into the practical domain. Some of the suggestions are more age-specific than others; I hope that the ideas inspire extending these and creating other applications of the concepts.

Unique Perspectives

People need to speak for themselves; they need to define the essence of their experience and their beliefs. While outsiders may apply general characteristics to a cultural belief and provide a different perspective, we also need to hear it from the viewpoint of the insider who experiences it. If we are not Muslims, we have an outsider's view of Islam; we end up describing it through research instead of through believers' eyes. Sometimes, we use our impression as the true meaning. While it is important to have a trustworthy outsider's view to enable a more global picture, we *must* also hear the insider's viewpoint to understand fully. For this reason, I have relied on examples and descriptions given by my international graduate students, by authors of biographical materials as well as ethnographic studies to augment the skeletal framework of the various topics. Different people have different experiences; culture is not a mold that limits possibilities. In fact, no two Germans or two Afghanis are alike, nor are two Anglo-Americans. Even as we absorb the ways of our own families, we each leave our imprint on that process. The family culture that I grew up in was somewhat different from my brothers', though the basic orientation remained the same. World events, family circumstances, my gender, and my personality particularized my upbringing even within our family. In my descriptions of general tendencies within a culture, I do not, by any stretch of the imagination, want to imply that all people of that culture believe or behave in the same way.

People ask why I don't highlight the similarities of cultures instead of looking at how we differ. They strongly believe that wars are fought, divisions exist, violence erupts because of differences, not because of similarities. I agree that similarities generally bring harmony. I am reminded of a discussion group I attended in the early days of interfaith inquiry when Protestant, Catholic, and Jewish laypersons gathered in living rooms for discussions about our faiths. Very early, my group decided that in order not to be divisive, we should talk only about our similarities. We ended up talking about our belief in one God, but soon had to shift to the weather and our children. I believe we need to celebrate distinctions; they make us unique. While I agree that terrible events occur between groups and individuals with different viewpoints, I believe that the reason they occur is not because of the *differences* themselves, but because of our mutual *lack of understanding*. Often we have not had a chance to talk in depth and without defensiveness with the person with whom we have a difference; we have not had the chance to offer them the respect to believe as they do, just as we would expect them to do for us. We have not had the opportunity to learn about others in meaningful terms, to know their dreams, hopes, fears, and frustrations. It is as if one person must be right and the other wrong—and we do not want to be on the losing side. Being open to different viable viewpoints is often hard to achieve. no right or wrong in cultures

As the United States becomes more diverse in its population and as the world community grows small, we need more opportunities to learn how others see us and how we see them; we need to search for answers to the hard questions of what makes us who we really are.

Beyond Tolerance

Reciprocal respect is crucial to the fabric of a diverse population in a democratic country. Respect for another person does not mean acceptance of that person's values as our own. To me, it means that I understand that a particular value gives meaning to that person's life though it may not give meaning to mine. I may value the intermingling of women and men professionally and socially, but I understand that other cultures have a different interpretation of the role of women. Mutual respect leads to a dialogue as opposed to a monologue. While we must teach immigrants what we value in this culture, we cannot demand that they or the world conform to our standards and values. We can expect that they agree to abide by the laws of the land, but our cultural values are not the same as our laws. Assimilation, total acceptance of the predominant cultural values, is only one of several ways immigrants relate to the dominant culture. We need to help all students learn how to live in this country, but all may not own the values that are commonly held here. The plurality of ideas and our mutual respect form the strength of our democracy and our diversity.

To engender this mutual respect, school systems, superintendents, school boards, education czars call for tolerance. But will that be sufficient? I suggest that we need to push beyond the *tolerance* of diversity. That may sound heretical, since *tolerance* has called heroes and martyrs to struggle with evil forces in political and educational systems, *tolerance* is on the lips of those who would see equity for all students in classrooms, *tolerance* is the clarion call of textbooks and magazines with strategies and stories. For me, however, the word carries the sense in which George Washington used it in the late eighteenth century: "Our first president, George Washington, wrote to a tiny Jewish community in Rhode Island that in this new nation, we will no longer speak of mere 'toleration,' because toleration implies that minorities enjoy their inherent rights 'by the indulgence' of the majority" (Dershowitz 2001). To me, *tolerance* implies attitudes of resignation, passivity, superiority; it should not be our ultimate goal. If we tolerate someone, we are not partners with them; if we tolerate something, we are not invested in it.

Instead, we need to move to the more powerful concept of *affirmation*, with confidence in the validity of our stand. This is not to say that we affirm or allow students' misbehaviors, insensitivity, hate, or acts of violence. As teachers, we are in a position to sketch the future, to shape the vision, and guide the hands that will create the blueprint of our society. For that task we will need to hold everyone to high standards of behavior and academics. Affirmation of the student's heritage or feelings and high expectations of civility and scholarship must co-exist. *Affirmation* suggests worth, creativity, empowerment. *Affirmation* invites an equal footing, a pro-active approach, a willingness to recognize more than "our" (i.e., the correct) point of view. Sociolinguist Deborah Tannen points out that many aspects of our dominant Anglo-American culture are always caught between two polarities: an adversarial framework. Opposition is at every turn; debating (an assumption of two sides) is expected. How much richer our lives would be if we saw issues "not composed of two opposing sides, but ... [as] a crystal of many sides" (Tannen 1998, 10). *Affirmation* of others' cultural foundations as valid for them would enrich all our lives and would empower *all* students in their understanding of the world.

Rabbi Hugo Gryn put it eloquently in an interview on BBC during the Gulf War Vigil, on January 18, 1991. He said that his tradition cherished the legend in which God is surrounded by ministering angels who sing and dance after the children of Israel crossed the Red Sea so miraculously, but notice that God is crying. "Are you not glad?" they ask. "How can I rejoice?" asks God. "My children are also drowning." *Affirmation* honors the other person.

Connecting with Students

A sharper awareness and a deeper discernment are the joy and blessing that the linguistic-minority children can provide for mainstream classroom teachers. Another "program night" is not necessary to make a connection with the student. Connections don't need programs. In my experience, a connection occurred when a mainstream teacher finally understood that in the Russian school system her ELL came from, seriousness was a mark of the student's interest and diligence. The student had been socialized that smiling a lot demeaned the process of learning. The teacher accepted the student's perception and stopped taking his demeanor as a personal affront; the student learned to relax a little (Clayton 1996). Connections happen when the student's background is validated; connections happen when the student is given an opportunity to talk about her homeland; connections happen when teachers are able to show the incomparable gift in our Declaration of Independence: that all people are created equal and have inherent rights. Disconnections will happen as the values and behaviors of linguistic-minority students clash with those of the teacher and the culture of the classroom. But with increased knowledge about possible causes, these disconnections can be taken as departure points for teachable moments, even when the ELL does not know much English. Mainstream students are ready and need to learn about the importance of non-verbal communication when an incident involving giggling, tones of voice, and group behavior signals to a newcomer that the students are making fun of him. This is not just a one-way street: Anglo-American students need to learn to live in a diverse world just as much as the linguistic or cultural minority students need to learn to live in the United States. In that teachable moment, the lives of all students can expand.

Use of terms

A brief comment is necessary about the use of some terms: Although the word "minority" carries a pejorative cast for many people, I have used it here in very specific cultural circumstances. Despite large groups of linguistic, racial, or ethnic populations, much of the dominant culture of the United States has an Anglo-American cast and most schools reflect the values of that dominant (not necessarily majority) culture. I am not suggesting that this is the way it should be; in fact, the purpose of the book is to help teachers understand how we might embrace a multicultural stance.

My dislike of the term "American" has caused considerable discussion. My guiding premise views the term as applicable to North, Central, and South America. We in the United States seem to have appropriated the term for ourselves; this to me seems preemptory since other countries are also included in the Americas. The dominant culture of the United States has the indelible mark of our mother country, England; hence the term Anglo-American. Even as a fledgling country, we had a fair amount of influence from other European countries; hence the term European American. I started to use that term but soon realized that European Americans did not use the term to describe themselves. Since the book looks at topics regarding immigrants and the dominant culture, I use the term Anglo-American to signify that dominant culture.

Reflections

Research on cultural issues has come a long way since my college days. We know now that cultures have different but valid ways of expression: The United States is notorious for "Come straight to the point," "Stop beating about the bush," and "Tell it like it is." Anglo-American thought patterns are linear, from point A to point B, as quickly as possible, please. My English professor's motto, his ABCs of English, was: "Accuracy, Brevity, Clarity." Other languages, Turkish among them, are more circuitous in their approach, with embellishments and subordinate clauses abounding. Those structures were still lingering in my writing for Freshman Comp. Despite my extensive experience and ease with English, certain structures of the language that had surrounded me from birth still clung to my inner psyche. That college experience is one the motivations for this book.

Since one of the goals of education is to prepare students for life, schools need to be a vehicle by which all students can become empowered in the dominant culture. Students do not need to give up one culture to be able to work within another. To grow up biculturally is possible; I know that from experience. Not only is it possible, it is a powerful gift. To ask children to give up their cultural conditioning is to ask them to shed their identity, to cast off their souls. Acknowledging children's cultural heritage and teaching them to access power in the dominant culture will help them grow to their full and true potential.

I invite you to read this book with your mind and your heart, with inquiry and reflection. I hope that you will increase your understanding of the English Language Learner's cultural voyage and also gain greater insight into your own beliefs and behavior. As you combine your insights about the challenges facing cross-cultural students and increasingly multicultural classrooms, may you also encounter a personal epiphany: an inquiring openness to other cultures, the vitality of different perspectives, and the core of your own identity.

Chapter One

Our First Language: Culture

No one calls his own buttermilk sour.

—Farsi proverb

Stanley has been here about two months; he arrived from China or Hong Kong, I don't remember. I can't say much for his linguistic abilities yet, but his math facts are phenomenal. He whizzes right along, so long as it is just computation. I know when he gets some language under his belt, he'll be just fine. The rest of the time, he just kind of muddles along; I don't understand why he doesn't come up to me to ask questions when he doesn't know what to do. Actually, that's my biggest problem now.

—(Celia, *a second-grade teacher*)

*I*t was November, and as part of my responsibilities as a teacher of English Language Learners (ELLs), I was meeting with classroom teachers whose students I shared. Celia had been teaching for ten years and had lots of experience with immigrant or sojourner children. She knew the steps of their linguistic development in English; she was not intimidated by their accents nor their shorthand attempts at making their wishes known. Two years of teaching in an international school with an English language curriculum had fanned her curiosity and interest in other countries. Recently, however, she had begun to question different aspects of her current and past students' adjustments to her classroom. Why did Anna always have trouble deciding what to do when given a choice of writing assignments? Why was Victor really unhappy when assigned to a group project? Why did Jaffar have a hard time being orderly in taking his turn or standing in line?

CELIA'S MUSINGS MADE ME THINK ABOUT THE ACCULTURATION issues immigrant students face in addition to learning a language. While some of the characteristics she delineated can certainly be personality traits, these behaviors can also reveal cultural traditions and values. As teachers with immigrant students, we often focus our attention on the linguistic part of these newcomers' lives and on the difficulty of matching their linguistic ability with our available resources to keep the student appropriately occupied. But a cultural side of the coin exists as well. We are accustomed to noticing visible aspects of different cultures: for example, different ways of dress or greeting patterns. Indeed, the explicit parts of a culture are the souvenirs we bring home from trips: the arts, clothing, and memories of quaint customs. In school, celebrations around the foods, holidays, and heroes of other cultures acquaint our students with a wider community. Harder to grasp are the invisible parts of culture: the attitudes, assumptions, and values. Often, when asked to define culture, my graduate students will mention behaviors, rather than the underlying foundation of those behaviors. And while the behaviors point to cultural assumptions, culture is deeper than the observable.

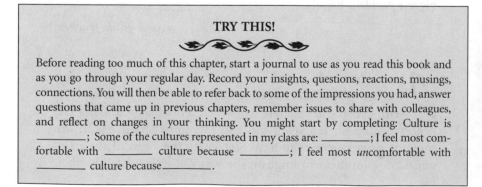

TRY THIS!

Before reading too much of this chapter, start a journal to use as you read this book and as you go through your regular day. Record your insights, questions, reactions, musings, connections. You will then be able to refer back to some of the impressions you had, answer questions that came up in previous chapters, remember issues to share with colleagues, and reflect on changes in your thinking. You might start by completing: Culture is _____; Some of the cultures represented in my class are: _____; I feel most comfortable with _____ culture because _____; I feel most *uncomfortable* with _____ culture because_____.

What is Culture, Then?

Celia's questions hinted at the implicit side of culture. Many definitions of culture vie for attention. One, written three decades ago, seems to speak to our technological society today: "a set of control mechanisms—plans, recipes, rules, instructions (what computer engineers call 'programs')—for governing behavior"(Geertz 1973, 44). Although the definition has been critiqued for, among other reasons, making culture seem too inflexible and static, the metaphor does suggest the foundational nature of culture. Not just the customs and traditions of a culture (the observable), but the actual underlying program (hidden) allows or defines behavior and thinking. Culture is all those patterns of thinking and behavior learned on mother's lap, by grandpa's side, in school, the grocery store, the synagogue, or day care. Renato Rosaldo has captured the extensive and permeating nature of culture: "[Culture] refers broadly to the forms through which people make sense of their lives, rather than more narrowly to the opera or art museums. It does not inhabit a set-aside domain, as does, for example, that of politics or economics. . . . Culture encompasses the everyday and the esoteric, the mundane and the elevated, the ridiculous and the sublime" (Rosaldo 1993, 26).

As Rosaldo indicates, culture is both explicit and implicit. Artifacts, music, art, food, and other material dimensions are one expression of culture. How "people make sense of their lives" is implicit and hidden. This book focuses on that implicit aspect of culture. When overlooked, it can cause consternation; when understood, it can be enlightening.

Descriptors of Culture

What are some of the implicit aspects of culture that have the most impact on a classroom? Let's look at the following characteristics:

- First, *culture is pervasive*; all areas of life are influenced or shaped by cultural forces. Culture is the underlying, assumed structure which gives shape to all we do and think and believe and value. The give and take of everyday life at home or at school is affected by our culture. In the classroom, in addition to the issues of choice, group-work, and orderliness that Celia was musing about, it can appear, for example, in attitudes toward the teacher, assumptions about help, expectations of peers, and parent interactions. Culture affects what we think, what we perceive, and how we behave.

- Second, *culture is shared*; it is not idiosyncratic. Culture is not only transmitted from generation to generation but also shared widely among people of that large (e.g., nation) or small (e.g., family) community.

Views on how life should be lived are inculcated in the young, becoming unspoken assumptions. Members of a society assign meaning and significance to some values or behaviors and not to others. That is to say, meaning and significance are understood and appreciated *within a context*; they are not intrinsic to the situation itself. For example, hand holding between members of the same gender means one thing in the Anglo-American culture of the United States and nothing more than friendship in many other cultures. The fact that culture is shared widely is not to say that there will not be countercultural people or groups. While adolescents may rebel at parental values and spike their hair or color it chartreuse, they do join another group, a micro-culture of other rebels with whom they share similar values. They may chose singular expressions, but they do join a group where they find coherent meaning, where the majority of the group has a similar outlook on life. Furthermore, when surrounded by a culture foreign to us, often we will try to seek out people with whom we share commonality in our basic assumptions, where we can do the important work of "reading between the lines" in a language we understand. The sharing of basic assumptions contributes to the reasons members of a particular racial or ethnic or linguistic group, for example, sit together in the cafeteria, as psychologist and professor Beverly Tatum points out. Issues of identity have become important for them; they seek the support of peers who share their unspoken assumptions, particularly if they are in the minority (Tatum 1997).

• Third, *culture is learned*; it is not genetic. Children learn culture from all the people and contexts that surround them as they grow up. The learning begins as soon as we are born, as we are socialized into the culture of the family. We learn how to communicate with others, what particular non-verbal signs mean, where we are in the hierarchy or in the equality within the family or society, what is good, not so good, and bad. Culture is learned, not genetic, because each culture, large or small, has created its own patterns of meaning among its members. That means, for example, that the classroom, the family, the bridge club, the health club, a religious organization, and a cocktail hour all have their own micro-cultures. These groups all have certain ways of behavior that are assumed and expected. Barbara J. Peters, a sociologist, was quoted in an article by Michelle Locke in the *Boston Globe* on January 18, 2001, about the disconnection felt by academics who had grown up in rural poverty and were now attending academic functions. In such a milieu, career moves often depend on small talk:

"Poor people, when we talk to each other, we sit down. We don't stand with a wine glass and a little plate of stuff trying to balance everything." Serious bridge players do not chatter through a bridge game; seasoned classical concert-goers understand that you do not clap between movements of a symphony; jazz fans know that each individual improvisation deserves applause. These micro-cultures all have assumptions about behavior that must be unearthed by those new to the situation. In a sense, all of us are multicultural in that we inhabit multiple micro-cultures in our daily lives; we absorb the culture of our home, and also learn, consciously or unconsciously, the culture of any number of other groups to which we belong as well as that of the larger society.

Classrooms have rules of behavior that have meaning for class members. Some of those rules are agreed upon by teachers and the students at the beginning of the year, and others are assumed. One of the morning rituals in a colleague's classroom was silent reading during the first fifteen minutes of the day. An immigrant student, not having had the emphasis on silent reading in her previous school (i.e., cultural) experience nor enough English to understand the schedule, started coming to school fifteen minutes later than expected. She thought that because students were all reading different books, school did not begin until the teacher took "control" of the class (Clayton 1996). The practice made sense to those inside the classroom community, but not to someone from the outside with a different conception of "school." Acceptable behavior at school, within the classroom, and in the school at large helps mold the students into good citizens with the values of the dominant culture.

• Fourth, *our own culture is often unknown to us.* Despite the fact that it is pervasive, shared, and learned, culture does not warrant much discussion in casual conversations with people of the same cultural group. Usually topics or interests shared within a cultural group (e.g., football, politics, ski conditions) are discussed interminably. However, culture is a topic that is not usually in our consciousness. People are not apt to say, "Isn't it curious how our emphasis on individualism pervades so much of life: My personal pleasure is important to me." Or, "I was struck the other day about our value of orderliness when I was in a line at the bus stop, at lunch, at the movies, at the department store, and then at the bank." Culture is like the air we breathe: we do not think much about it until we are unable to fill our lungs. When we come into contact with a cultural value that is not ours, we might begin to ask what is happening. But that process is meaningful only if we are aware of the basic tenets of the cultural foundation on which *we* stand, so that we can understand why the conflict is occurring. Anthropologist Edward Hall writes: "Culture hides much more than it reveals, and strangely enough what it hides, it hides most effectively from its own participants. Years of study have convinced me that the real job is not to understand foreign culture but to understand our own" (Hall 1973, 30).

- Fifth, *culture is dynamic*; it changes over time. Think about some of the values and behaviors of the 1970s, for example, that are no longer valid in the new century: In the United States, generally, women were expected to marry young and raise children within a two-parent family, the husband was the only one who worked outside the home, and children were expected to be seen and not heard. Current statistics show that the median age for a first marriage for a woman rose from 20.8 in 1970 to 25 years in 2000; in 1998, in fifty-one percent of married couples with children, both spouses worked (U.S. Census Bureau), and from life experience, we see that children are front and center at all times. Cultures change over the years, more quickly now than in the past, due to technological innovations leading to instantaneous global impact. When we read about other cultures, we need to pay attention to the era being portrayed; the books may be describing what was true decades ago, but not how it has changed in our exponentially shrinking world.

- Finally, *culture is the root of our identity,* closely allied with all that makes us who we are and what we believe. It encompasses our very being. In my experience, linguistic minority students are extremely eager to blend into the class as quickly as possible and to be accepted by classmates. To do that, they try to shed as many of the visible, more superficial signs of their cultural upbringing as possible. This pressure to assimilate into the crowd brings real tension to the home, where the family sees constant attacks not on their "ethnicity" but on their very souls. To force children to disregard such an integral part of their heritage does incalculable harm; to validate their culture brings joy, and to ask them to share it means increased understanding for others. Research shows that with a strong foundation in one's own culture, the process of learning about another can be an additive, rather than a subtractive process. Bruce Feiler, in his insightful and humorous *Learning to Bow*, details the clash of Anglo-American and Japanese assumptions, beliefs, values, and customs. He comments to his Japanese colleagues at the end of his year of teaching in a Japanese high school: "I am an American. I look, think, and act like an American. Sometimes, however, when I am with you, I can think and act like a Japanese. . . . The problem I face is knowing when to act like you and when to act like me" (Feiler 1991, 209). This comment comes from an adult who was able to be objective and grounded enough to detail what was happening to him. It verbalizes the blessing and the dilemma many children face who do not have the words or maturity to explain their confusion.

The Two Sides of Ethnocentrism

Having been surrounded by assumptions, attitudes, beliefs, and values from birth, we take them for granted. Growing up within the safety provided by the familiar, we assume that our experience is good, right, and true. This process results in *ethnocentrism, the belief that our ways are the center of the universe and hence superior.* Ethnocentrism initially provides the ground for our identity. Given the socialization of our youth, a basic and natural human response is to protect our values when opposed by others.

However, ethnocentrism can take on a negative cast when we impose or judge people of other cultures by our beliefs. "[C]ultural identity represents the bright side of ethnocentrism, but when such cultural bias is used to support negative and capricious evaluation of the new and strange, then it is very dark" (Damen 1987, 214). Ethnocentrism blinds us to the authenticity of others' realities. We are so rooted in what we have been taught over the years that it is difficult to recognize that others may experience the world differently. We find it hard to admit that other perspectives are valid. This concept applies not just to individuals but also to whole nations. Stewart and Bennett, professors of psychology and communication respectively, write about ethnocentric self-perception of cultures: Many in the United States assume, for example, that all people who come to this country will want to stay here; most Japanese assume that because they are so different, no one can understand them, nor they anyone else; many Europeans assume that the pinnacle of civilization is to be found in Europe. All of these assumptions can lead to interpretations of disrespect (Stewart and Bennett 1991). Professor Jaime Wurzel points to the struggle to burst out of the restraints ethnocentrism inflicts: "The powerful spell of culture will not let us easily accept the existence or validity of other cultures. We will hold on to our own as long as we can, for there is a painful loss in admitting the relativity of our reality and the validity of others" (Wurzel 1988, 4). Often, disbelief and then defensiveness jump out as first responses when we come in contact with the realities of other cultures, resulting in "How can they think that?" and then, "Well, our way is certainly better."

Some students have asked about the influence of ethnocentrism when growing up under colonial rule. Professor of women's studies Leila Ahmed gives voice to one aspect of that experience. She speaks of growing up in her homeland, Egypt, in the last days of the British Empire: "For me now there is no doubt that, at least implicitly, English was valued above Arabic in ways that would have marked it, in a child's mind at least, as being somehow innately a 'superior' language. . . . I think we heard Arabic music, too, as somehow lesser. . . . We grew up believing that some world over there was better, more interesting, more civilized than this world here" (Ahmed 2000, 23, 24, 154). Half a world away, anthropologist Cathryn Clayton documented the attitudes of people growing up under a different colonial power. During four hundred years of Portuguese rule in Macau, many Chinese kept their particular Chineseness intact, with feelings of reluctant appreciation or irrelevancy or antipathy toward the colonialist Portuguese. Monica, a Chinese acquaintance, commented, "Here in Macau, we live more naturally, we do things as we used to do them and don't try to force an unnatural break with our past" (Clayton 2001, 394). Growing up under colonial power produces different results. On the one hand, in Egypt the negative aspects of ethnocentrism ruled the lives of the Egyptians; they felt inferior to the British. On the other hand, in Macau the Chinese were able to preserve their personal and cultural identity throughout the centuries.

Ethnocentrism, then, is a universal process as well as an inevitable one, since each culture enculturates its young to the values and ways of the culture. People can learn to recognize it, become aware of its presence, and reduce its negative influence, but the condition is inherent to humanity. Wurzel lists seven steps that lead from an ethnocentric view to a multicultural view:

- *Monoculturalism*—we assume that our ways are universal;
- *Cross-Cultural Contact*—we start to have some contact with other cultures but still assume our cultural patterns prevail;
- *Cultural Conflict*—we experience varying degrees of tension between others' cultural assumptions and our own;
- *Educational Interventions*—effective education dissipates the tension and improves contact;
- *Disequilibrium*—we absorb the new information and decide how to act upon it;

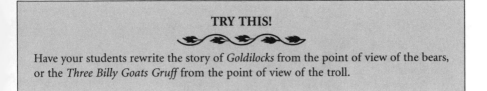

TRY THIS!

Have your students rewrite the story of *Goldilocks* from the point of view of the bears, or the *Three Billy Goats Gruff* from the point of view of the troll.

- *Awareness*—we recognize the depth of culture and begin to work with the concept; and finally,
- *Multiculturalism*—we recognize and appreciate cultural differences; we embrace a new cognitive as well as psychic worldview (Wurzel 1988, 5–10).

In the Classroom

While we may bend over backwards to accommodate our cross-cultural students and the cultural heritages they represent, ethnocentrism can creep into the classroom in subtle ways. For example, maps! Maps convey a lot about our attitudes regarding the validity of others' realities. Many traditional wall maps (still found in numerous school systems) are based on the Mercator Projection of 1569, which was created in Germany for navigational purposes during the European colonial expansion. Working out of that ethnocentric bias, the Mercator projection shows Europe to be larger than South America, when in reality South America is 3.1 million square miles larger. It distorts the size of nations in favor of those with white populations—Scandinavia is shown to be larger than India, whereas India is about three times as large. Also, the equator is drawn two thirds of the way down the map, compressing the whole of the Southern Hemisphere into the bottom one third of the map (Peters Projection 1983). The Peters Projection, on the other hand, is a map created to represent accurate land areas. It corrects the above inaccuracies, as well as others, but has problems with elongating countries near the equator. It looks odd to those who have grown up with the shapes of countries as depicted in the Mercator map. Fortunately, some recent world maps using newer projections, such as those published by the National Geographic Society, are now available and highly appropriate for classrooms. The controversy around these maps points to the fact that we can view the world in several ways, that flat wall maps can distort reality to meet the needs or bias of the creator. Publishers also do this when they put their country in the center of the map, with all other countries fanning out to either side, regardless of national boundaries. For example, with the United States in the center, as

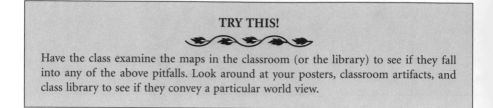

TRY THIS!

Have the class examine the maps in the classroom (or the library) to see if they fall into any of the above pitfalls. Look around at your posters, classroom artifacts, and class library to see if they convey a particular world view.

on many maps in our schools, Russia gets cut in half. This makes a statement to all, but particularly to the Russian students in our classes. Of course, a flat map must be cut somewhere, but the point is that our choices of such basic educational tools may prolong some hidden ethnocentrism.

Ethnocentrism can also creep into the classroom in the attitude that "Children are the same the world over." That may be true physiologically, but because of the cultural conditioning that occurs around the world, that is where the similarities end. Approaching immigrant children with the attitude that they will be just like Anglo-Americans does a disservice to those who are different from the dominant culture. They can't meet our unspoken assumptions if they don't know what those expectations are. If we expect them to be just like dominant-culture students, we ignore the culture that makes them who they truly are and we are blind to both the children's uniqueness and our own.

Difference and Deficiency

Ethnocentrism promotes judgments about the rest of the world relative to our own culture. Since the culture surrounding us is all we know and are familiar with, anything outside that sphere is unfamiliar and thereby judged to be inadequate. That is, we unconsciously judge the unfamiliar by our own, thought-to-be-universal, standards. Thus, since we think that what we believe is "normal and natural," anyone who does not share our values and beliefs or behaves in unacceptable ways is considered *deficient*. People who speak with an accent or who wear a *hijab* are often deemed inferior. "That child couldn't tell me how many brothers he has," or "She obviously does not understand the meaning of the story; she just answers the recall questions," can also imply a deficiency approach, not just to the children's skills, but to their mental acuity as well. Students carry with them the ways they have been taught at home and in school. They may be working out of their own cultural upbringing in which cousins are part of the family and stories are recounted with specific attention to details. While they might not be at the standards expected in this classroom, for us to make generalizations about what they cannot do, instead of validating what they already do know, blinds us to the existing structures of their knowledge. That knowledge exists; it is just different from the Anglo-American expectation. Instead of looking at these children as somehow being deficient, we need to see them as *different*, acknowledging the existence of their cultural truths. In fact, professor of education Christine Bennett suggests viewing cross-cultural children as representing *alternatives*, rather than as being different. She writes, "Alternatives connote the coexistence of worthy options, and open us to the various ways our students have learned to perceive, evaluate, believe, and behave" (Bennett 1999, 238).

Accepting differences does have limits, however, since one can ask just how far to carry that acceptance. Should the Nazis or the KKK enjoy such acceptance? Of course not. Fortunately, philosophies that condone religious bigotry and racial, ethnic, or other discrimination are considered unethical and unlawful around the world. We are not alone in condemning torture or murder or evil dictatorships. However, we must also acknowledge that many countries do not have the unlimited individual rights that we do in the United States. The delicate balance lies in knowing how and when to respect cultural differences and how and when to propose alternative strategies to achieve the goal of human dignity.

We must zealously guard against situations in which "cultural difference" becomes a euphemistic catch-all for racism. These days, many people describe the problems of diversity not as race or religion, but that of culture. We may hear that the Hispanic *culture* makes people lazy or insolent or poor; or after September 11, that the Arabs' *culture* or Islam makes them all terrorists. Exchanging the word "culture" for the term "ethnicity" or "race" or "religion" seems to be a more acceptable way of registering complaints; the complainer is not branded a racist or a bigot. However, that ascription often carries the same generalization, intolerance, and hatred that racism and bigotry carry.

Stereotyping

Stereotyping is another universal phenomenon, a natural tendency, which all people share. In order to simplify the information that is accosting us everyday, we categorize: athletes, teenagers, senior citizens, to name just three. If we did not do this, our experience of the past would be unable to help us deal with the present. The problem is that in stereotyping, we put people into categories of generalization that end up describing all members of one group: Academics are absent-minded; blondes are dumb.

When it comes to perceptions of those outside our sphere of experience, our ethnocentric tendencies protect that which is familiar to us and therefore valued by us; all else becomes suspect. The categories become broader, the sources (word-of-mouth, TV) unquestioned, the information incomplete, the judgments more fixed. In one study I conducted, teachers in a bilingual Chinese program and a bilingual Russian program were passionate in their dismay at the stereotyping of all Chinese and Russians. For the Chinese teacher, it made a great difference whether the student came from mainland China, Hong Kong, or Taiwan, because socializations were different in each of those places and the children would have widely differing expectations and experiences. For the Russian teacher the child's socioeconomic background was important due to major social differences between the classes in her so-called classless society (Clayton n. d.). Very often our stereotypes are handed down to us through our primary socialization, and are perpetuated through lack of further experience or correct information.

The dangers of stereotyping were demonstrated when Arabs were immediate suspects in the bombing of the Murrah Federal Building in Oklahoma City in 1995, due to the first attack on the World Trade Center in 1993. The fact that it might have been a radical, home-grown Anglo-American was initially never considered. Many Arab-Americans suffered physically and psychically after this event; all Arabs were put into an intolerable generalization based on the crimes of a few. The anti-Arab violence, anti-Muslim hate crimes subsequent to the tragedy of September 11, 2001, have been an embarrassment to a country that was built on the premise that all people are innocent until proven guilty, are equal before the law. We know that *all* cultures have people who act in immoral ways; none should be judged by the acts of the fanatical few. However, fear limits our chances for favorable contacts that would dispel negative attitudes. As teachers, we need to monitor our own attitudes and continue our efforts to encourage better understanding between individuals or groups, introducing one or two individuals to each other to help break a myth or dispel misconceptions.

But what of positive stereotyping? That is, seeing broad groups of students in a positive light. Many Southeast Asian-Americans (a stereotypic term, since many differences exist among them) have fallen into the stereotype of the model student (behaviorally) and/or the whiz kid (academically). While we may be complimenting them by considering them smart or well-behaved, lumping all Southeast Asian-Americans into that category does a disservice to them individually. Lost within the glow may be other issues that will go unnoticed. Students may fail to meet the high expectations and

> ### TRY THIS!
>
>
>
> Gather a list of stereotypes with your students. Begin the list with stereotypes close to home and then spread out to other cultures. The object is to sensitize students to how easy it is to stereotype and to help each other when a stereotype slips out unintentionally. If they can hear stereotypes about themselves, they might see how untrue and hurtful they are. Keep the list available in a prominent place in the classroom so that students can add to it throughout the term. Conclude the study by discussing ways to destroy stereotypes. This activity can be done at all grade levels.

thereby feel even more anxiety. They may be set up for resentment among classmates. Their model behavior may mask other problems. Our expectations may contribute further to stereotyping.

Reflections on Celia

Let us consider again Celia's comments at the beginning of this chapter. A caring, astute teacher, she nonetheless had underestimated the role of culture, ethnocentrism, and stereotyping in addressing the problems of her student. Her collapsing of China and Hong Kong into one unified whole disregarded the context of the student's heritage. While China has many large, urban areas, the socialization of children in Hong Kong is strongly permeated by an international influence. A child from rural China would be at even more of a loss in urban United States than one from Hong Kong. Celia also seemed to be bordering on the assumption that given his math accomplishments, Stanley would be a whiz in English, once he learned it. In actuality, he may have more linguistic problems than computational problems. Since Stanley *did* have one language under his belt already, might her use of "some language" indicate an ethnocentric assumption that English is the only language of note? Additionally, coming up to the teacher to ask questions is not a universal expectation. Graduate students of mine from China and South Korea explain that in their cultures, students do not ask the teacher questions; they do not want to insult our ability to explain, nor incriminate themselves in exposing the fact that they did not understand. Unaccustomed to showing their ignorance or emotions in public, they are expected to answer their questions through their own hard work. Furthermore, in some cultures, children are taught not to complain; asking for clarification might be interpreted as a complaint. This situation is further exacerbated when we, expecting the stereotype of obedient and quiet Southeast Asian students, may not perceive that a problem exists. If Celia understands this background, she may be able to give Stanley more direction, or cautiously allow him to struggle up to a point just prior to frustration. Many immigrant students coming into our schools are ready for much more guidance and direction than they find. As a bridge to independent learning, we may have to start with more guidance and back away as the student understands not only more English but also the culture of the classroom. If we can understand the patterns of other cultures, we will have the flexibility to interpret our own responses and make use of teachable moments.

LINGUISTICALLY AND CULTURALLY DIVERSE CHILDREN ARE EAGER TO BLEND IN with their classmates as quickly as possible. However, in the early days of their arrival, before the pressures of assimilation mount, they may bring in differently spiced lunches or unusual offerings for "Sharing time." These concrete items of a different culture are harbingers of the invisible layers of the cultural assumptions they have acquired over even a handful of years. These assumptions also come daily to the classroom in their backpacks, along with other classroom necessities.

Chapter Two

Carried by the Current: Socialization

What is learned in the cradle lasts until the grave.

—Hungarian proverb

My teacher keeps asking me why I am absent so many days. I am absent because I must take care of my brothers and sisters while my mother looks for a job. My teacher does not understand how my mother cannot let me come to school. Now my teacher wants my mother to come in to talk with her. I have to come in too because my mother does not understand English well and I must translate.

—(Rosa, *an immigrant sixth grader*)

*I*t is always hard to believe that others do not value what we value, be it a national political candidate, a local environmental policy, a family religious tradition, or a personal life decision. While we may get accustomed to the variety of opinions intrinsic to democracy, education as a fundamental right and necessity is non-negotiable, especially for a teacher. Rosa's comment, above, seems incomprehensible; in order to succeed in life, she must be educated, which translates into her coming to school in a consistent fashion. If a family does not value education, then the child will not succeed; Rosa will either get a social promotion or fail the year. Frustration was palpable when Rosa's teacher and I talked about the upcoming appointment: How could she work with a family who did not value education? How could Rosa's family, who had left Guatemala several years earlier for the sake of their children, not understand this necessity?

The Meaning of Socialization

In trying to answer that question, I found myself thinking about the ways in which we acquire our beliefs and assumptions. Socialization is the way in which a person becomes a member of the family, the community, and the culture. It is not the process to become a universal human being, but to become a particular person (Geertz 1973). Starting at birth, socialization is the process of absorbing what is acceptable in the family with regard to beliefs and practices: what is good and what is evil, what to say and how to say it, whom to honor and how to address them, what is good to eat, whom one should marry, whom to avoid, whether to show emotions, and all such attitudes and conventions. In other words, socialization is learning how to live, soaking up all of the assumptions that are shared by the family, the community, or the culture: learning the fundamental perspective on and practice of life within the specific culture. "William, you can see that I am talking to someone else, you'll have to wait"; "Jane, say hello to Mrs. Clayton"; "Jenny, if you can't share the cotton candy, I'll have to take it away"; "What a butterball you've become, Chris"; "Wow! Todd did best in the class on the spelling test!" These comments, typical of those made by adults in the Anglo-American culture, socialize children to believe in the tenets that underlie the comments: maintaining orderliness, respecting others, sharing possessions, being slim and athletic, and valuing competition.

To put it more succinctly, socialization, according to professor of psychology Çiğdem Kağıtçıbaşı, "is for competence. Competence refers to what is culturally valued and therefore shows variation across cultures" (Kağıtçıbaşı 1996, 35). She goes on to point out that differing needs produce differing capabilities: In Kenya, eight-year-old children can cook dinner for the family; in the United States, in Cambridge, MA, eight-year-old children can retell a story, each of these eight-year-olds unable to easily do what the other has been socialized to do. Across the oceans, in a Hawaiian-American community on Oahu, the major goal of socialization is to teach children how to become contributors to the family. This differs from the traditional goal of socialization in the United States, which is for the child to become a confident, competent, and autonomous individual (Gallimore et al. 1974). Additionally, within the same larger culture, each new family makes decisions as to which values to pass on and which to change. What is the same across cultures is that the family, nuclear or extended, teaches ground rules, the truths that pertain to the specific culture. What is different across cultures is the content of those particular truths.

In addition to the family as a primary socializer, schools play a role as secondary socializers for children. Educational, religious, or cultural institutions shape children by transmitting the values that must be learned to be able to function effectively within the culture. Historical events mold the family or the nation and will shape the ways an individual will respond to his surroundings. In the United States, the Vietnam War kindled young people's questioning attitude toward authority in the 1970s. Additionally, environmental factors also shape the way a culture adapts its life style. Children growing up in rural Alaska see myriad nuances in snow unknown to those who think in terms of "light," "heavy," and "slush," or "powder," "corn," and "groomed." Those growing up in the Pacific Islands learn to "read" waves of infinite variety. In both places, these skills have a tremendous impact on livelihood and survival.

However, due to the implicitness of the socialization process, we sometimes forget that not everyone is socialized the same way we are. Differences between cultures are sometimes fairly obvious. Yet, as many of us know, differences can exist within one culture as well. The Amish or those living in Chinatown are conspicuous examples, of course; but consider as well the differences between urban and rural children. Each has been socialized into a particular culture (a competence regarded highly within their culture), absorbing the mortar that binds the group together and becomes invisible.

Though each of us has the option of whether to conform to or rebel against cultural ways, conformity is the characteristic response of the human

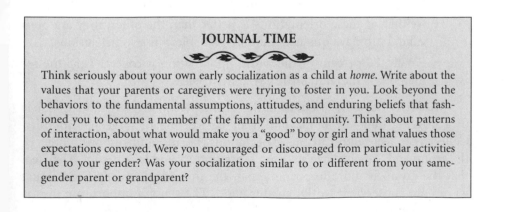

JOURNAL TIME

Think seriously about your own early socialization as a child at *home*. Write about the values that your parents or caregivers were trying to foster in you. Look beyond the behaviors to the fundamental assumptions, attitudes, and enduring beliefs that fashioned you to become a member of the family and community. Think about patterns of interaction, about what would make you a "good" boy or girl and what values those expectations conveyed. Were you encouraged or discouraged from particular activities due to your gender? Was your socialization similar to or different from your same-gender parent or grandparent?

condition. Though true in all cultures, some value it more than others. Conformity is necessary to bind a culture—be it a micro (bridge-group) culture or a macro (Anglo-American) culture. In Japan, the signal emphasis on conformity produces the saying, "The nail that sticks up gets hammered down." Children from some Asian countries, where the group is more valued than the individual, have a hard time being singled out (even for praise) since that separates them from the group. However, even in a country such as the United States, where the individual is prized more than the group, a propensity to conform exists. For example, having the "right" clothes and paraphernalia, especially for that first day of school, is highly important not only for most students but also for some parents. The non-conforming individual stands out, and if not by personal choice, then quickly tries to comply with the majority, in order to be considered part of the group. "Stop doing that, everyone is looking at you," is a common comment from parent or friend. High school graduation speakers often exhort seniors to "Be your own person" rather than to follow the crowd. In this culture a paradox exists between the basic need to conform and the foundational value of individualism.

In this chapter, I would like to first discuss the general parameters of two distinct approaches to socialization, then look at how these approaches shape children and families, and, finally, apply the dimensions to the classroom.

Collectivism and Individualism

One of the most helpful ways of understanding how cultures differ from one another is to look at the orientation of the culture toward the individual and the group. The two major orientations are *individualism* and *collectivism*. But first, some important points:

- Both orientations exist within each individual and each culture, and though one usually predominates, there is flux between them.
- Neither of these orientations is better than the other; they are both valid; both have qualities that are valuable and also deleterious.
- Finally, 70 percent of the world's population is collectivistic; the remainder is individualistic (Triandis 1995).

Collectivism is the orientation that sees a person primarily as a member of a larger group—be it the family or co-workers or larger community. Collectivists feel bound to the expectations, norms, and responsibilities of the group and thereby have a strong sense of duty and loyalty to it. They feel that the group is more important than the individual and that individual wishes are subservient to the greater good. The group's importance means that maintaining relationships and harmony stand paramount. The breaking of a relationship carries an extremely heavy weight.

Individualism, on the other hand, emphasizes the individual who is not strongly bound to a group. The individual's preferences, needs, rights, and identity are paramount. With a solid sense of independence, individuals decide whether particular relationships are worthwhile to maintain. The individualist attitude leads more to doing what pleases one, rather than to responsibilities for the common good.

Molding to these orientations starts at birth. For example, in many homes in individualistic cultures, the baby is placed in a separate room, has her own crib, has her own toys (which she is taught to share, but are still hers, primarily), and in a short time is urged into making her own decisions about clothing or activities. These orientations are pervasive throughout our interactions and we are usually unaware that our practices are reflecting anything more than getting through the day. Just two of many examples in adult life, which show the breadth of our assumptions: In an individualistic culture, the shopping process is short and focused on the exchange of money for goods. In fact, when the salesperson has a lengthy conversation with the shopper ahead of us about the family or the week's problems, we get impatient. In a collectivistic culture, on the other hand, the relationship with the shopper is very important; lengthy, personalized conversation and coffee (or tea) help achieve this goal. Another example is the relative emphasis on history. Collectivists, due to their group consciousness and the importance of ancestors, consider history to be more important than individualists who are more focused on themselves (Triandis 1995). When I was questioned by a friend from a collectivistic culture about (what I considered) minutiae of an academic institution where I worked, I had to plead ignorance. He was nonplussed that I did not care about the historic details of the group to which I belonged.

Further Exploration into the Concepts

Important in understanding the breadth and depth of individualism and collectivism are the three constructs of *self, goals, and obligations* (Triandis 1995). The first construct, *self*, shows the priority of the particular orientation. As mentioned earlier, collectivists value the group and the individualist values the self. For example, an immigrant child calling us by the title "Teacher" rather than by name does not indicate that the student does not know or care about us; she is honoring our affiliation with the group (which has a great deal more honor than is common here in the United States). Individualistic teachers tend to chafe at this nomenclature, since in the United States we try to think of particular identities, not group. The second construct is *goals*. In collectivistic cultures, the group defines goals which members adopt as their own; the group goal takes precedence should any tension arise between the individual's and group's wishes. In individualistic cultures, not only does the individual set his own goals, but he will find ways of accomplishing his preferred goal, despite the opposition. Within the classroom, this may be seen when a student from a collectivistic culture has difficulty in setting or deciding on personal goals for the year (as some teachers ask their students to do) or even in deciding what topic to write about. They are accustomed to being told what the group is to do. And finally, the third construct is *obligation*. Where the group sets the goals, the members carry out their duties as a matter of course; everyone assumes that each person will work for the common good and fulfill obligations not only to the group as a whole, but also to others within the group. The understanding is that all work together until the work is finished; the group benefits from the contribution of each member. In individualistic cultures, the individual decides what to do based on how much benefit will be derived from fulfilling that duty. Often, clear lines are drawn around each person's responsibility; obligation is to her own goals. For example, in my experience, students from collectivistic cultures are far more apt to help within the classroom—cleaning up or other classroom duties— than are students from individualistic cultures. This occurs not just in elementary or secondary schools, but at the graduate level as well.

Let me reiterate that we are talking about general tendencies within a culture: Not all collectivistic or individualistic cultures will value or behave in the same ways from person to person or from situation to situation. Indeed, both of these tendencies exist within each individual as well. Additionally, this orientation is not something we think about very often, at least not until we come in contact with a different perspective. We do not go around introducing ourselves as a "collectivist" or an "individualist." In fact, I smiled when a student told me that in his upbringing his parents did not know about these two different orientations, as if they might have made a conscious choice. That is the point. We are brought up in accordance with the values of our parents and grandparents and generations beyond them. We are socialized, unwittingly and generally, toward one or the other orientation. However, knowing about these different orientations can help us understand different behaviors in the classrooms of children who come from other cultural backgrounds. We must remember, however, not to pigeonhole a student with an "Aha! You are from a collectivistic culture, therefore you will probably prefer working in a group." That would be blatant stereotyping. We can observe the student in many different situations or, where possible, ask his preference.

Values that Influence Child Rearing

Since the family is the primary socializer, knowing some of the prevailing assumptions is useful. Figure 2–1 by Jaime Wurzel illustrates important aspects of family life, each on a scale. Families are formed (subconsciously, usually) around a series of values; they can land anywhere on the scale for each feature. They may be oriented, for example, more toward the nuclear rather than the extended family, and then be more adult- than child-centered. "Right" and "wrong" do not exist here. Cultures or families or individuals might have a zigzag profile, though ordinarily most will stay closer to one end of the scale than the other. Analyzing the categories can help us understand a family's (and hence the student's) perspective.

Figure 2–1

Family Orientations and Child Rearing Values (Wurzel)

Family Structure	Nuclear ◄——————————————► Extended *What is the categorization of a family?*
Family Orientation	Democratic ◄——————————————► Hierarchical *How is authority categorized?* *How is power structured within the family?*
Role Orientation	Open ◄——————————————► Fixed *How are age and sex categorized within the family system?*
Activity Orientation	Child Centered ◄——————————————► Adult Centered *Are activities centered around children or adults?*
Control Orientation	Indulgence ◄——————————————► Discipline *What are the tools used to reinforce good or bad behavior?* Reasoning ◄——————————————► Physical / Verbal Positive Reinforcement ◄——► Negative Reinforcement
Personality Orientation	Independent ◄——————————————► Dependent *Is separation subtly or directly encouraged?* Assertive ◄——————————————► Compliant *What kind of individual behaviors are directly or indirectly reinforced?* *What is the value categorization of childhood?*
Relational Orientation	Competitive ◄——————————————► Cooperative *What interactional behaviors are reinforced by the family structure?*
Cognitive Orientation	Analytical ◄——————————————► Global *What cognitive behaviors are reinforced?*

FAMILY STRUCTURES

In collectivistic cultures, the extended family is the norm; often the family lives with other relatives—if not in the same household, at least very nearby. Though not identified as such, *inter*dependence is encouraged at all ages. Parents are not the only ones responsible for the upbringing and socialization of the child. Strong ties of loyalty to group members bind them in a way that seems unusual to individualistically-minded people. Many of my graduate students from an individualistic culture who are married to people from a collectivistic background have complained about the amount of entertaining they are expected to do for kith and kin visiting from "the homeland." The graduate students consider these people to be only tangentially connected to their spouses and feel that the relationship is being exploited. Indeed, more than once, I have found myself in the position of entertaining (i.e., providing housing, food, and activities) the friend of a collectivistic friend for extended periods of time. In no way is this considered exploitation; such hospitality would be expected of any member of the in-group and is reciprocated bountifully when the visit is reversed. The impact of family orientations can be felt in the classroom. I remember, early in my career as an ESOL teacher, trying to get a kindergartner to list his brothers in an "All About Me" booklet. He said he had five, while according to school records, he had two. I worked hard trying to narrow the count down to what I knew was "real." He was adamant that he had five. Only many years later did I learn that cousins lived in town who were regularly at his home; they were part of the group to whom he felt tied, and thereby he considered his brothers.

In individualistic cultures, the family orientation is usually more nuclear. Family members are often scattered across the country or the globe since individual needs and preferences take precedence over the family and the job market may supply a good opportunity at the other end of the country.

FAMILY ORIENTATIONS

In collectivitistic cultures, authority in the family and the community is vertical and hierarchical. In many traditional families (though not all), the father has the responsibility to determine the direction of the family, to give necessary permissions, and to be the "public face and voice" of the family. Author Sattareh Farman Farmaian describes her father in the early twentieth century. His noble birth meant a slightly larger household than usual: "In [my childhood] my father watched over the welfare of more than a thousand people whose very survival depended entirely on him: wives, children, countless paid servants, secretaries, craftsmen, and laborers, as well as many faithful elderly retainers and old soldiers who had served him in the past. For the shelter and protection of all these people, as well as of their families, he alone was responsible" (Farman Farmaian 1992, 5). While some of these traditional ways are changing, strong belief in authoritarianism, benevolent or absolute, still rules. This attitude contrasts remarkably with the pervasive distrust of power and authority of the contemporary, egalitarian United States' culture. One of the legacies of the Vietnam era is the tendency to shrink away from the exercise of authority in families and classrooms.

We see the tension between an individualistic teacher and a collectivistic student in a number of different ways. First, for the collectivistic student, we teachers are included in the hierarchy of authority. When I was teaching in a middle and high school in Turkey in the early 1960s, one of the most difficult concepts for new, U.S.-trained, Anglo-American teachers was the teacher-student relationship. Many of these new teachers approached the profession with the then-current, more relaxed attitude (similar, said one, to a camp counselor). This informal attitude caused a lot of bewilderment for the Turkish students and, therefore, discipline problems for the teachers. Students coming from some collectivistic backgrounds will have difficulty adjusting to the more casual teacher image. While some cultures (e.g., Hispanic) look for a warm (though not "a buddy") relationship with the teacher in elementary schools, others (e.g., Chinese) are accustomed to a more authoritarian relationship. In comparing United States' and Russian schools, a Russian fifth-grader commented, "[In the United States,] you don't have to address a teacher as if he is your commanding officer" (Clayton 1996, 92). The dependence on authority may mean that the student will need more direction than we are accustomed to giving. On the flipside, however, the conferred authority, if used effectively, may mean fewer problems with boisterous students.

Second, as researchers Ronald Gallimore and others found in Oahu, the teacher's wish for negotiation with the student (about a paper, a project, or behavior) may further confound the student. In Oahu homes, the young person was not allowed to negotiate with the adult authority figure; decisions of authority were accepted without argument. Hence, a student from a similar background may see the attempt at negotiation as the mark of a teacher with weak authority (Gallimore et al. 1974). The student may expect a more definitive, authoritative stance.

ROLE ORIENTATIONS

Age and sex roles within the family are fairly rigid in collectivistic cultures; however, the roles of the parents and children in individualistic cultures are apt to be more flexible, particularly in recent years. Many immigrant children are accustomed to having more "adult" responsibilities since in their countries they do not have the inclination or economic wealth to support the luxury of "childhood." Children take care of younger siblings, take public transportation alone to activities, and run errands for parents at the grocery store. These capabilities are somewhat reminiscent of an earlier time in the United States, showing how cultures change over the years. As elementary students, collectivistic children may flourish when given greater responsibilities than are typically given to English Language Learners (ELLs). Since gender roles tend to be more fixed than fluid, immigrant students may have more hesitation working one-on-one with an opposite-sex student than dominant-culture students do.

ACTIVITY ORIENTATION

Within collectivistic cultures, activity generally revolves around the whole family, instead of separate activities for the children. Whether it be a walk around the neighborhood or day trip to visit relatives, parents set the agenda and the children participate along with the adults in the same agenda. In schools, these expectations from home might limit the student's participation in all the extracurricular activities that occupy the time of of today's young people. It might also mean that family plans outrank soccer practices. The modern-day, Anglo-American family is becoming much more child-oriented than in previous decades, for a number of reasons. The common complaint of the suburban mother today is having to arrange for, or be, a taxi for her children as they get transported from one activity to another, every day of the week. For many dominant-culture families, life revolves around children's extracurricular schedules—including the tension-producing scheduling of practices that take place Friday evenings or Sunday mornings, making parents decide whether sports or religion is more important for their children's development.

CONTROL ORIENTATION

The continuum for reinforcing good and bad behavior reflects cultural values as well. Many collectivistic cultures (though certainly not all) have not inherited or adopted the European Enlightenment's emphasis on logic, so are not as likely to reason with a young child as many (especially modern, Anglo-American) parents do. Conversely, in many different cultures or even pockets within the same culture, physical discipline continues to be acceptable. Though unacceptable to us, we must acknowledge that others assume it's an acceptable way to teach values. However, physical discipline must stay within reasonable limits for correcting behavior. The jump to severe and abusive treatment is not far and cannot be tolerated. As teachers we need to be careful not to jump to conclusions about what we might consider abusive treatment by the family since, for example, some forms of coining—a health treatment—end up with red marks on the body. Another control tool in the family is the use of positive or negative reinforcement. Praise is used often in many Anglo-American families; parents will distract toddlers rather than say "No!" In many other cultures, parents are more quick to point out imperfections; children are compared to a model to emulate and are shown or told how they fall short, how they can improve. Constant pressure to do better is the norm. In fact, for Arabs, "Children are taught that conformity with an acceptable social image is the most important reason for modifying behavior" (Nydell 1996, 94). In the classroom, students of other cultures may look for a succinct verbal directive as to how they are to change their behavior; they may need more guidance as to how they can improve.

PERSONALITY ORIENTATION

In collectivistic cultures, with the emphasis on the group, children grow up dependent on their parents and usually more compliant rather than assertive. Young adults, no longer in school, often live at home until marriage, and even after that. To be an autonomous individual or family is not the mark of success. Behaviors nurtured from birth include subservience to elders, and group- rather than individual-mindedness. In individualistic cultures, assertive behavior is usually reinforced in the process of socialization. For example, in the Anglo-American culture of the United States, children are encouraged to initiate conversations with their elders (instead of waiting to be addressed) and are usually consulted as to their preferences. Furthermore, "Don't be a doormat!" or "Stand up for your rights!" convey parental expectations for their children's behavior with their peers.

RELATIONAL ORIENTATION

Collectivistic cultures thus favor cooperation rather than competition. Harmony within the group is important and cooperation brings that about more than competition. In more individualistic societies, children tend to be socialized to be competitive rather than cooperative. The competitive culture of the United States thrives on descriptions with superlative adjectives: the biggest or best or longest or highest or most expensive. In the last decade, however, we teachers in dominant-culture schools in the United States have been using much more cooperative learning because we are finding that learning is enhanced when students collaborate. Additionally, an economic factor has also supported this trend: business and industry are looking for people with teamwork skills. Some of us also hope that this increased collaboration among students will help alleviate the increasing sense of entitlement in this country among people who feel that their own, particular needs are paramount.

COGNITIVE ORIENTATION

The final aspect of Figure 2–1 is the spread of cognitive orientations. This will be discussed more fully Chapter 4, Learning Styles. However, the language involved in everyday behaviors at home is part of the socialization process and reinforces particular learning orientations in children. The types of questions asked, the modeling of story telling, and everyday types of interactions, for example, all contribute to the shaping of a learning orientation (not to be confused with cognitive abilities).

LET ME REITERATE THAT NO CULTURE OR FAMILY OR PERSON IS strictly at one end of the continuum or the other; both collectivistic and individualistic orientations are present, though one usually predominates. The dominant culture may be at one end of the spectrum; minority cultures (family or community) may continue to practice traditions at the other end. Or, with increasing exposure to the dominant culture, they may have moved closer to the dominant culture than their ancestors' position. Age (we tend to have more collectivistic tendencies as babies and as senior citizens), affluence, rural/urban settings, and exposure to mass media are all factors in determining our responses to life situations. While sometimes we change for particular instances, at other times, we gradually shift across the entire paradigm. Many collectivistic cultures are finding more individualistic tendencies in their populations as the world shrinks and globalization prevails; many individualistic families and institutions are choosing to incorporate more collectivistic practices due to what they perceive as unhealthy effects of extreme individualism.

TRY THIS!

Farman Farmaian describes her childhood in Iran in the 1920s and 1930s: "We Iranians, who value the family above all else and spend our whole lives within its hot, protective walls, know that from it we derive our very being, our deepest and most meaningful sense of self. Through it we define who we are, to the world and to ourselves. As long as the family is intact, secure, and complete, we know that we are somebody instead of nobody" (Farman Farmaian 1992, 93). Use this description to generate a discussion in class about the importance of family in the lives of the students. How does her statement differ from the dominant culture of the United States? How do the students place themselves across a continuum of the importance of family? Would they give up personal goals for the benefit of the family? Would they be willing to move far away from their parents and siblings? When are times that they are fairly individualistic or fairly collectivistic or are they pretty consistent?

Collectivism and Individualism in the Classroom

As a secondary socializer, schools play an important role in socializing children to be effective in their culture. The primary difference between schools in collectivistic or individualistic cultures is that in a collectivist society, the goals or values of the school and family are very closely allied; the parents expect the help of schools in the moral as well as the academic instruction of their children. In research with the parents of some of my elementary students, Chinese parents from Hong Kong felt that the primary goal of kindergarten should be discipline—an inner "discipline that will help my daughter resist bad influences." The father felt that since he was home only two days of the week and the child went to school five days a week, the school's role in achieving this inner strength was extremely important. He felt that the freedom for the student to speak up in class and say what she thought was a lack of discipline. In addition, he wondered if we could warn parents about "bad" children in the classroom so that families could keep their children away from such influences. An Iranian father likened a student to a frog living half his life in the water and half his life on the land, and therefore both environments (school and family) had the responsibility to shape and nurture the student.

Although some Anglo-American teachers and parents might puzzle at the above comments, schools do communicate the values of the predominant culture. Warning families about troubled children would not occur in classrooms in the United States. However, we do pass on our values within our classrooms; our attitudes and actions often convey the values of the society of which we are products. In the Anglo-American culture, the importance of independence, self-reliance, and individualism is conveyed in every corner of the classroom. Some of the ways will be explored more fully in Chapter Eight, Classroom Culture. However, here, looking at some processes that occur in the classroom will help delineate more clearly some of the junctures where collectivistically nurtured children may struggle in our individualistically oriented classrooms, or where, as teachers, we may experience some attendant problems.

In the following comments, I want to convey where some exchanges or expectations may be problematic. I am not suggesting that we carry the total burden of negotiation in the classroom; the students need to do their share. However, some of this information may assist our efforts to be compassionate teachers promoting understanding. If we understand the origin of the behavior, it will help in two inseparable ways: One is that we may be less judgmental in our response to the behavior; the other is that we will realize how to best help the student become acquainted with the ways of the majority culture—a crucial step in helping an immigrant child. Using some of the categories mentioned by Triandis (1995), I see the following applications to classroom situations:

DECISION MAKING

Because dependence is valued and expected, collectivistic children may not be accustomed to making decisions on their own. They generally receive a great deal of guidance and consultation. This issue may arise in any number of situations where decisions are expected, be it a book from the library, the choice of a work-partner, or the lunch menu. A Brazilian parent complained that her daughter had not done well in decision-making early in her year in the United States; she had made some poor choices since she was not used to making decisions. It had been a difficult adjustment, but she had learned.

AGENCY

Because of this dependence on elders, collectivistic students *may* also not be as assertive on their own behalf; they may expect the adults in authority to settle problems that come up (whereas in the Anglo-American culture, the students may be told to "settle the issue among yourselves"). The collectivistic student has been socialized to be sensitive to relationships within a group and therefore to be less assertive (or even conscious) about his feelings. For collectivistic parents, the ideal child is one who obeys what she is told to do. Indeed, in many collectivistic cultures, even adults expect to receive verbal reminders, which to them indicate caring and connectedness between people, not nagging (a more individualistic interpretation).

PRAISE

Some students from collectivistic cultures may feel uncomfortable with public praise. Since they are conditioned to be part of a group, this type of credit singles them out. In a recent study, Chinese, Japanese, and Brazilian parents and teachers varied in their reactions to their children being singled out. A Chinese teacher commented: "In China, it is very different. We put [tests, homework, classwork] up in 1,2,3, . . . order. If you are the best, you are on top. If you are on the bottom, that is the way it is. We don't think it will make the person feel bad. It is because the top person studied hard. That is why some parents keep asking classroom teachers what standing their child is." Japanese and Brazilian parents were more on the side of shunning public praise, feeling that their children would stand out from the group (Clayton n. d.). The only way to know for sure is to ask the child or the parents about their attitude or watch for body language toward this tactic of public praise.

DISAPPROVAL

In many collectivistic cultures, where group consciousness is more significant than in individualistic cultures, shame is used as a strategy for expressing disapproval. "What will others think? How could you do this to your family's honor?" are common responses to the inappropriate behavior in a collectivistic culture. Strong ties to the group make shame a tool of displeasure. That means that children are socialized to respond to social criticism, not self-criticism. The person's perception or apprehension of group disapproval directs behavior. To bring shame in any way, large or small, to the family name is a great tragedy. In that way, children are taught to think more highly of others' opinions of them than to cultivate their ability to self-judge (positively or negatively). Students may be reluctant to volunteer answers in class for fear of bringing shame to the family name if their response is incorrect. Since the approval that is sought is that of adults, the students may also have trouble in judging a peer's work, feeling that they do not have the authority to do so.

Guilt is more common in individualistic cultures. Guilt emanates from self-judgment and self-criticism. It may involve another person, but the individual's perception of herself, not her relation to the larger group, usually shapes guilt. Instead of "What will others think?" the question is more likely to be, "What will I think about this, how will I feel?"

SUPERVISION

Because of the prevalence of adults in and around children in a collectivistic culture, the assumption is that children will be closely supervised at all times. Collective activities or games are encouraged rather than individual ones; children are not left alone to play or to study. If parents allow their children to play at another's home, many will want to accompany the child. Most parents from collectivistic cultures want to help with their children's homework at night. The amount they can help depends, among other considerations, on their literacy in English. Many have not yet achieved this skill and must repeatedly face the growing separation of their children from the family's world. Another difficult adjustment for immigrant parents (who do or don't know English) is the practice of their elementary-age children not bringing textbooks home so that the parents can know what is being studied.

SELF-PERCEPTION

From my experience, the emphasis on individualism in the dominant-culture schools in the United States can be seen as early as kindergarten, or earlier, where students are assigned the project of making a booklet, "All About Me." This whole booklet is about the individual's preferences (*my* favorite color, activity, food, etc.). While there may be information about siblings, grand-parents, or parents, that information is tangential to the major thrust of the book, which is the author. A collectivistic child might miss questions about relationships to others, or might not be as ready to boldly state his own pref-erences. A parent from a collectivistic background might ask about the ob-ligations or duties that the child might have toward other members of the family or community or nation.

Japanese graduate students have told me that in Japan (a predominantly, though not exclusively, collectivistic society), no equivalent term exists for "I." A variety of different words are used to refer to the self, words that have to do with the speaker's gender, age, and status within the group. Another example of the importance of the group, this linguistic difference may mean that the newcomer does not have the sense of self that Anglo-American teachers may be accustomed to in individualistic students. The collectivistic students' identities are bound up with that of a group, not themselves.

SOCIAL RELATIONS

Professor Kağıtçıbaşı reports that Japanese mothers, similar to American and Israeli mothers, value independence in their children. However, for the Japanese mothers, independence means that the children are capable of in-teracting with other children in sensitive and trusting ways (Kağıtçıbaşı 1996). What a great example of the same word having different meanings for peo-ple from different cultural backgrounds! Children from collectivistic cultures are accustomed to much more parental control than are children in individ-ualistic cultures. They interpret it as a demonstration of love and may, in-deed, miss it if removed. Transferring that authority image to us, the student from a collectivistic culture may feel a lack of caring if we allow the student the usual (from an individualist's perspective) freedom to work at her own pace or to choose for himself the order in which to accomplish classroom tasks. The more direction we can give early in the year, the easier it will be for the student to settle into the learning process. Many collectivistic stu-dents, transferring their group-related tendencies, also look to us for a closer relationship than individualistic students usually do.

PRIVACY

Great fluidity and connection within the collectivistic group means little, if any, sense of privacy. This has far-ranging implications: Socially, without meaning to be intrusive, a student may think it acceptable to read another student's essay or listen to a private conversation we may be having. A pleas-ant comment that this conversation is just with this person and that we will have a chat with the "intruder" in a short while (about any topic) should help fill the need to be included and, at the same time, help the student learn the ways of the majority culture.

Another implication involves physical property, which may be understood to be largely communal property. This may apply to toys of the very young, or to using others' books or belongings without asking the owner first. An explanation (and probably constant reminders) that in this culture we need first to ask permission before using others' possessions will help the student learn what is expected.

Finally, issues of privacy have implications for intellectual property: If something is published, many cultures feel that it then belongs in the public domain. Giving credit to the original author is not considered necessary. The exposure of "pirated" textbooks, compact discs, and software, particularly in China, has aggravated tensions between our two countries. To "own thoughts" sounds as absurd to them as their seemingly libertine acts do to us. Understandably then, many newcomers approach this whole topic from a very different perspective. *All* students (even at the university level) need instruction, clarification, or at least reminders before a major project that will involve research into published materials.

RESPONSIBILITY

Students coming from collectivistic backgrounds have always had the group—family or beyond—to relate to. This group reliance applies to getting things done, taking blame for inappropriate behavior, and learning new tasks. It may be quite a jolt to have to work alone, to be singly responsible for the final product, or, for examaple, to be left alone to learn a computer program.

Triandis makes the distinction, "Collectivists tend to explain failure by lack of effort, and individualists by task difficulty or bad luck" (Triandis 1995, 157). This comment reminds me of a childstudy with an Indian parent who insisted that his daughter simply needed to work harder in order to do better, while her classroom teacher felt that she needed extra help from the Resource Room, where a program could be modified to fit her particular needs. The stigma of being "learning disabled" (bad luck, individualists would claim) and what that label would mean in the Indian culture fueled the parent's insistence that he would personally see to it that his daughter worked harder. Nothing would persuade him to the contrary.

MORALITY

For collectivists, because the cohesion of the group is paramount, morality is behavior that will support that solidarity. Specific rules, rather than abstract principles, define morality (Triandis 1995). Not telling the truth has a different complexion in collectivistic cultures, especially if it will save face or maintain a relationship. To break the harmony or jeopardize a relationship, particularly in an in-group, is as much an anathema to collectivists as misrepresentation is to individualists. Individualists tend to opt for "honesty at all times," though as anyone knows, white lies also creep into those interactions as well. Who has not said, "Oh, you look great," in order to boost a friend's morale, or expanded the truth to get out of a social invitation? Generally, however, since connections to others are not as crucial to identity, individualists feel that honesty is the best policy at all times; some choose it over maintaining a relationship. Maintaining that relationship is what compels students from collectivistic backgrounds to share their test answers with friends who need their help. Not to share information is to reject and jeopardize the connection, the strong web of friendship. For individualists, lying is seen as breaking a principle, not a relationship, and hence, a major offense.

IN ALL OF THESE SITUATIONS, THE STUDENT'S BEHAVIOR, SO baffling and perhaps even challenging to our authority, may not be what it seems. The act or attitude arises not from malice but from her own set of cultural practices. Because the student has been socialized to assume these practices are the norm, she needs to be shown what the normative behavior is for the new environment. However, disparaging the student's background usually produces more resistance than compliance from the student. An acknowledgment that some rules are followed at home and other rules prevail in school and in the dominant society will help the student grasp the benefits of being bicultural.

Color Blindness

Many people (teachers among them) comment that children all laugh, they all cry, they all hurt. Wouldn't just loving them all, as an eminent educator professed to doing thirty years ago, be the answer to the diversity in our classrooms today? Without minimizing or disparaging the inordinate amount of love needed by teachers (and children) these days, I would suggest that not only is it a difficult ideal to reach, but also the effort is based on a false foundation. Human emotions are pretty much the same; children do all laugh, cry, and hurt; but the causes of those emotions can differ from culture to culture. How they were socialized will determine how they will react to certain situations. They may have been taught not to show emotions, to defer to authority, or to approach education in a very serious manner. I feel strongly that to be "colorblind" (feeling that white/black/tan, we are all the same) is to do a disservice to the student. Colorblindness presumes that all

JOURNAL TIME

Many people of the dominant culture, particularly, don't agree with the previous perspective. They feel that all students should be treated the same; that cultural differences should be minimized in order to achieve harmony. How do you feel about taking the backgrounds of your students seriously? Do you see harm in doing so? Do you see gain? Are there parameters you would impose on how much influence backgrounds should have? What kind of balance, if any, would you want?

children have come from the same background with the same assumptions and privileges, as well as skills and needs, that they have the same understanding of the ground rules of the dominant culture. Being colorblind denies the very identity of people who are not brought up the same way as we were; it taps into our subconscious ethnocentrism. Chaos need not reign in the classroom as we try to affirm the many different cultures swirling around us. As a student in one of my graduate classes pointed out from her experience, "Some teachers really allow you to have both cultures; they teach you the dominant one but they don't denigrate the one you come from."

Reflections on Rosa

Let us return to the problem Rosa presented at the beginning of the chapter. It could be that Rosa's mother does not care about education, but highly unlikely, given the sacrifices the parents made to come to the United States. More likely her cultural priority (as well as an economic one) assigns Rosa's primary obligation to her family, not to her individual ambition (i.e., even education). These cultural priorities change from one collectivistic culture to another: For example, for Koreans, education is a top priority. Rosa's situation would be rare in a Korean family. Rosa's teacher is confronted by two major issues here: One is the difference in priorities and how to address that; the other is the use of a child as a translator. Criticizing the mother about negligence of her daughter's education will not accomplish a long-term change. We do not easily give up values to which we have been socialized, particularly if attempted by external agents. Primary socialization has a very strong hold on one's development; one changes more profoundly as the result of personal choice. Solutions that are compatible with the priorities of the immigrants will yield more results than insisting upon the Anglo-American priority. Helping the mother access possible community resources (ideally of her own culture) will honor her collectivistic assumptions.

Communicating with the mother about her reasons for keeping Rosa out of school, about the benefits of consistent attendance and the legal ramifications of not doing so, and then showing her possible ways to achieve that goal can pave the way for a win/win solution.

The second issue is the use of the student as translator for even such informal meetings. Within this particular issue loom two factors: first, the cognitive act of translation, and second, the relationships within the family structure. Translation is more than just a linguistic exercise. Even if it were just that, the possibility exists that the student may not have enough English vocabulary to completely understand or say what the parent or teacher wants. More importantly, thoughts are not translated word for word. Some concepts or words do not exist in other languages: For example, the concept of privacy does not exist in Arabic. It takes a great deal of knowledge of a language to translate the nuances and the true meanings that are being expressed by either adult participant. It also takes a great deal of maturity on the part of the student to talk about himself in an objective way in a conversation between his parent and his teacher. He is put in an untenable position between them. Second, being the translator changes Rosa's role within the family. Coming from a collectivistic culture, Rosa is in a hierarchical relationship with her parents. The hierarchical lines of authority and dependence shift with this act. If the child translates—and many do for various parental appointments—the parent becomes dependent on the child instead of vice versa. This can increase conflict within the family at a time when all energies should be devoted to issues more important than role reversals. If at all possible, an adult translator would be better to do this adult job, even if the bilingual adult is not within the school system, but a friend of the family or a volunteer from the community.

Socialization runs so deeply and quietly that we tend to think that everyone else flows in the same current we do. As teachers we need to see beyond the banks of our own experience and point the way for our immigrant students to effectively navigate two or more streams.

Chapter Three

Points of View: Values

A single bamboo pole does not make a raft.

—Chinese proverb

I asked Sayora's mother to come to see me the other day about her daughter's adjustment to the U.S. and to school. I was pleased to be able to tell her how well Sayora is doing. What was totally unexpected was the mother's reluctant confession about the problem Sayora is having with her classmate who lives in the apartment above them. The girl, who is Anglo-American, has been taunting Sayora in class and out. I told the mother that I would get the two girls together to talk it out, but the mother did not want her daughter involved in the discussion.

—(Ed, a fourth-grade teacher)

*E*d was clearly frustrated by the turn of events. Though fairly apprehensive, Sayora had been making progress in acclimating to his class. The people of Afghanistan had become much more real to him through her haunting eyes and tentative nature. Refusing to stereotype any culture, but particularly all

Afghanis after September 11, he resolved to better understand her background. He found himself scanning the newspaper more often for any bits of news about her people and digging for books at the library to learn her country's history. In class, he tried to involve her as best he could and asked some girls to help her out in the cafeteria and at recess. He could see it was a lonely struggle she had to endure, but he felt that she was coming along. It was a shock, then, when Sayora's mother very hesitantly shared this problem with him and resisted her daughter's involvement in the projected conversation. She couldn't seem to tell him why she did not want her daughter in the mediation; it was obvious that she was uncomfortable with it. Naturally, he was baffled at her obstructing his attempts to resolve the issue.

DEEP-ROOTED BELIEFS BY WHICH WE LIVE CREATE OUR VALUE systems. These preferred principles guide and organize our lives. Passed on through the generations, we usually accept, sometimes modify, and sometimes rebel at the values taught by our families. As we saw in Chapter Two, values are transmitted within families as soon as children are born. Parents and grandparents socialize children intentionally as well as incidentally to important beliefs, expectations, and assumptions.

Recently, the increasing diversity in our country has shown the need for a new emphasis on respecting people with values different from our own. The school's role in teaching values has recently come into sharp focus in the United States. In a school system in which I did research in 1992, each school had devised, with the help of teachers, parents, and administration, a list of "core values" for the school. As a principal of an elementary school said, "These are values that the students should take with them when they leave this school; that they should absolutely hold on to; that would be quickly identifiable to a stranger coming into the school" (Clayton 1996, 13). One of the three main components was "respect for others and the celebration of diversity," which the school community determined as necessary in the student population. Schools have taken on not only the transmission of the values of the dominant culture but also the transformation of xenophobic attitudes.

In a February 15, 1998, Sunday *Boston Globe* article on "Values 101," Brian MacQuarrie stated that private schools had started shifting more than 15 years previously to more emphasis on moral and ethical development, in addition to academic goals. The article quotes Steve Clem of the National Association of Independent Schools: "This is work we've always done, but now more schools are accepting that this is work we have to do. . . . You don't just teach what the Greeks thought respect meant. You integrate that into what respect means in the classroom." Time constraints as well as additional stresses on parents in modern life were the reasons given for this increasing need. However, both administrators and parents interviewed for the article struggled with the role of the school in such issues, with some parents feeling that such discussions were invasive and some administrators feeling that there were limits to what schools could do. The issue exemplifies the tension and the dynamism of a multicultural society, where some basic tenets must prevail in society and differences must be honored in the homelife of each student and teacher.

Schools in Pluralistic Societies

The role of the school as a secondary socializer is much more clear-cut in a culture that is homogeneous rather than pluralistic. In the former, school and family are unified in their expectations and in the values of the society; generally the values of school and home do not necessitate a "shift away" and a "shift back" between them. However, in pluralistic cultures, morality may be a more complex issue and navigation around differences of opinions, trickier. In a culture as pluralistic as the United States, learning to respect those with whom we differ is even more imperative. The need to transform values in response to changing times falls on all institutions within the culture: the family, schools, religious organizations, and community groups. The transformation is not to a particular perspective, but to a generic attitude of civility; "respect" does not mean that we *accept* the values of others as our own, but that we acknowledge their existence and importance to others. Sitting at the dining room table to eat with my husband and our guests may be right and true for me; for my friend from Sri Lanka, serving her husband and guests but eating in the kitchen may be the right way for her. To understand that belief when we visit her home, however uncomfortable it may make me feel, is to show respect for her values. Lack of understanding and respect leads quickly to stereotyping. The ethnic profiling and hate crimes targeting anyone who looked like a Middle Easterner subsequent to the September 11 attacks in the United States make such a transformation toward greater respect all the more urgent.

Differences with people who do not share our beliefs, as Ed experienced with Sayora's mother, can be quite a jolt. They can also be a moment of revelation if we can get away from the Right/Wrong seesaw and quell our natural defensiveness long enough to consider a different perspective. Throughout the world people approach life in a variety of ways. How they do that is based on their values, on what they judge to be good or bad, right or wrong. Values differ not only from culture to culture but even from person to person within the same culture, due to socialization and context. While we say that we believe in honesty, or decency, or fairness, these concepts may have different meanings to people shaped by their different contexts. And due to our socialization, values are accepted without questioning. People think of values as "the ways things naturally are." Values are *not* behaviors, but the foundation (rules and norms) from which behavior emerges and by which it is judged. A friend who teaches English to adult immigrants in New York City said to me in 1999: "I always teach something about culture in my classes. For example, I teach about subway culture. I get so upset when I am on the subway in New York City. It is objectively good to give your seat to a pregnant woman or a man with a cane. It is objective. Why don't people do that? My students learn they must." This friend's "objective" truth clashes with a prevalent emphasis in New York City as well as much of the United States on personal comfort or an infinite sense of equity. If people are equal, or my comfort is as important as another's, then why should I give up my seat? Furthermore, some argue that if they give an older person their seat, they are often met with a withering "No, thank you." (The emphasis on youth in the culture of the United States trumps again.) Since we have absorbed assumptions of behavior from the cradle on, the possibility that someone thinks differently may not enter our minds. In the New York City subway, equality seems to rank over deference more than my friend would like.

Exploring Proverbs

One way to find out about a culture's values is to look at its proverbs, the wisdom of the ages, which grow out of the historic, social, ethical, and religious essence of a culture. Generally regarded as pithy sayings, they encapsulate a well-known truth. "Don't count your chickens until they are hatched"; "You've made your bed, now sleep in it." As cultures change over the years, sometimes a proverb is considered antiquated: For example, "Little children should be seen and not heard" meant more to the 1950s patriarchal Anglo-American families than today; likewise "A penny saved is a penny earned" reflected Puritan frugality. Finally, not only do values and proverbs change, but also the actual importance of proverbs differs from culture to culture: Those for whom the past is important tend to use proverbs more freely in their speech and writing.

Proverbs point to similarities across the cultures, as in "Kind words would entice even a serpent out of its hole" (Turkey) and "You can attract more bees with honey than vinegar" (USA), as well as to contrasts as in "Too

> ## TRY THIS!
>
>
>
> A two-step activity: Ask students to gather proverbs from family members or other adults. Make a list in class and, in small groups or large, identify the value in each one. Discuss the meaning of each in the current times. The second step, for an older group, involves students bringing to class proverbs from a culture different from their own. In small groups they can explore the unusual (to them) images used (e.g., holding back a lion, as in the above proverb), talk about the value that the proverb expresses, and see if it is a different value or the same value expressed differently (in terms more meaningful to that particular culture). Share the results with the class.

many cooks spoil the broth," (originally England) and "Helping each other, even boys can hold back a lion" (Ethiopia). One can look for specific lessons that are taught in different ways. For example, Professor Vivian Zanger points out, "The importance of being cautious is communicated in seven different ways by the following proverbs: 'Turn the tongue seven times, then speak' (French); 'Have an umbrella before getting wet' (Japanese); 'Before you drink the soup, blow on it' (Arabic); 'First weigh [the consequences], then dare' (German); 'If you don't know the ford, don't cross the stream' (Russian); 'Be careful bending your head—you may break it' (Italian); 'Look before you leap' (English)"(Zanger 1985, 31).

A Helpful Framework

While investigating proverbs can be an enjoyable as well as educational way of learning about the values of cultures, it does not provide a very systematic way of understanding a basic framework for that culture. Looking at the concept of value orientations offers insights into our own and others' assumptions and conduct.

Believing that people have convictions about what is "best, right, or true," anthropologist Florence Kluckhohn developed a cognitive framework for value orientations and their variations in the 1950s (Kluckhohn and Strodtbeck 1961, 12). Her paradigm continues to have value to this day, since it examines the deepest levels of values. It provides a window on how different cultures perceive issues common to all humanity, which, in turn, demonstrates that no one solution is better than another, but simply a different approach. It also gives an opportunity to see how variations within the orientations relate to each other and to the whole. If we have a basic understanding of the range of those value orientations, we are better prepared not to make inferences about a person's response to a situation. Knowing the types of patterns that exist will help us keep from interpreting issues in light of our own cultural values. Though the framework does not encompass all values or all variations that could be found within a culture, it provides a systematic look at major orientations and some clear differences that can exist.

WHAT ARE VALUE ORIENTATIONS?

Consider this description of Iran in 1915, where a fundamental attitude of fate ruled some people's lives: "The idea of a community's organizing in such a way to save itself from disaster was a revolutionary concept in Iran, where help only came by chance to people in trouble, either through alms or the kindness of some rich protector" (Farman Farmaian 1992, 39). The account exemplifies a basic orientation to life. Kluckhohn and Strodtbeck categorized the values which determine our approach to life into five orientations and three variations within each orientation. Every society develops values in order to have internal coherence, to guide actions, and to shape attitudes. These principles result from the interaction of cognitive and affective elements and our innate desire to make sense of our lives (Kluckhohn and Strodtbeck 1961). In other words, not just the mind or the heart but also an internal drive for meaning within each person combine to shape these values that determine how to respond to everyday situations. For example, do you feel anxious if you are not keeping busy and getting a lot done, or do you prefer having time to visit friends, read, or play an instrument? Your response could indicate your basic attitude toward what gives meaning to life, toward the ultimate reason we are on this planet. Our values are the foundations of our beliefs about how life should be lived. Generally a dominant orientation exists within a cultural group. Variations of the orientation are shaped not only by different contexts within or across cultures but also by our own particular preferences or idiosyncrasies. For example, despite the fact that the dominant culture in the United States expects punctuality, we probably know of people within that culture who are seldom on time; their inability to organize their life, or any number of such reasons, makes them late, even though they know the expected norm. The important concept to remember is that, as Kluckhohn and Strodtbeck point out in each chapter, the variations within each orientation are found in each culture. Where cultures differ is in the ranking of a particular value for that culture.

You may ask, "Isn't honesty a universal value?" Yes, it is, but *where* it ranks in that culture's hierarchy of values defines its salience. Some societies may place more importance on other values, such as avoidance of confrontation, deference to authority, or loyalty to family and friends. Describing a conversation between an aunt and niece about a devious secret, writer Amy Tan puts it this way: "I am laughing, confused, caught in endless circles of lies. Or perhaps they are not lies but their [sisters'] own form of loyalty, a devotion beyond anything that can ever be spoken, anything that I will ever understand" (Tan 1991, 524–525).

Before we look at Kluckhohn's model, let me state some of its important assumptions. Then, in each discussion of the five different orientations, I will suggest where the dominant culture of the United States stands within the orientation. Last, we will look at how these values might apply to dominant-culture classrooms.

BASIC ASSUMPTIONS OF THE FRAMEWORK

The Kluckhohn framework is grounded in three basic assumptions: "1) There is a limited number of common human problems for which all peoples at all times must find some solution; 2) While there is variability in the solutions to all of the problems, the variety is neither limitless nor random, but within a range of possibilities; and 3) All the alternatives of all the solutions are present in all societies at all times, but are differentially preferred." Societies have a dominant profile as well as variant ones, and there is rank ordering in both profiles (Kluckhohn and Strodtbeck 1961, 10). That final assumption of the framework is very important, as it warns against assuming that cultural groups have a homogenous value system.

The model does not describe succinctly any one specific culture; instead it gives a framework for understanding the differences that may exist between cultures and within cultures. Indeed, a certain dynamism exists in the contrapuntal tension between dominant and subcultures in the United States. Even as the framework makes it clear why people may have disagreements (if they come from opposite ends of the scale), it also makes it harder to stereotype anyone. One exciting aspect of the framework is that it can be applied not only to the larger culture but also to smaller cultures, for example, to schools or businesses, by asking the same questions to find out the attitudes and values that shape the organization.

THE ORIENTATIONS

The framework asks five basic questions, each with three variations. I have used Kluckhohn's orientations and variations, italicized below, to explain the variations, then to explore the variety of values of the dominant culture of the United States. Finally, we will examine how they might appear in dominant-culture classrooms.

Human nature: What is the Character of Human Nature?

Evil (mutable or immutable): Human nature is basically evil; it has the capacity to remain as such or to change. We need to be wary of others.

Neutral or Mixture (mutable or immutable): Human nature is either neutral or both good and evil; it also has the capacity to remain the same or to change. We need to be fastidious about whom to trust.

Good (mutable or immutable): Human nature is basically good; it has the capacity to remain as such or change. At their core, people are really trustworthy.

This first orientation describes the belief people have about fundamental human nature, ranging from Evil to Good. The question of being changeable runs across all three variations in this orientation, which does not appear in the other orientations.

This orientation also introduces us to the reality of all variations within one culture. In the United States, for example, some people ascribe to the Puritan-based belief within Christianity that people are inherently evil; many believe that both good and evil exist in people, and finally, despite the September 11, 2001, attacks, many continue to affirm attitudes of optimism toward human nature. "Innocent until proven guilty" even puts this attitude into our legal system; we aim to think the best about a person until proven otherwise, though this attempt does not always prevail. People's basic goodness toward each other is often very evident in natural disasters, where folks pitch in to help each other out. Of course, most of us could name instances that do not bear out this belief, including examples of racial, ethnic, or cultural crimes. In essence, examples can support all three variations, which is the point. There is no right or wrong, just variations within the same orientation.

Additionally, differences also exist in whether people are basically set (as opposed to changeable) in their nature. If we support social programs in the United States, such as prison reform and drug rehabilitation, we believe that people are changeable (Kohls 2000). Edward Stewart and Milton Bennett, professors of psychology and of communication respectively, comment, "Perhaps no people in history have believed as firmly as Americans in the ability of education to improve the individual"(Stewart and Bennett 1991, 114). On the other hand, many in the United States believe in the death penalty because they feel the prisoner incapable of reform. On the September 2000 primary ballot in Massachusetts, a referendum question asked whether those arrested for drug possession should be put in rehabilitation with monies collected from drug-related crimes or be put in prison. Prison won. Perhaps the intended desire was punishment first and then rehabilitation; nevertheless, the possibility to change was secondary. Across cultures, people will place themselves in different variations—and indeed, may find that they change from one variation to another, depending on the context.

Person-nature: What is the Relation of [People] to Nature?

> *Subjugation to nature*: People are at the mercy of outside forces.
>
> *Harmony with nature*: People feel integrated with nature.
>
> *Mastery over nature*: People have control over most aspects of nature.

This second orientation explores the range of beliefs between dominance by outside forces and our dominance over those forces. The first variation, that of being at the mercy of outside forces, might be characterized by a taxi driver I encountered in a suburb of Istanbul, Turkey, in 1961. He precariously wove through traffic in a 30-year-old car at (I felt) an unconscionable speed, muttering a phrase in Turkish that best translates as, "Let's hope for the best." Fate, not the driver, was going to determine the outcome of the ride. The earlier description of life in Iran in 1915 also expressed this variation. The second variation in this orientation can be characterized by those living in total harmony with nature, be it the planting cycle, or Japanese architecture and flower arranging, or the deference of Indian tribes to Mother Earth, Sister Moon. Domination of nature is the core of the third variation: Bridges, space exploration, stem cell research, and the Hong Kong airport (built on a landfill) all illustrate some of the ways that people can have mastery over nature.

The prevailing attitude in the United States about a person's relationship to nature is generally that of dominance; that attitude, emerging out of the Enlightenment period, has enabled incredible feats including vaccines, space exploration, early prediction of dangerous storms, and the like. To shape our destiny, we manipulate external forces as much as possible to achieve our ends. Stewart and Bennett state, "For Americans, human beings are unique, having a quality that is absent in all other forms of life: a soul. It follows that no other forms of life in the physical world possess souls, so they are conceived of as material and mechanistic. . . . In many cultures, human beings are just one form of life differing from others only in degree" (Stewart and Bennett 1991, 113). Changing the course of rivers, cloning sheep, and discovering the human genetic make-up are further illustrations of positive results of this assumption that we can dominate and control nature. While we may long for the more simple life of our ancestors, they were, also, determined to subdue the earth, as clearly indicated by the differences between the Pilgrims' and Indian tribal attitudes. The centuries have changed, but the dominant variation remains.

Time: What is the General Attitude Toward Time?

> *Past-oriented*: People revere the past.
>
> *Present-oriented*: People feel neither the past nor the future are as important as the present.
>
> *Future-oriented*: People look to the future for their fulfillment.

The third orientation explores fundamental attitudes toward time and the course of human life. In the first variation, people focus on the way things were; they do not particularly care about change, they prefer to maintain and restore traditions. While this may be attributable to some ancient societies with ancestor worship, modern societies which have had royalty or aristocracy (e.g., Great Britain) or who have major emphasis on tradition tend to be in this classification as well (Kluckhohn and Strodtbeck 1961). This is not to say that these cultures close their minds or their borders to new technologies, but that traditions, preserving and honoring the past, play an important role. Not just the presence of royalty or aristocracy determine where this variation is met. Attitudes toward traditions can be found, for example, in some houses of worship in the United States where new forms of worship are creating nostalgia for the traditional. Elsewhere, "family traditions" or "rural traditions" or "traditional values" guide the lives of many people. Alternatively, cultures that pay little attention to what has happened in the past and also regard the future as both vague and unpredictable comprise the second variation. That prompts them to fully live in the present, without interest in reliving the past or planning for the future. Neither the past nor the future necessarily means "better" for them. And finally, the third variation focuses on the future. While the past is somewhere in the background, most energy is expended on providing for the future. Change is generally regarded as good; being "old-fashioned" is not a compliment.

In this time orientation, the dominant culture of the United States is pretty much in the *future-oriented* category. "Thinking about tomorrow" and "Tomorrow . . . is only a day away" express in song the fundamental dominant-culture belief. We save money for college when our children are still in single digit ages; we plan conferences, meetings, or vacations months and sometimes years in advance; we save for our retirement as soon as we land our first job; we strive for a better future for ourselves and our successors; we steer our children at young ages into activities that will enhance their futures. Progress and change are closely related to this futuristic view. At our core, we believe that change is good: we commonly hear, for example, "Oh, the change will do him good," or "We need a new approach to this problem." Children are taught to not be content with what is at hand but to always strive for something better. To be successful in meeting new demands required by change and progress, people must be willing to abandon not only the present but also the past.

Activity: What is the Modality of Human Activity?

> *Being*: Being is more important than doing.
> *Being-in-becoming*: Inner development fulfills the goal.
> *Doing*: Activity defines us.

The fourth orientation is not an "active/passive" dichotomy, but rather a fundamental attitude about how you express your existence. In the *Being* variation, worth is not indicated by what you do, but rather who you are. In the second variation, development is paramount: While being is more important than doing, a sense of personal growth and introspective self-development must occur to become an integrated whole (Kluckhohn and Strodtbeck 1961). Our son once asked a friend he hadn't seen in a while what she'd been up to. "Oh, evolving," she mused. The third variation stresses the importance of accomplishing tasks. Work is an end in itself; career advancement is paramount. Identity often revolves around work.

The dominant Anglo-American culture falls fairly clearly into the category of *doing*. Anglo-Americans always keep busy—even to the extent that we try to "look busy" if not totally immersed in work. An elderly New England friend used to complain that when she went to the beach, all she could see were people lying around doing nothing; she always took her knitting. Our vacations are filled with activities, our children's extracurricular schedules need intricate planning, and our work often becomes equated with our personhood. One of our first questions of a newly met person is "What is your work?" or if we are sensitive to the economic nuances of that question, "What keeps you busy all day?" We have the need to "get things done," or to "do something about it." This attitude has meant that decision-making and problem-solving rank high in the dominant culture. Children are given many opportunities for decision-making, even at an early age (beginning, for example, with the color of their socks for the day); having choices is considered a fundamental right. Decisions are made, plans are carried out, and usually visible and measurable results are produced. This attitude also leads to an intense competitiveness that can be unfamiliar and even extreme to those from other cultures. While shelves in bookstores in the United States groan with the weight of all the books on self-development and indicate great interest in that variation, on the whole, we are a culture more tuned to "doing" that can be measured by external rather than internal standards. Even with self-development books, we "do" what is recommended.

Relational: What is the Relation Among People?

Lineal: Authority travels down the line; people's rights depend on their place in that line.

Collateral: Relationships are lateral; people make decisions on their own after consultation with others from any of the groups to which they belong (e.g., family, friends).

Individualistic: Equality prevails; individuals control their own lives.

This final orientation explores the dimensions of authority within a culture, with the understanding, as in all orientations, that all three variations will be found in any society. The variation labeled *lineal* describes groups where lines of authority are clearly established, leading to a sense of continuity through time. Positional order and succession are important; status is achieved usually through birth family, rather than personal merit. As novelist Isabel Allende comments about two generations before hers in Chile: "In those days, Chile was like a *millefeuille* pastry. It had more castes than India, and there was a pejorative term to set every person in his or her rightful place. . . . It was easy to descend in the social hierarchy, but money, fame, or talent was not sufficient to allow one to rise, that required the sustained effort of several generations"(Allende 1995, 6). If the image of the first variation is vertical, the image in the second is horizontal. In the *collateral* variation, connections to groups and subgroups are recognized, but so is the importance of consulting with others before making big decisions. He has both the collectivistic sense of the lineal as well as the independence of the individualist. She makes her own decisions, but often in conference with others. The third variation, *individualistic*, can be found even in collectivistic cultures. This variation stresses the autonomy of the individual, the egalitarian (as opposed to authoritarian) attitude even of those in positions of authority. Individuals are expected to voice their particular points of view and decisions are achieved through majority rule (even in the family, where parents and children get an equal vote). The individualist believes in attaining status through his own merit—though we all know that this note of meritocracy may be hollow, even in the United States.

The dominant culture of the United States, as discussed in the last chapter, is predominantly individualistic. Again, large or small pockets of a more collectivistic nature nestle in, but overall, an individualistic attitude dominates. An increasingly egalitarian attitude that scorns all authority makes it difficult for Anglo-Americans to understand the hierarchical organization or status differences in other cultures. Though seemingly more prevalent now than a generation ago, the egalitarian attitude has a long history in the United States. Author David McCullough describes the debate in the fledgling government of the United States over the title for the president. John Adams echoed the traditions of England and some legislators in expressing that "President" seemed too ordinary, since it was the title for the head of any number of organizations. This position was one of distinction and should be honored with "dignity and splendor." However, the newer perspective, voiced by James Madison, was that "[t]he more simple, the more republican we are in our manner, the more national dignity we shall acquire." "Mr. President" won over "His Highness." Even our constitution proclaims,

TRY THIS!

Note that many of these boxes have been something to *do*! What does that say about the dominant culture of the United States? Look at Advice Columns in your local paper, paying attention to the cultural values that are being expressed by both the inquirer and the responder. Have students watch cartoons to discover the values that are encouraged by the characters.

"No title of nobility shall be granted by the United States" (McCullough 2001, 404–407).

One of the benefits of this framework, as mentioned earlier, is that it can be applied to micro-cultures, such as schools or businesses. Kluckhohn used it to look at the subculture of women's roles in the United States. By using this framework "she showed that women's roles historically have expressed 'variant' rather than 'dominant' values in American culture. She posited that individualism—with man as autonomous free agent—was a dominant male value, while women as wives and mothers were oriented toward group goals. Where the valued personality type for males was the 'person of action,' that is the 'doing personality,' for women, it was the philanthropist type, dedicated to community improvements and family morality" (Spindler and Spindler 1990, 54). While this comment may not hold as true these days as it did when it was originally published in 1961, the application of the framework to the subculture of women shows its widespread usefulness. Also, while we each can think of people who do not fall into the "traditional" male or female roles, from the glimmers of recognition in my graduate-level classes, it would seem that vestiges of habitual roles remain. Cultural values are foundational and do not change easily or quickly.

INTERACTIONS BETWEEN MACRO- AND MICRO-CULTURES

Both dominant and variant cultures have an impact on each other; the dominant culture does not paint everyone with its own color. In this country, newcomers need to learn how to handle the dominant-culture power structures for access to the economy. Beyond our borders, technology has spread the Anglo-American culture far and wide in the world. However, influences go the other direction as well. The Anglo-American culture has been influenced by both macro- and micro-cultures: extreme individualism is being countered by more emphasis on living and working cooperatively; rampant materialism has experienced a few inroads by those who feel that life is more than physical goods; the appeal of Islam and Buddhism has grown; women have brought a different perspective to major corporations; gay and lesbian communities have had an impact on the definition of families; and Christian theology has felt strong reverberations from the liberation theology that began in Latin America. Neither individuals nor societies can live wholly in one variation. People have their own ranking of values which grow out of their particular context.

The Framework Applied to U.S. Classrooms

Having considered the orientations within the framework and the place of the dominant culture of the United States in the different variations, let us explore the meaning of the framework for the values of the dominant-culture classrooms of the United States.

HUMAN NATURE

Our approach to children is fairly dependent on this orientation and its variations. Generally, in our classrooms, we focus on the good in a child; we talk about helping her achieve her potential, about supporting his creative skills, or about finding ways for them to achieve their best. If a weakness is discovered, we seek programs to compensate. As teachers, we expect the best—or are begged to do so—and more often than not, we are rewarded for our high expectations. An example of this orientation comes from our own family, when our children were in middle school. At a meeting for parents at the beginning of the year, the vice-principal described the school policy in words to this effect: "Middle school children are at an age when they will want to try out various behaviors as they try to figure out who they are. We want them to do that in a context where if they fail, or make a mistake, they will be able to learn from their experiences." In other words, children were seen as a mixture of good and evil—but eminently changeable.

On the other hand, some teachers see middle and high schoolers especially as untrustworthy and incorrigible. Their attitudes that students can't be expected to achieve due to their background, culture, race, ethnicity, or disability would indicate their feelings that the student cannot change. While we all find students who like to blame "the other" for failure ("the dog/computer ate my homework"), there may be students, particularly girls, who feel truly constrained by "the other," that is, by cultural expectations communicated from home. We must acknowledge to them that value clashes between school and home may exist, but that we and they need to work together to see how to help them take advantage of the many opportunities this country is known for, without alienating their family values.

PERSON-NATURE

Our educational system is imbued with the dominance-over-nature variation. Science Fairs are the epitome of urging the young to make new
discoveries. Accessing the Internet, space exploration, eating out-of-season-
fruits for lunch, "the greatest mall on earth," and medical achievements are
all markers of our sense of dominance over nature. We will need to be sensitive to the dismay or confusion of newcomers from lands (even within the
United States) where subsistence fishing, hunting, or farming is practiced.
Students may have different beliefs concerning the causes or cures of illness
(e.g., "The most common cause of illness [among the Hmong] is soul loss"
(Fadiman 1997, 12)). Or they may view natural disasters as punishment for
hubris. Evil spirits are an integral part of the belief system for many people.
Our attitude of dominance over nature means that we can accomplish many
feats; it also gives rise to an attitude of waste. The abundance of paper or
pencils in class; the use of disposable cutlery, cups and plates in the cafeteria; the (bi-) annual box of new crayons; food fights all indicate a disregard
of natural resources. The experience of a Russian immigrant student is also
illustrative. Told by his art teacher that the design he had drawn in the middle of his paper was much too small, instead of crumpling up his paper (as
many of his Anglo-American classmates did), he continued with his design,
knowing that the smaller would be incorporated into the larger (Clayton
1996). He brought a different perspective to the relationship between people
and the earth. Looking at folk tales—many of which deal with this topic of
our relationship to nature—would be an effective way to see what we can
learn from other cultures about this orientation.

TIME

Reflecting the larger society, schools are fairly well imbued with a sense of
the future; traditions are few and far between in most educational institutions these days. In the curriculum, history has taken a back seat in the last
few decades; attention at ceremonies marking history is often cursory; many
students do not see a reason for honoring something that "does not have
meaning for us" (Memorial Day or Convocation Day in high school or college, for example). We are expected to make lesson and field trip plans well
in advance; often we do not consult the previous records of students in an
effort to start afresh; "Back to School" nights for parents are advertised a
month or more in advance. When I was trying to make some plans with a
Russian bilingual teacher to meet some Russian parents at a school function,
I wrote a letter to be sent home, detailing the plans for the meeting two weeks
ahead. I found out that she did not send it out until one week before the
event, because "Russians do not plan that far in advance; one week is all they

manage." If a problem emerges with particular parents who do not seem to be able to make a meeting, one of the first things to do is to ascertain why: It may not be a different orientation to time, but may be due to very practical issues. If, indeed, planning that far in advance does not seem to be part of their lives, then we can either get another parent to remind them or offer to bring them, or send additional reminders home at particular points along the way (e.g., three days before, the afternoon before).

ACTIVITY

Professor of education Jaime Wurzel sees applications of the activity orientation in many different forms in the classroom: A *doing* orientation may be reflected in verbal output, whereas *being*-oriented people are more likely to be reflective, quietly absorbing all that is happening; *doing* wants to get the task done quickly and efficiently, whereas *being* needs to make sure personal contacts and positions of authority are honored. *Doing* may be oriented more to the product, while *being* is oriented to the process, which means that the usual products of class—papers, exams, reports—are measures of competence as opposed to social interaction, personal effort, loyalty, and respect for the teacher (Wurzel nd). Once again, acknowledging where the students' values lie and appreciating the positive aspects of different variations go hand-in-hand with making sure that the students understand the values of the dominant culture. While we need people who pay attention to the personal side of getting a job done, immigrants need to be able to prove their competence in the dominant culture even if it differs from their personal orientation.

RELATIONAL

The variations in the relational dimension range from *lineal* to *individualistic*. Since many aspects of the individualistic variation have been discussed in the previous chapter, I would like to apply here four of the categories of social relations identified by Stewart and Bennett (1991): obligation, informality, friendship, and confrontation.

- *Obligation* to others includes a variety of practices; one of them, the idea of reciprocation around social events or gift giving is no longer very strong in many parts of the dominant culture of the United States—certainly not as strong as in some other cultures. Arriving empty-handed for an evening meal and leaving with sincere thanks are considered acceptable and practiced widely. A return gesture, while welcome, is often not seen as obligatory. The way of life in most of the rest of the world revolves around a profound sense of reciprocity and obligation, which can go on for generations between families. All of this is to say that people from other cultures have a different way of looking at the act of saying "Thank you." It took a number of visits from Sri Lankan friends (who had not lived in the United States) for me to understand why no one expressed gratitude for our hospitality: In their view, verbal acknowledgment would have been insulting because of the underlying bonds of relationships. In other words, we were considered part of the in-group, and to thank us would have implied a distant relationship. This attitude holds true in many parts of the collectivistic world. Stewart and Bennett observe that "In parts of India, no expression of 'thanks' exists; social conventions have not required its invention. A social act is seen as the fulfillment of an obligation or a duty and requires no verbal acknowledgment" (Stewart and Bennett 1991, 95). Back in the classroom, after ascertaining that the student may not have the custom of the quick "thank you" in her culture as prevalent as it is here, teaching her the etiquette involved in small acts of kindness in the classroom or on the playground would be an important step in helping her acculturate to the dominant culture.

- *Informality* in relationships is one indicator of the sense of equality in the dominant culture of the United States. This informality is visible not only by our dress, lack of protocol, and our conversation, but also, less visibly, in our body language and in our assumptions. For example, in recent years I have seen teachers invite elementary students to call them by their first names. That means that those in authority do not want to take on the aura of power. Authority took such a beating in all segments of life during and after the Vietnam War that even those who are in positions of authority often try to allay their power. In an egalitarian situation, some people may call everyone by their first names; in an authoritarian one, they may not. It is disrespectful. To demand an immigrant student to call us by our first name, similar to looking us in the eye, is asking him to be rude, just the opposite of our request. For his future in this country, the student will need to eventually learn the direct gaze or the absence of titles, but we must also realize what the student is being asked to do. Acceding to that request results in not just a verbal act, but in a psychological turnaround, a seismic shift in which internal plates need to find a precarious new balance. Not all people from authoritarian cultures are comfortable with this informality. Students from many cultures are astounded by teachers and students who drink water or coffee in class (to say nothing of eating in higher level education classes), or by teachers who use the desk/table as a prop to lean against during lectures in high school. Also, in many cultures for a student to have his hands in his pockets while talking to a teacher is insulting. These examples are given not to curtail or change the behavior that is reflective of this culture, but to point out the little ways our values come across. Knowing the differences between the more formal structures of other cultures and the informal ones of this culture might help in understanding some students.

- *Friendship* is another area of social relations that has a different expression in the individualistic culture of the United States. Friendships are often formed through common activities in which people are involved, and continue through those same or other activities (Stewart and Bennett 1991). Anyone who has been to a large party at a friend's home can identify with the little groupings of people from the different interests of the person's life, such as the "office group," "the exercise group," "the church group," and the like. Since individualists shy away from *inter*dependence, even "best friends" in adulthood tend to be of a more light-hearted nature rather than a true mutual interdependence. Many of my international students note the profusion of diverse, multiple, but fairly superficial friendships in the United States. They sense a reluctance by the Anglo-Americans to become involved and to enter into a more solid relationship. Once a deeper friendship does form, that reluctance may not end. French-educated anthropologist, Raymonde Carroll, points out the different meanings that the concept of "friend" can have: "[T]he axiom 'friends help each other' is valid both for Americans and for the French. Yet. . . misunderstanding arises from different presuppositions. . . . 'X is my friend, he is therefore going to offer to help me' (French side); 'X is my friend, he will therefore ask me to help him if he needs me' (American side)" (Carroll, R. 1988, 78). This observation corroborates the view of many with an individualistic bent who do not want to burden their friends with their troubles; rather they tend to seek professional help or support. Cross-cultural students may have more restrictions or expectations around their budding friendships: They may not be involved in many activities through which to meet people; school may be their only source. Gender issues may loom, as may jealousies if the friendship is shared among many. Due to differing emphases in collectivism, friendship seems to be considered a more sacred phenomenon than is generally viewed in the Anglo-American culture.

Carroll continues her observations with the pressures placed on young children to "make friends," commenting that the child's requirement for friendship is agreement which means that two-way friendships dissolve when disagreement erupts (e.g., "You're not my friend anymore"). This different attitude toward friendship may be a difficult transition for the cross-cultural student who may understand friendship to be based not on "doing," but on "being," involving more interdependence, having more depth, and being a more substantive part of their lives.

• Finally, *confrontation*: In the dominant culture of the United States, people generally like to get to the source of a problem immediately: They assemble facts and address issues directly. As I mentioned earlier, Anglo-Americans usually prefer a direct mode of communication. While we sometimes may skirt around issues or find extremely tactful ways of getting our point across, generally we do feel it important to face the person with whom we have a problem. Intermediaries are not in our vocabulary or on the horizon for most Anglo-Americans. In many other cultures of the world, intermediaries serve an important function either for their personal influence or for negotiation. Describing her family in Iran, Farman Farmaian comments, "If there was a problem in the family, you had to choose someone to intercede for you. For instance, if I didn't like the color of a dress my mother was sewing for me, I never went to her myself, but would send Jaby [her older sister] to explain how I felt, thus avoiding the sin of disrespect to a parent" (Farman Farmaian 1992, 86). In other situations, a person with influence is asked to represent someone, in the hope of effecting a favorable decision. While that strategy is also quietly sprinkled across the United States, it pours across collectivistic cultures. What is less practiced in the United States is the concept of "saving face" (avoiding shame) which is paramount in other cultures. Delicate issues where rejection or embarrassment may be possible are conducted by third parties so that neither of the involved parties may lose face with the other. Very often, Anglo-Americans do not pay enough attention to how serious this is to cross-cultural students. If a cross-cultural student is too embarrassed to ask us a question, she may send a friend to ask in her stead. Or, a ploy used not only by many cross-cultural students but also by dominant-culture students is to imply that the question comes from a third party, when, indeed, it is her own. For us to respond with, "Tell your friend to come and see me" does not always have the intended effect of showing interest. The student may not be able to face the real or imagined embarrassment

---

JOURNAL TIME

Write down your reflections on your values within each orientation and note where you fit into the variations. Think back to a misunderstanding you may have had with someone (student or colleague) to see if different variations may have been the cause of the problem. Describe how each variation shaped both responses. Being able to *cognitively* explain the reason often helps take it out of the emotional realm, which can lead to better understanding.

---

by talking directly with us; the cover of anonymity may still be necessary. We can try a variety of strategies to be more accessible to the student, to create ways of interaction that will build up trust, such as taking deliberate steps to create a sense of community in the classroom, engaging students in individual conversations about their lives and recalling the shared information at a later time, or remembering to follow up on promises. Of course, the severity of the situation will demand certain procedures, but we must be alert to the keen sense of saving face, which is internalized by many cross-cultural students.

Reflections on Sayora

In the opening vignette, Sayora's mother had difficulty with the suggestions Ed made regarding his meeting with Sayora and the other student. The mother may have wanted to protect her daughter from further hurt and humiliation, she may not have wanted to extend any kind of contact with the Anglo-American girl, she may have wanted to avoid conflict at all costs, or she may not have wanted a one-on-one situation for her daughter who was already feeling very vulnerable. Possibly, also, Sayora's mother came from a culture which did not value a bold-faced approach, a culture in which these sorts of issues are settled by elders who are wiser, or by intermediaries who can absorb whatever anger may be expressed without taking it personally. Ed, on the other hand, acted suitably for a dominant-culture teacher in the United States by trying to get to the source of the problem between the two girls and rectify it. In an effort to solve the problem—and we of the Anglo-American culture are known to be good at that due to our emphasis on logic and rationalism—Ed wanted to bring the two girls together. His assumption was that each would state the problem as she saw it and then arrive at some understanding regarding future behavior. In his straightforward manner, he may not have understood the need nor had the time or patience for a more indirect, deflective approach. In such a situation, instead of stating what the solution was to be, Ed might have inquired of Sayora's mother how she would deal with the problem. In reality what happened was that after understanding that this would be far too difficult a step at this early stage in Sayora's acculturation, Ed put aside the dominant culture's immediate answer, and not only talked directly with the offending student but also sensitively opened up one of many discussions with the whole class about respecting those who are different. Obviously, everyone gained from this teachable moment.

When we understand the framework for the range of values that exist, objectifying a clash of values becomes easier. We can become less defensive; the other person's behavior does not become a personal affront. As teachers, we have an obligation to help our students, at whatever level, to truly understand each other and to work toward a world in which respect and affirmation will replace taunts and jeers. At stake is not just a personal or local wish but a global goal, the creation of a world where respect prevails for those who are different, where conflict is replaced by understanding. We have a rare privilege to shape that view. As teachers, we can do no less.

Chapter Four

Making Connections: Learning

One is equally indebted to one's teacher and to God.

—Turkish proverb

I am having a very difficult time with my project. I keep trying to ask the teacher about it, but she doesn't pay attention to me. I wanted to study with Anne but she is working on a different project. I helped her for a while, until the teacher told me I must do my own work. I know that both the teacher and Anne think I am not a good student, because I bother them. I don't understand what I am supposed to do; perhaps my English is not yet good enough.

—(Maria, an immigrant fifth grader)

*M*aria seemed to be wandering in a wilderness as she roamed the classroom. As if from oasis to oasis, she would go from one desk to another, wanting to be helpful; often others found her intrusive. She had a hard time focusing on her own work. When Sarah, her English and science teacher, compared notes with Jim who taught math and social studies, they found that she behaved similarly in both classrooms. Sarah felt she seemed excessively clingy, always wanting input from her; Jim thought she was reluctant and unwilling to venture off and accomplish tasks on her own. Originally, they had wondered if she had been placed incorrectly in fifth grade; she seemed so immature. They were astonished when I related that she felt ignored. She had come from a classroom of 40 in her country, so Jim and Sarah felt that their classrooms of 21 must seem pretty individualized to her. However, in discussing the issue with the ESOL (English to Speakers of Other Languages) teacher, they found that Maria did well in that environment. The small size of the ESOL class enabled a closer teacher-student contact than was possible in the mainstream classroom. When Jim or Sarah did work with her one-on-one for a while, she seemed to understand and continue, but she craved a very high level of connection with them, which understandably they did not feel they could continue indefinitely. In non-curricular responsibilities she was a great asset, ready to take on any jobs that needed to be done in the classroom. While it was easy and possible to blame the lack of English for Maria's problems, Jim, Sarah, and the ESOL teacher concurred that Maria's English was not the issue.

Underpinnings of Learning

Environment, as well as culture, tells us what to pay attention to and what to ignore, and shapes what we see or hear and how we organize information. Anthropologist Edward T. Halls mentions an example: "the direction and smell of the wind, together with the feel of ice and snow under his feet, provide the cues that enable an Eskimo to travel a hundred or more miles across *visually undifferentiated waste* [emphasis in the original]" (Hall 1969, 79–80). Various studies have shown that though the perceptual processes are similar, people are sensitized by their environment to see different details more prominently (for example, round huts vs. rectangular skyscrapers, or distant horizons vs. car details). Their language trains their eyes to go across a line or a page in a particular direction. Also, the color spectrum contracts to fewer distinctions than what we have in art classes in the United States. As students who speak Trukese (western Pacific islands) learn English, they also learn to distinguish between, for example, blue and green. For them, the same word answers the questions: "What color is the sea?" and "What color is the grass?" (Stewart and Bennett 1991). Who is to say that one interpretation of the spectrum of color is the only one, the right and true one? White is usually "white" until you try to match the white paint on your walls. While commonality runs through actual perceptual processes, some differences in conceptualization result from our natural and cultural ecology.

If culture has an influence on perception, what about on intelligence? A story from the 1970s illustrates that point. "An anecdote sometimes told in introductory anthropology courses describes an educational psychologist who set out for Australia many decades ago to test the intelligence of the aborigines. He expected to be able to account for their 'backwardness' by showing that their intelligence was not up to standard. He arrived in Australia with his IQ tests under his arm, rented a Land Rover, and set out across the outback to find his subjects. As he drove through the desert, his Land Rover failed him, his supply of water ran low, and he set out on foot in growing desperation; eventually he collapsed in the barren land. Two passing aborigines came upon him shortly thereafter. Scooping sand not two feet from where the psychologist's head lay, they exposed a spring and gave him water. Revived, he signaled that he was hungry, and one of the aborigines threw a stone, killed a rabbit, and fed the psychologist. The point of the story, of course, is that the Western educational psychologist very visibly failed an aboriginal intelligence test" (Gumpert and Harrington 1972, 262). Socialized for competence within our culture, we find that what is learned in one culture may not be at all important in another. Even in the United States, children learn to tell stories with great elaboration in one micro-culture of the Piedmont Carolinas, while in another, they learn that they must tell only factual events in correct sequence, and refrain from fictionalizing (Heath 1983). Culture is not determinative of the learning capability of a student, but a shaper of the approach, or gestalt, that the student brings to the classroom and to the subject matter.

Approaches to Learning

The concept of how we learn, sometimes referred to as learning styles, has been receiving much attention in recent years, as evidenced not only in the number of books, articles, and centers on the topic but also in the more than 1.2 million (as of January 2003) websites on the Internet. This abundance means that one can find many different perspectives on how a student might learn best, that a variety of ways exists to think about the concept. What exactly is a learning style? In 1979 a national task force sponsored by the National Association of Secondary School Principals included in its definition that learning styles are a fairly consistent combination of behaviors that are instrumental in perceiving, interacting, and responding to learning situations. Three strands weave together to create our own personal learning styles: *cognitive, affective*, and *physiological* (Griggs 1991).

THE COGNITIVE STRAND

The *cognitive* strand contains the ways in which an individual receives, processes, stores, and retrieves information. In the United States, we generally believe that all students do not respond uniformly to material that is presented; an effective teacher will use different methodologies to present the material, for example, switching between direct, verbal instruction, multimedia presentation, group work, individual research, and the like. This is not a common practice or belief throughout the world. Speaking out of the experience of her own children, Gail Benjamin, anthropologist and professor, comments that in Japan, educators feel that "[a]ll children can learn, all should learn the same basic lessons, and *the same sets of teaching techniques can be effective with all children* [italics mine]" (Benjamin 1997, 223). Since socializations are different across cultures and social class, in the multicultural classrooms of the United States, it would follow that children will present numerous learning styles as well. Some will have been taught to imitate, some to memorize, some to explore, some to elaborate; some learn by listening, and some by doing.

THE AFFECTIVE STRAND

The *affective* strand of learning styles consists of emotional and personality characteristics related to attention, locus of control, interests, willingness to take risks, persistence, need for structure, and sociability. All of these factors are familiar to us, though perhaps not as a component of a learning style. As we all know, some students seem to need more structure than others; some need to have directions explained more than once (or twice or thrice or ten times); some seem to be more oriented to friends than many of us would like. More often than not teachers say that student inattention requires us to repeat directions. While that may be true in many situations, the cause also could be the student's innate need to have directions explained in a *different* way (i.e., more individualized explanations, or written instead of oral directions).

THE PHYSIOLOGICAL STRAND

Finally, the *physiological* strand involves two different parts: the preferred modalities (visual, auditory, tactile, kinesthetic) and the environmental context of light, temperature, noise level, and room arrangement. Differences in learning modalities naturally prompt us to present material in more than one mode. For example, presenting material on the overhead projector or on PowerPoint at the same time as presenting it orally is helpful not only for English Language Learners in class but also for others who may be visually oriented. The spoken word disappears so quickly that these students may not have the time to process the entire content of what is being said. Being able to follow along visually gives a considerable boost. Regarding the environmental context, professor of education Wilma Longstreet acknowledged a habit from her youth, rediscovered when she was writing her doctoral dissertation. Admitting what was considered an inefficient study pattern, she had become dependent on having the television on as she did her homework. In graduate school, she found she was unable to concentrate in complete quiet. To accommodate her need for visual stimulation, she wrote the dissertation in the reading room of the university library (Longstreet 1978). For her, it proved to be a very efficient way!

BEYOND THE THREE STRANDS

Some more points about learning styles: First, learning styles can change over the years. For example, as we all know, young children need to move about, but learn to become more visual or aural (and sedentary) as they progress through the grades. This is not to say that kinesthetically oriented students are not found in higher grades, but that others may move away from being purely kinesthetic as they mature. Furthermore, some international students in my classes point out that schooling in the United States makes them more analytical than the education in their homelands. This point resonates with me personally, since in my early schooling critical thinking was non-existent. That was another non-linguistic, cultural adjustment I had to make upon entering school in the United States, though that disconnect was not clear to me at the time.

Second, one's position on an instrument that measures learning styles does not involve a value judgment. The various instruments simply show how we prefer to learn, and as such are tools to accomplish more effective teaching as well as learning. We can better match teaching strategies with the needs of the student and the student can be empowered by understanding how she learns best. Different measurement models assess different dimensions of learning styles: the influence of personality, information processing, social interaction tendencies, and instructional preferences (Griggs 1991). Hence, one instrument will not give a holistic picture. Organizing teaching around the students' preferred styles of learning, instead of having students always adjust to our dominant—or only—style of teaching requires flexibility from us. This is not easy, but who ever said this was an easy profession? The point is, however, that students whose learning style differs from the dominant style in the classroom should receive some instruction in their preferred style at some point. Indeed, research has shown that grade-point averages rise when students are taught in their preferred learning styles at the elementary, secondary, and college levels (Dunn and Griggs 1995).

Third, generalizations about learning styles must not fashion a student into a mold, but rather must comprise one part of a puzzle that needs other pieces to be complete. "One way to ameliorate what can be the overly deter-ministic tone of this research is to speak of *learning preferences* instead of *styles*. In this case, the implication is that numerous factors influence how people learn, and that in fact all individuals differ in some ways from one another in how they learn [emphasis in the original]"(Nieto 1999, 65).

Understanding learning preferences is another way of getting to know our students better, which may help us uncover what may be affecting the learning process. Furthermore, when the student understands her preferred style, she can acquire coping mechanisms to use in different contexts; she is empowered to become a partner in the learning process.

Learning Preferences and Culture

If learning preference theories help us understand how we, individually, meet and interact with information, what, then, is the role of culture? Learning is more than an individual effort; it is influenced by culture. Anthropologist Edward Hall states: "[P]eople reared in different cultures *learn to learn* dif-ferently. Some do so by memory and rote without reference to 'logic' as we think of it, while some learn by demonstration but without the teacher re-quiring the student to do anything himself while 'learning.' Some cultures, like the American, stress doing as a principle of learning, while others have very little of the pragmatic. [Some] even guide the hand of the pupil"(Hall 1973, 48). Thinking back to family orientations in Chapter Two, we can see how, for example, a child brought up in an authoritarian-structured family might learn differently from a child brought up in a democratically oriented one. In the authoritarian family, generally the child remains quiet in the pres-ence of adults, does not ask questions unless asked directly, never questions decisions made by a figure of authority, and does as he is told. Professor Howard Gardner writes of a family experience in a Chinese hotel when two approaches to learning clashed. He and his wife were delighted to have their one-and-a-half year old son explore how to fit the room key into the key hole; the Chinese, upon seeing that the child was having difficulty with the task, would go over and guide the child's hand (Gardner 1989). Within the United States, researchers have shown that differences exist across the nation, for example, in rural and urban communities, in Native American tribes. Women in the United States have many different ways of learning, ways af-fected by their views of the world, ranging from dependence on objective au-thority to subjective intuition, from outside power to inner reflectiveness, from knowledge which is received to that which is constructed (Belenky et al. 1986). A small piece of research I did showed that these descriptors also applied to a cross-cultural group of women. Clearly, how we learn is connected to culture and generally one learning style will predominate in schools of the dominant culture. However, having said that, we must not allow culture to dictate; not everyone in one culture will learn the same way.

Child development, a crucial factor in education, is also culturally shaped. Piaget's theory may not be as universal as originally thought, though data are still inconclusive. Piaget has stated that sequential stages at particular ages define intellectual development: the sensorimotor stage in infancy; the pre-operational stage from about age two to seven; the concrete operational stage from about seven to eleven; and finally, the formal operations stage which starts anywhere between eleven and fifteen years of age and lasts through adulthood. Some research has shown that, while the stages are sequential, cultural factors such as the use of language or the level of education can accelerate or delay the age at which those stages occur (Dasen and Heron 1980). This information works as a little reminder that we must be careful in our judgments in class or in IEP (individualized educational plans) meetings, that we must not assume that all students will measure up to the same point on the yardstick at the same time.

Social class has also been proposed as a major player in the field of learning styles, due to the impact that economic and educational levels provide. Given the definition of culture as ways that provide meaning and cohesion within a group, social class is a culture in itself. For example, computers play a role in children's lives in homes of the wealthy and the middle classes. This will have repercussions particularly in places where computers are not a part of school furniture, especially since computers are seen to foster greater analytical thinking. Studies have shown that parents from high- and low-income groups have different expectations of their children. For example, over three different studies, Turkish low-income parents put obedience and positive social relations as primary expectations of their children, while high-income parents did not. The low-income parents valued a social rather than cognitive understanding of competence (Kağıtçıbaşı 1996). This difference is repeated in other cultures as well.

However, some educators do not want to take culture into consideration. Believers in this viewpoint think that ethnic, racial, or cultural differences should not play a part in how we view students, that too many decisions may be made with these considerations in mind. They fear that once tendencies are presented, we will be tempted to use them for stereotyping which, for example, might become determinative of student capability. They believe that the relationship between culture and learning becomes oversimplified and thereby misinterpreted. And they are right in some situations. Nieto tells of alarming teacher practices such as making Hispanic students share books when there were not enough (whereas non-Hispanics were each given one), denying them leadership positions, withholding from them choices permitted to non-Hispanics, all due to a stereotypic stranglehold about their cultural backgrounds (Nieto 1996). Such practices, including those of low expectations for particular students (e.g., defined by race/ethnicity/cultural background), are unconscionable especially since we teachers are dedicated to preparing the youth of society.

Opponents of the culture/learning style connection make a second point: that newcomers must learn the style of the dominant culture for their future success. I find this concern difficult to defend, since many Anglo-Americans learn in a variety of non-dominant ways. No one is asking that, for example, independent work should be thrown out altogether, but rather that there should be diversity in methodology. We do not all learn best when sent off to explore a topic on our own. Furthermore, being taught solely in the dominant cultural style also brings up the school's role in the assimilation process. While students need to be exposed to and prepared for the dominant culture they will participate in upon graduation, we need to *help* them, not hinder their learning in the process. Finally, an attempt at a uniform methodology also brings up the issue of substituting uniformity for educational equity. Educational equity demands not that all students are taught or treated the *same*, but that they all are offered equal opportunities to develop their potential, which may require different treatment.

A third point of controversy against making a culture/learning style connection is the possibility of confusing differences in ability with deficiencies, not only by the teacher but also by the student. Achievement disparities should necessitate inquiry into learning styles. Students who learn in ways that are different from the majority present a mandate for us to diversify teaching strategies. These same students need to be assured that we all learn differently; that, with practice, they will have the advantage of becoming bicognitive, and that we will honor their differences through our teaching as best we can.

Being aware of cultural tendencies to better inform teaching as opposed to using them to constrict a student's potential are two very different paths.

Field Sensitivity and Field Independence

Field sensitivity and field independence are two learning styles that demonstrate the influence of culture. These theories (originally developed solely for visual perception and called field dependent and field independent) had been around for two decades, when, in 1974, professors Manuel Ramirez and Alfredo Castañeda expanded the theories to include more than just the cognitive aspect and related the theories to a cultural world view. Imagine a college class we attend together. The professor divides the class into two groups; she meets with one group regularly throughout the semester. After a few weeks of basic instruction she sends the other group off to independent work. In that second group, you are really excited. You will be able to explore a topic that you have been curious about for quite a while; you don't have to abide by another's schedule; you love the freedom and independence you have been given. And I? I am delighted to be in the first group. I cannot fathom going off on my own: I wouldn't know where to begin the research and I would miss the relationships provided by the group. I am sensitive to and need the group context. You exhibit some of the characteristics of a field independent learner and I, a field sensitive learner.

In very general terms, field independent learners usually prefer to work alone, have good analytical abilities, notice details, and are task oriented. Field sensitive learners, on the other hand, prefer to work in a group, may learn by watching rather than doing, see the whole picture rather than details, and are relationship rather than task oriented. Of course, most people are not exclusively one or the other, but may have more tendencies in one field than the other. Ramirez and Castañeda showed in their work with Mexican-American and Anglo-American children that these proclivities were shaped by the early socialization of the student. Having been brought up in a context of extended families and group orientation, the Mexican-American students were more field sensitive than field independent. The Mexican-American children exhibited more cooperative than competitive tendencies; they indicated a greater need to interact socially than did the Anglo-American students who had been brought up to be individualistic. Ramirez and Castañeda point out that these two different and equal cognitive styles do not preclude each other; development of both is possible over the years, particularly, for example, by bilingual students who tend to become bicognitive (Ramirez and Castañeda 1974). Also, most people are not at the polar ends of the continuum, but somewhere in an amalgam of both, zigzagging from one tendency to the other, early socialization having strongly influenced inborn propensity. Lest some think that since Mexico is a predominantly collectivistic culture and therefore all students from collectivistic cultures will enjoy group work, let me share that graduate students from both South Korea and Nigeria (both predominantly collectivistic cultures) have commented that they do very little group work there. And Anglo-American students have told me that in high schools in the United States (predominantly individualistic), students enjoy working in groups, so long as the work load is equal and individuals each do their share.

STUDENTS WITH FIELD SENSITIVE / FIELD INDEPENDENT TENDENCIES

Understanding that this is just one among many learning theories, let us look at it in more detail. In further work, Castañeda and Gray (1974) devised some descriptors of these different learning styles. In addition to alerting us about different ways in which students might approach the task, the teacher, or peers, these guidelines can be used for observation purposes, to determine where a student might be on the field sensitive/field independent continuum without resorting to testing the student. Links can be seen to Right/Left Brain as well as to Global/Analytic learning theories, among others. The chart below summarizes field sensitive/field independent students' preferences.

Figure 4–1

Field Sensitive and Field Independent Students (Castañeda/Gray)

	Field Sensitive Behaviors	Field Independent Behaviors
Relationship to Peers	1. Likes to work with others to achieve a common goal 2. Likes to assist others 3. Is sensitive to feelings and opinions of others	1. Prefers to work independently 2. Likes to compete and gain individual recognition 3. Task oriented; is inattentive to social environment when working
Personal Relationship to Teacher	1. Openly expresses positive feelings for teacher 2. Asks questions about teacher's tastes and personal experiences; seeks to become like teacher	1. Rarely seeks physical contact with teacher 2. Formal; interactions with teacher are restricted to tasks at hand
Instructional Relationship to Teacher	1. Seeks guidance and demonstration from teacher 2. Seeks rewards which strengthen relationship with teacher 3. Is highly motivated when working individually with teacher	1. Likes to try new tasks without teacher's help 2. Impatient to begin tasks; likes to finish first 3. Seeks nonsocial rewards
Characteristics of Curriculum That Facilitate Learning	1. Performance objectives and global aspects of curriculum are carefully explained 2. Concepts are presented in humanized or story format 3. Concepts are related to personal interests and experiences of children	1. Details of concepts are emphasized; parts have meaning of their own 2. Deals with math and science concepts 3. Based on discovery approach

Relationships to Peers. Socialization and values play a major role in the shaping of learning preferences. Students coming from contexts where the group has had precedence will naturally be more group-oriented than those coming from contexts with strong individualistic tendencies. Hence, students with field sensitivity basically are very tuned to the social context of their situation, not just in the sense of socializing, but to the feelings and opinions of others. Often they cannot make a judgment about their own work without the input of others. I am reminded of a college friend who always knew when he had handed in a good paper; I, more field sensitive, could never make that statement. Field sensitive students are apt to feel a responsibility, as well as a genuine interest in helping others in their group to achieve a group goal. Cooperative learning has tried to address this aspect of a field sensitive approach to learning. However, sometimes it has its own field independent imprint on it as illustrated by high school groups whose members demand equal work loads. Along the same lines, I was amused to learn from one of my international graduate students about a collaborative project her husband had done at work. Accustomed to being part of a larger group in his home country, he was quite surprised when, at the conclusion of the project, each member of the group was asked to put his name on the section he had written (the individualistic transmutations of a collectivistic custom).

As conditioned as the field sensitive student is to the group, the field independent student is conditioned to working alone and/or getting recognition for work that she has done. The social aspect of work is often, though not always, quite secondary to getting the work done efficiently. Attention to warm relationships in the peer group is less important than the task.

Personal Relationship to the Teacher. The relationship with the teacher is also important to a field sensitive student. For example, as a child in a Turkish elementary school, a few of my (Turkish) classmates and I would get together on Turkish holidays to visit our teacher's home and "pay our respects." And the sense of privacy is different between those who are socialized to a group and those who are socialized to self-sufficiency. Seemingly "prying" questions, some immigrant students may ask (like, "How did you meet your husband? How long have you been married?") are not meant to invade privacy; the students are working out of a different world view with different boundaries of personal space and information. The school in which I taught in a suburb of Istanbul, Turkey, had dorms for ten to fifteen students in a room. The number was not a problem since the students were used to being members of a larger group. I would dare say that most of the students would have had as much trouble adjusting to a double or single room in the United States as

Anglo-Americans might have had adjusting to fourteen roommates. As a dorm teacher (living in the dorm building, but in a separate faculty suite), I found that the students craved any kind of attention we could give. Going for walks, going to the movies, playing basketball or softball, and listening to (Western) music were all ways in which the relationship between the students and teachers could grow. The primary interest for the students was to establish a relationship with the teacher; incidentally, this connection provided a way to learn about each other's culture.

Teachers in the United States are now legally constrained to keep their hands off of students, even when a pat on the back or a hug might be needed. We try to find other ways to express those feelings of support. However, after a certain age, most field independent students are no longer seeking that kind of contact, especially in school. Contacts with us are usually limited to understanding our expectations or the task. Opportunities to make connections with teachers are possible through extra-curricular sports or other events, but even there they are limited in scope. Having been socialized to independence, most Anglo-Americans don't have the innate need for greater connection, or to connection beyond the immediate family.

Instructional Relationship to the Teacher.   A collectivistic culture tends to have an authoritarian structure, which also transfers to the classroom. A field sensitive student from such a culture may be accustomed to being shown how, then imitating the patterns of the more knowledgeable authority figure. Instead of being left on their own to figure things out, as field independent students prefer, field sensitive students look for guidance. This can be particularly true if the student is a newcomer and does not know the language or the culture of the classroom. In many collectivistic cultures, the title "Older Brother" or "Older Sister" carries some privilege and a lot of responsibility to show the way. In dominant-culture classrooms of the United States, if an older student is not available to help out, at least a knowledgeable *and* interested peer would be of help. But this peer relationship would never completely replace having direct contact with us whenever possible.

The field independent student, having been socialized to make decisions very early in her life, is usually eager to try out new ideas on her own and very eager to finish ahead of everyone else. Somehow in the dominant culture of the United States, being smart has become conflated with understanding and accomplishing tasks quickly. Hence the urgency. Hall comments about the dominant culture in the United States, "the person who learns fast is valued over the one who learns slowly. Some cultures seem to place less emphasis on speed" (Hall 1973, 51). Naturally, this speed is also linked to a competitive atmosphere that tends to suffuse the classroom.

TRY THIS!

Many teachers use different kinds of puzzles to create a change of pace in class: for example, hidden pictures, hidden words, brainteasers, or computation problems. Use a variety of these and notice if particular students have difficulties with particular types. Allow students to find the answers in whatever way they want to: e.g., working with someone else or working alone. What work habits do they prefer? Do they see details quickly? Do they enjoy the process? If the students are old enough, discuss and list as a class the strategies they used; urge them to keep track of their own strategies for future reference, particularly if they had difficulty with any part of the activity. Help them identify how they seem to work best and how they can cope when confronted with tasks they don't seem to like.

CURRICULA THAT COMPLEMENT FIELD SENSITIVE / FIELD INDEPENDENT STYLES

The last section of Figure 4–1 leads into Figure 4–2, explaining the kinds of curricula that appeal to these different tendencies. Most field sensitive students learn faster when they are given examples rather than theories. Insofar as possible, the more the material is humanized, the more quickly the field sensitive students will be able to understand it. That is to say, stories rather than a listing of facts will intrigue them more. They are more comfortable with being told rather than finding out for themselves.

Field independent students tend to prefer details, graphs, and formulae rather than stories. Since details are important, dates, facts, and figures loom large on interest's horizon. For many in the United States, quantification has an aura all its own. "To some foreigners the description of, say, the Washington Monument in terms of statistical information devitalizes the experience of seeing it. Americans are known to tourist guides in foreign countries for asking questions about size, cost, or age . . . while visitors from other cultures (including Europeans) tend to ask questions about history or aesthetics" (Stewart and Bennett 1991, 126).

Neither one of these tendencies is better than the other; nor are they mutually incompatible. As stated earlier, most people are a mix.

FIELD SENSITIVE / FIELD INDEPENDENT TEACHING STYLES

Shifting now from learning to teaching styles, many teachers are surprised that our own learning style influences much of our teaching style. Of course, we adjust our style to the students: First graders do not sit for lectures. But what is our balance between small group work and independent seat work?

Figure 4–2

Field Sensitive and Field Independent Curricula (Castañeda/Gray)

	Field Sensitive Curriculum	Field Independent Curriculum
Content	1. Social abstractions: Field sensitive curriculum is humanized through use of narration, humor, drama, and fantasy. Characterized by social words and human characteristics. Focuses on lives of persons who occupy central roles in topic of study, such as history or scientific discovery. 2. Personalized: The ethnic background of students, as well as their homes and neighborhoods, is reflected. The teacher is given the opportunity to express personal experiences and interests.	1. Math and science abstractions: Field independent curriculum uses many graphs and formulae. 2. Impersonal: Field independent curriculum focuses on events, places, and facts in social studies rather than personal histories.
Structure	1. Global: Emphasis is on description of wholes and generalities; the overall view or general topic is presented first. The purpose or use of the concept or skill is clearly stated using practical examples. 2. Rules explicit: Rules and principles are salient. (Children who prefer to learn in the field sensitive mode are more comfortable given the rules than when asked to discover the underlying principles for themselves.) 3. Requires cooperation with others: The curriculum is structured in such a way that children work cooperatively with peers or with the teacher in a variety of activities.	1. Focus on details: The details of a concept are explored, followed by the global concept. 2. Discovery: Rules and principles are discovered from the study of details; the general is discovered from the understanding of the particulars. 3. Requires independent activity: The curriculum requires children to work individually, minimizing interaction with others.

JOURNAL TIME

Looking at the charts of FS/FI students and curricula, take a few moments to think reflectively about how *you* learn best. Where do you put yourself as a student? And then, consider thoughtfully your teaching style. What are your strengths? What might you need to work on? Can you identify what you really need to pay attention to? Who, in class, do you have a difficult time connecting with? Could a mismatch in teaching and learning preferences be a clue? Make notes of all these so that you can look back at a later time to see if you still feel that way, or if you have changed.

Or, for example, do we tend to emphasize instructional goals over social goals, details over global concepts, or lectures over group discussions? We need to know our own learning preferences so that what we think is a "natural" way of teaching will not inadvertently conflict with or be unresponsive to the learning preferences of the students. While adopting strategies or modalities that are not our strengths is not easy, as teachers we need to offer a variety of methodologies so that at some point all students will feel comfortable. One of the causes of teacher burnout is the feeling of a constant uphill battle in the classroom: We just do not seem to be on the same page as some of the students, and that problem takes a disproportionate amount of our time. A mismatch of learning preferences and teaching styles may be one clue. If we can identify our own preference and also go about trying to expand our repertoire of pedagogical interaction, we may be able to find a comfort level for more of the students and thereby for ourselves. Castañeda and Gray have listed some teaching methodologies associated with the general characteristics of the two domains as seen in Figure 4–3.

The question arises as to whether "good teaching" in general would not answer the dilemma of accommodating various cultural preferences of learning. If the idea that good teaching includes keen sensitivity to different learning styles, then good teaching may cover the needs that cross-cultural students bring to the classroom. However, good teaching in the dominant culture of the United States often emphasizes field independent characteristics, with peripheral attention to students who may be field sensitive in their orientation. Professor Leonard Davidman states the point: "[I]nquiry-oriented teaching strategies that promote a critical, open-minded posture toward established knowledge, and which encourage learners to question the claims of authorities such as teachers, textbooks, and media pundits, could be construed as cultural assaults by students and parents who believe that the content of some books (e.g., the Bible and the Koran) should never be

Figure 4–3

Field Sensitive and Field Independent Teaching Styles (Castañeda/Gray)

	Field Sensitive Teaching Style	Field Independent Teaching Style
Personal Behaviors	1. Displays physical and verbal expressions of approval and warmth 2. Uses personalized rewards which strengthen the relationship with students	1. Is formal in relationship with students; acts the part of an authority figure 2. Centers attention on instructional objectives; gives social atmosphere secondary importance
Instructional Behaviors	1. Expresses confidence in child's ability to succeed, is sensitive to children who are having difficulty and need help 2. Gives guidance to students; makes purpose and main principles of lesson obvious; presentation of lesson is clear with steps toward "solution" clearly delineated 3. Encourages learning through modeling; asks children to imitate 4. Encourages cooperation and development of group feelings; encourages class to think and work as a unit 5. Holds formal class discussions; provides opportunities for students to see how concepts being learned are related to students' personal experiences	1. Encourages independent achievement; emphasizes the importance of individual effort 2. Encourages competition between individual students 3. Adopts a consultant role; teacher encourages students to seek help only when they experience difficulty 4. Encourages learning through trial and error 5. Encourages task orientation; focuses student attention on assigned tasks

questioned"(Davidman 1995, 7). Furthermore, Professor Christine Bennett states: "To equalize opportunities for success, it is imperative to use unequal teaching methods that respond to relevant differences among students" (Bennett 1999, 205). Immigrant students are not the only ones who bring different learning profiles to the classroom; that is, a class full of "same-culture-students" has innumerable learning differences as well. Therefore, thinking about our own teaching styles and learning how we can accommodate those who do not learn the same way we do benefit the whole class.

Looking at Multiple Intelligences

Another perspective on the approaches that students bring to class is that of multiple intelligences (MI). Howard Gardner, a professor in education and medicine, believes that people have a range of ways in which they show their abilities. He has set forth, most recently, eight categories:

- *Linguistic* describes a person who is gifted in the expression and nuances of his or her own language and possibly in other languages as well.
- *Logical-mathematical* defines a person's keen understanding of underlying causal principles in logic or numbers.
- *Spatial* delineates a person who easily visualizes the spatial world.
- *Bodily kinesthetic* characterizes the ability to use the body skillfully.
- *Musical* portrays a person with extraordinary musical understanding.
- *Interpersonal* represents the ability to understand other people.
- *Intrapersonal* defines a person who operates out of a good and clear understanding of self.
- *Naturalist* depicts an extraordinary interest, expertise, and sensitivity to the natural world.

Thomas Armstrong, an educator, psychologist, and champion of MI, lists four key points about this theory:

- Each of us has all intelligences, each of us with a unique configuration of the eight.

TRY THIS!

This project can be done in two separate steps, or together, depending on the age of your students and your own inclinations. The first step helps you better understand your students: Hand out a list of these different intelligences and their core components (as listed in the Figure 4–4) and have the students place themselves in the categories they feel describe themselves. Or, if your students are very young, use it as an observational tool. With their names on these pages, you can then use the pages to help you in your preparations for teaching strategies.

The second step aims to broaden the students' appreciation of the contributions of non-Anglo cultures: Ask the students to identify people who have achieved prominence in each of the intelligences (e.g., Evgeny Plushenko in bodily-kinesthetic, Sandra Cisneros in linguistic, etc.). The project can be expanded to have separate columns for different cultural groups, rather than just one column including all groups. Students can bring in newspaper articles over a period of time about their nominations. (This project was inspired by Thomas Armstrong 2000, 125.)

- Given the right circumstances, all eight intelligences can be developed to some competence.
- In most people, the intelligences work together (e.g., being on a kick-ball team requires not only kinesthetic but also interpersonal, spatial, and linguistic intelligences).
- Each particular intelligence may be displayed in any number of ways (carpet weaving may be valued more than baseball in one culture, both of which are bodily-kinesthetic intelligence) (Armstrong 2000).

Figure 4–4, developed by Armstrong, is a summary of the theory, including some examples of each, the developmental attributes, and the ways in which the particular intelligence is valued in a culture.

THE RELATIONSHIP BETWEEN LEARNING STYLE THEORIES AND MULTIPLE INTELLIGENCES

What is the relationship between learning style theories and MI? Armstrong refrains from making a direct connection with any one learning style theory, commenting, "MI theory has a different type of underlying structure than many of the most current learning-style theories" (Armstrong 2000, 10). Connections can be made between the two concepts, but in reality, they are two different paradigms. One connection that can be made is culture. The impact of culture runs through both the field sensitive/field independent theory and MI theory. Howard Gardner uses a definition of intelligence that supports the idea that children are socialized to competence within their society, which would differ among cultures. He defines intelligence as "the capacity for (1) solving problems and (2) fashioning products in a context-rich and naturalistic setting" (Armstrong 2000, 1). That is, the aborigines who saved the educational psychologist's life in the earlier story were solving problems particular to their context. The definition of intelligence is set not in the single trajectory familiar to school systems, not in the discrete (and possibly irrelevant or unknown) tasks on intelligence tests, but within familiar environments. In other words, intelligence is not a unitary concept, but multiple skills, aptitudes, and abilities. Culture is foundational to Gardner's theory: Students bring with them intelligences that are valued highly in their culture, having acquired those preferences passed on from generation to generation. These may be the valued abilities of the macro-culture, or the student's particular subculture (e.g., students from Appalachia, within the macro-culture of the United States). For some students, storytelling may be culturally valued, in others it may be navigating the desert, or singing and dancing intricate dances. Intelligences that are valued more will be more

Figure 4–4

Multiple Intelligences Theory Summary Chart (Armstrong)

Intelligence	Core Components	High End-States	Developmental Factors	Ways That Cultures Value
Linguistic	Sensitivity to the sounds, structure, meanings, and functions of words and language	Writer, orator (e.g., Virginia Woolf, Martin Luther King, Jr.)	"Explodes" in early childhood; remains robust until old age	Oral histories, storytelling, literature
Logical-Mathematical	Sensitivity to, and capacity to discern, logical or numerical patterns; ability to handle long chains of reasoning	Scientist, mathematician (e.g, Madame Curie, Blaise Pascal)	Peaks in adolescence and early adulthood; higher math insights decline after age 40	Scientific discoveries, mathematical theories, counting and classification systems
Spatial	Capacity to perceive the visual–spatial world accurately and to perform transformations on one's initial perceptions	Artist, architect (e.g., Frida Kahlo, I. M. Pei)	Topological thinking in early childhood gives way to Euclidean paradigm around age 9–10; artistic eye stays robust into old age	Artistic works, navigational systems, architectural designs, inventions
Bodily-Kinesthetic	Ability to control one's body movements and to handle objects skillfully	Athlete–dancer, sculptor (e.g., Martha Graham, Auguste Rodin)	Varies depending upon component (strength, flexibility) or domain (gymnastics, baseball, mime)	Crafts, athletic performances, dramatic works, dance forms, sculpture

Figure 4–4 (continued)

Intelligence	Core Components	High End-States	Developmental Factors	Ways That Cultures Value
Musical	Ability to produce and appreciate rhythm, pitch, and timbre; appreciation of the forms of musical expressiveness	Composer, performer (e.g., Stevie Wonder, Midori)	Earliest intelligence to develop; prodigies often go through developmental crisis	Musical compositions, performances, recordings
Interpersonal	Capacity to discern and respond appropriately to the moods, temperaments, motivations, and desires of other people	Counselor, political leader (e.g., Carl Rogers, Nelson Mandela)	Attachment/bonding during first 3 years critical	Political documents, social institutions
Intrapersonal	Access to one's own "feeling" life and the ability to discriminate among one's emotions; knowledge of one's own strengths and weaknesses	Psychotherapist, religious leader (e.g., Sigmund Freud, the Buddha)	Formation of boundary between "self" and "other" during first 3 years critical	Religious systems, psychological theories, rites of passage
Naturalist	Expertise in distinguishing among members of a species; recognizing the existence of other neighboring species; and charting out the relations, formally or informally, among several species	Naturalist, biologist, animal activist (e.g., Charles Darwin, E. O. Wilson, Jane Goodall)	Shows up dramatically in some young children; schooling or experience increases formal or informal expertise	Folk taxonomies, herbal lore, hunting rituals, animal spirit mythologies

developed, though others will also be present. Naturally, once again, educators must not stereotype all students from a particular culture, or equate one culture with a particular intelligence emphasis.

Individuals, as well as cultures, exhibit the impact of valued intelligences. In individuals, some of these intelligences are more developed by *"crystallizing experiences"* when a particular interest is acknowledged by the individual as well as by significant others. Other interests wither with *"paralyzing experiences"* when initial attempts within a particular intelligence are diminished by others (Armstrong 2000). When I was about ten an artist/teacher friend of my parents put me in front of a window, with an easel and oil paints, to paint what I saw. I sat down protesting that I did not know how to paint; she demurred and said everyone could do it. After an eternity, she came back, looked at the easel and commented, "You really can't paint, can you?" or at least words that communicated that to my very vulnerable mind. I was not challenged by her words; I was paralyzed. Even today, my spatial intelligence is not expressed through any artwork, though an aptitude test in high school indicated I should be an architect.

MULTIPLE INTELLIGENCES TEACHING STYLES

Naturally, in our teaching, we tend to emphasize the intelligences where we are strong. If you have a developed spatial intelligence, you perhaps draw pictures on the chalkboard; a developed, logical, mathematical intelligence enables you to engage in Socratic questioning easily and regularly. A cursory glance at Figure 4–5 will no doubt yield many nods or mental checkmarks; perhaps our eyes go first to those types of practices that we naturally employ. Another step would be to see how many checkmarks are within each category, that is, to try to understand where our preferred style lies, so that we might be able to thereby include styles that resonate with other intelligences. Since Gardner insists that we have all intelligences and that some are simply more developed than others, we *can* expand our repertoire and our ability to wield control of the class by students actively engaged in learning through their various preferences. Armstrong's chart suggests ways in which we can try to accommodate those various intelligences.

Whether through learning styles or multiple intelligences, the cultural stamp helps create student preferences. Some children will have grown up learning by observation, not exploration; some will have learned to be submissive to authority, not assertive; some will have learned to depend on group support, not rely on their own ideas; some will need close identification with the teacher, not independence; some will have kinesthetic or spatial intelligences more developed than linguistic; some will respond to Socratic questioning, while others will prefer visual stimulation. There exists a richness in

Figure 4–5

Multiple Intelligences Summary of the Eight Ways of Teaching (Armstrong)

Intelligence	Teaching Activities (Examples)	Teaching Materials (Examples)	Instructional Strategies	Sample Activity to Begin a Lesson
Linguistic	lectures, discussions, word games, storytelling, choral reading, journal writing	books, tape recorders, typewriters, stamp sets, books on tape	read about it, write about it, talk about it, listen to it	long word on the blackboard
Logical-Mathematical	brain teasers, problem solving, science experiments, mental calculation, number games, critical thinking	calculators, math manipulatives, science equipment, math games	quantify it, think critically about it, put it in logical framework, experiment with it	posing a logical paradox
Spatial	visual presentations, art activities, imagination games, mind-mapping, metaphor, visualization	graphs, maps, video, LEGO sets, art materials, optical illusions, cameras, picture library	see it, draw it, visualize it, color it, mind-map it	unusual picture on the overhead
Bodily-Kinesthetic	hands-on learning, drama, dance, sports that teach, tactile activities, relaxation exercises	building tools, clay, sports equipment, manipulatives, tactile learning resources	build it, act it out, touch it, get a "gut feeling" of it, dance it	mysterious artifact passed around the class
Musical	rhythmic learnings, rapping, using songs that teach	tape recorder, tape collection, musical instruments	sing it, rap it, listen to it	piece of music played as students come into class

Figure 4–5 (*continued*)

Intelligence	Teaching Activities (Examples)	Teaching Materials (Examples)	Instructional Strategies	Sample Activity to Begin a Lesson
Interpersonal	cooperative learning, peer tutoring, community involvement, social gatherings, simulations	board games, party supplies, props for role plays	teach it, collaborate on it, interact with respect to it	"Turn to a neighbor and share . . ."
Intrapersonal	individualized instruction, independent study, options in course of study, self-esteem building	self-checking materials, journals, materials for projects	connect it to your personal life, make choices with regard to it, reflect on it	"Close your eyes and think of a time in your life when . . ."
Naturalist	nature study, ecological awareness, care of animals	plants, animals, naturalist's tools (e.g., binoculars), gardening tools	connect it to living things and natural phenomena	bring in an interesting plant or animal to spark discussion about topic

this variety, begging to be tapped, if we can take the time to identify what those strengths are. That is not an easy task, given our workload these days, but jotting down some personal observations each day or using observational checklists of learning styles or multiple intelligences will help put some of the puzzle pieces together. Indeed, Armstrong suggests even using misbehavior of students to help identify their learning preferences or developed intelligence: "The strongly linguistic student will be talking out of turn, the highly spatial student will be doodling and daydreaming, the interpersonally inclined student will be socializing, the bodily-kinesthetic student will be fidgeting, and the naturalistically engaged student might well bring an animal to class without permission!. . . These intelligence-specific misbehaviors, then, are a sort of cry for help—a diagnostic indicator of how students need to be taught" (Armstrong 2000, 21–22).

Testing and Assessments

The profound influence of culture speaks to the difficulty of using standardized testing. Schools in the dominant culture of the United States prize linguistic and logical-mathematical learning and standardized tests expect demonstration of those abilities in very particular forms. Standardized tests gauge a slice of learning, in a moment of time, in a uniform way. How can instruction be standardized when the influence of culture is so profound? Standardized tests hinder our creativity to teach to students' learning preferences and strengths since the material must be covered in a way that will match what will be asked on the test. We then are no longer in charge of the class; the test is. And seldom has that type of curriculum improved the actual learning in the classroom. Improved test scores may have resulted, but not actual learning, since true learning preferences cannot be accommodated. Essays, research projects, lab work, and student-centered discussions are just a few of the methodologies that must give way to the hegemony of the test.

In addition, often students will need practice on how to take such a test. Immigrant students come with different ways of exhibiting their grasp of the material. The standardized form then becomes not a test of the material, but of "test taking." International graduate students of mine, who have enough English proficiency to have passed the exam to get into a university in the United States, often have a difficult time simply figuring out *how* to fill out anonymous course evaluation forms distributed by the administration, presumably a "stress-free" task.

Teacher, resource, and instructional inequalities as well as lack of support services are among the reasons why standardized tests cannot be really standard. If schools and instruction are not standardized, how can student performance measure up? The standardized test becomes a test of schools, not of students, but the students are denied a diploma if they do not measure up. Also, unfortunately, standardized tests often lead to unfair segregation of poorly performing students and to increased drop-out rates, when efforts should, instead, be placed on expanding teachers' understanding of student learning styles to effect increased learning.

The increasing use of portfolios, performance in any of their multiple intelligences, and completion of particular tasks are a most welcome sight as a way to document student achievement. A wide variety of authentic assessments can use criterion-based measures, enable students to exhibit their skills within contexts that demand those abilities, take into account their preferred learning styles, and provide benchmarks of how they have progressed.

Cultural Responses to Learning Disabilities

In the United States, if a student is having continual problems in class, usually some kind of testing is initiated to discover the problem. Then, with caregivers present, the results are discussed with suggestions for remediation. After all of this professional input, the caregivers are asked what they want to do. Anglo-American parents attend these meetings with an attitude shaped by dominant cultural values: that humankind can fix anything; that the school department (through taxes) is responsible for the child's education, and that the learning disability does not imply a lack of effort, but a unique genetic configuration. While parents would rather not have their child diagnosed as learning (or behaviorally or emotionally) challenged, in the dominant culture of the United States, the "problem" is often regarded within a medical framework, as a diagnosis that is treatable. Parents from many other cultures have a very different outlook. These parents may have attitudes that differ from the dominant-cultural attitudes of the United States toward human dominance over nature, or about the particular challenge facing their child and how to handle it; they may not trust the educational system; or mismatched perceptions about effort vs. inner wiring may be at work. Furthermore, if the disability is seen as a supernatural phenomenon, schools are the last place this would be "treated." Even the gathering of information by school personnel or the expectation that parents will be an important part of the remediation is fraught with different cultural perspectives. If school personnel and teachers know of these possibilities or, preferably, the specific attitudes of the particular culture, sensitivity and clear explanation can be practiced at every point of contact on this important topic.

Reflections on Maria

Maria, of the opening vignette, was extremely fortunate to have teachers who were not willing to accept the easy answer (not enough English). Indeed, hers was a cultural, not linguistic issue. She came from a culture where the group, not the individual, was the operating norm, and looked to others to accomplish a common goal. She had grown up with close connection to those in authority; she craved that as much as an Anglo-American student might crave some independence to do things alone. She was obviously not accustomed to working on her own and needed some very concrete steps spelled out for her as to what she needed to do first, second, third, and so forth. To wean her from "excessive" dependence (so it seemed to Jim and Sarah), teachers could begin with a one-on-one effort for the first few steps, then weave the personal contact with a written checklist, then balance the two approaches a little more to a more independent style with many words of encouragement. Obviously this learning curve is more than a two-week project. Maria would then be able to learn content and a different learning style. Small learning groups might be most welcome to her, but she should also learn how to address the unwritten, unspoken, and, I daresay, unrecognized assumption of field independent learning in many of the dominant-culture classrooms of the United States.

In order to be effective, we must accept the challenge of teaching the multi-faceted learning profiles of our students. Though it will not cure all the problems in education, attention to the impact of culture on learning is a very relevant factor in the needed reformation in our schools. The important approach is one that does not negate but builds on the cultural strengths which students bring to class—an approach which enables them to become bicognitive in addition to bilingual and bicultural, in order to be successful in any school or society in the world.

Chapter Five

Expressing Our Essence: Verbal Communication

There is no shame in keeping silent if you have nothing to say.

—Russian proverb

I know my teacher does not like my stories because there are lots of red marks on my paper. She says that I do not tell my story the right way. Last time, I wrote about something that happened to me so I know that I told it the right way. But she said that I wrote about too many extra things. I don't understand.

—(Juan, *an immigrant fourth-grader*)

*J*uan and I were having a casual conversation in the school-yard; we had met the previous year and were now catching up on life in fourth grade. He was a lively, energetic, outgoing, pleasant addition to any class. Well-liked by both peers and teachers, he was known also to a larger circle through his after-school sports activities. He had arrived from Venezuela three years before, when his father was transferred to the United States for business. His parents were most enthusiastic about the experience of living cross-culturally for their children. Juan was a hard working student; however, both Juan and his teacher were perplexed about his writing skills. Victoria, his teacher, could not understand where she had failed him: The class had worked on sentence and paragraph building, the importance of topic and supporting sentences. He was an avid reader. Nonetheless, when writing he invariably brought in extraneous details that he felt contributed to the context, but she felt littered the terrain. When she talked with him about the report—or story—he seemed to understand what she was trying to convey, the straight path she was looking for from beginning to end, but the next time his attempts did not show the improvement she hoped for. Since he was otherwise a good student, she wondered if there was "something more" behind this inability to write clearly.

Stirrings of Literacy

One could say that Juan started acquiring his writing skills at birth. In the multitudinous routines of the day, a caregiver's interactions with the child help him make sense of the environment and help him learn to interact in verbal, functional, and social ways. From infancy we absorb and spout language. We learn to talk through the variety of spoken exchanges, through reading, listening to or telling stories, through learning the correct language for particular situations (Schieffelin and Ochs 1986). We learn not only the grammar of the language but also the cultural values that underlie the interactions. For example, we learn that the language used on the playground may not be acceptable in the classroom; we learn that words used with peers may not be appropriate in interactions with Grandmother. As parents in many different cultures, we go through interminable and ubiquitous processes to teach our children the politeness particular to our culture. We learn far more than the surface structure of our language.

Understanding that routines instill linguistic and social competency comes easily; that common, everyday interactions also shape a child's participation in the written word comes as more of a surprise. Pointing out road and store signs or reading cereal boxes are simple examples of how, through the variety of the written language that surrounds them, children begin to understand the fact that print carries meaning. However, anthropologist Shirley Brice Heath points out that interactions as "common" as the bedtime story are culturally defined. Through that event and throughout the day, parents who ascribe to the dominant middle class culture of the United States generally and unconsciously involve their children in the types of verbal exchanges that are replicated in dominant-culture schools. The bedtime story is not a "common" occurrence even across the United States and interactions in and around various literacy events at home differ widely.

In her study of three communities in the Piedmont Carolinas, Maintown (white, middle class), Roadville (white, working class), and Trackton (black, working class), Heath found that the three communities had different patterns of language use and thereby in the language socialization of their children. The children from Roadville were exposed to language through emphasis on learning to ask specific, direct questions, to recount factual events in correct sequence, and to refrain from fictionalizing. Children from Trackton, on the other hand, were surrounded by stories that were told instead of read, were encouraged to tell and elaborate their own stories, and to see analogies in their daily experiences. Both sets of children had rich backgrounds in language, but neither group did as well in school as the Maintown children, who, through exposure at home, had internalized the skills that were more directly related to the linguistic expectations of the school culture (Heath 1982). We will look at those expectations more specifically later in the chapter. For now, let's focus on the fact that children are socialized to many different styles of spoken and written language from the moment of their birth. As teachers, we need to remember that a single, unilinear model of the development of reading and writing which happens when the child gets to school can no longer be taken as the norm. By the time they enter school, children come with a substantial background in interpreting some of their written and spoken environment (Heath 1986). In this chapter, we are considering verbal messages, both spoken and written; In the next chapter we will look at the important role of non-verbal communication.

High and Low Contexts, and In-Between

Many of us have seen couples married for a long time who are able to finish each other's sentences or who can intuit what the other needs, or twins who need only a few words to express their thoughts to each other. In these situations, words and sentences are collapsed and the context carries much of the shared meaning. This form of communication is considered high context. Yet again, there are other situations in which an issue is explained in immense detail, for fear someone might not understand it. Nothing is taken for granted; the surrounding context plays almost no role. That is an instance of low context.

High and low contexts are a conceptual framework created by anthropologist Edward T. Hall that applies to many components of culture; here we will focus only on communication. As we all know, context is quite intermingled with language. A word has a different meaning depending on the context. I am reminded of a colleague from the United States when I was teaching in Turkey: A Turkish student asked for clarification of a word she had come across in her reading. The word was spelled S-O-B. My colleague paused for some time as she tried to think of the best way to explain the meaning and usage of this bit of slang. Finally the student offered some help. She asked, "Does it have to do with crying?" Hall points out that computers cannot work alone as translators because computers cannot yet fully convey the context of the words; they only "know" syntax and vocabulary (Hall 1977).

Going beyond single words in a sentence, context in our current consideration refers to the amount of assumed or shared information that surrounds an interaction. Some cultures in general rely more on the words (low context) and other cultures depend more on the surrounding context (high context). Anglo-Americans, for example, tend to assume that words are the way to get across a message; they rely on logic and clearly spell out their thoughts. Otherwise, too much could be misunderstood. Japanese, on the other hand, have been socialized from birth to be not as explicit and thereby allow the other person to arrive through intuition at what is intended. They feel that using many words repeats the obvious (Hall 1984). High and low contexts apply not only to macro-cultures but also to smaller units such as communities, families, and individuals.

As with all the other models in this book, no group or person exists exclusively at one end of the continuum or the other, though some are generally high context and others are generally low; and still others are a mixture. Hall points out that simply being from similar contexts (e.g., high, as are both French and Japanese) does not mean that people will operate in the same way. While the French prefer subtlety, they also enjoy lively discussions; the Japanese are more reserved (Hall 1990). Without assuming that all people within a culture will behave in the same way, let us look at some tendencies that can be seen in some cultures.

In low-context cultures such as much of the United States, Germany, Switzerland, Scandinavia, and other north European countries (Hall 1990), the main function of speech is to express one's personal ideas logically and persuasively; expression of self is the ultimate goal. Usually, what is said is more important than who said it. That is, the message is more important than the messenger. Since people tend to have fairly loose connections with others and have many different groups to which they belong, each interaction needs to establish the background. One of Hall's examples is of a courtroom in the United States. In courts, contextual information is seldom allowed: "Answer the question: Yes or No." A newspaper article recently quoted a lawyer who was hired by the opponents of a particularly heart-rending healthcare case: "The bottom line is business is business; the particular facts are not terribly relevant." Only established facts, stripped of all contexting background, are admitted as evidence.

In the high-context courtrooms of France, as a contrast, "the court wants to find out as much as possible about the circumstances behind the surface acts that brought people before the bench" (Hall 1977, 107–108). In high-context cultures, context plays a very important role. Hall lists Japanese, Arabs, and Mediterranean peoples among high-context people who "for most normal transactions in daily life . . . do not require, nor do they expect, much in-depth, background information. This is because they keep themselves informed about everything having to do with the people who are important in their lives"(Hall 1990, 6–7). In high-context cultures, then, the unspoken information that surrounds a message is vital. The attitude toward communication is holistic: Words are inseparable from the person saying them. "In contrast to the Western significance of eloquence and self-assertion, the general attitude for Japanese people toward language and verbalization is that fewer words, supported by the *aesthetics of vagueness* are better than more words" (Ishii and Bruneau 1988, 312). This attitude arises out of their emphasis on self-restraint, reserve, and consensus rather than individual expression. The aim of speech is to promote harmony rather than the speaker's own unique contribution. People will talk around the topic, expecting the other person to grasp the central point, without relying on the demeaning act of verbalizing it. A high-context person will expect the other to know what is bothersome, without having to explicate it.

Neither of these contextual systems is better than the other; both have strengths that contribute to human life and are expressions of the organization and values of their cultural ways passed down through the generations.

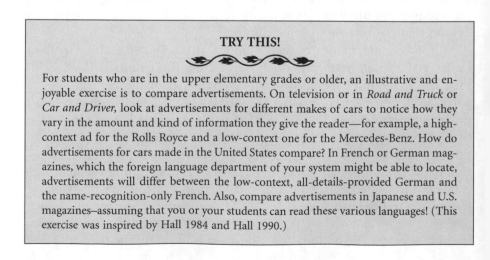

TRY THIS!

For students who are in the upper elementary grades or older, an illustrative and enjoyable exercise is to compare advertisements. On television or in *Road and Truck* or *Car and Driver*, look at advertisements for different makes of cars to notice how they vary in the amount and kind of information they give the reader—for example, a high-context ad for the Rolls Royce and a low-context one for the Mercedes-Benz. How do advertisements for cars made in the United States compare? In French or German magazines, which the foreign language department of your system might be able to locate, advertisements will differ between the low-context, all-details-provided German and the name-recognition-only French. Also, compare advertisements in Japanese and U.S. magazines—assuming that you or your students can read these various languages! (This exercise was inspired by Hall 1984 and Hall 1990.)

JOURNAL TIME

Reflect on your classroom practices and write down in detail how you communicate in different circumstances. Are there times when you assume that everyone knows what is to happen and how (e.g., doing, handing in, grading homework assignments; fire drills, lunch time)? Are there other times when you are in a low-context mode and need to explain the science experiment in great detail? The high-context situations will be most difficult for the ELLs, since they may not share the assumptions built up over the years in dominant-culture schools and may be struggling, as well, with their grasp of English.

CONTEXT IN DOMINANT-CULTURE CLASSROOMS

A dominant-culture classroom in the United States is usually a low-context situation; we give explicit directions and do not expect students to intuit what we expect. The year starts with detailed directions, for example, for content or behavior during "Class Meeting" time. As the year progresses and the workings of the class are understood more fully, we may collapse the announcement simply to "Class Meeting." However, generally speaking, in Anglo-American classrooms, much verbal expression is expected from teacher and student alike; debates encourage verbal facility; we invite students to express themselves; expectations are clearly defined; supporting evidence is crucial. From birth on, in the Anglo-American cultural style which is reflected in mainstream schools in the United States, children are taught the "logical" order of telling a story and what details are necessary.

Students coming from high-context cultures, in interactions with peers or teachers or giving reports, may not state what they consider obvious. In many Asian cultures, if you talk a lot, the value of what you say is lowered. Also, for high-context communicators, the emotional aspect of the situation may have much more emphasis than "the facts." Many high-context students will probably be much more tuned to being polite and making sure that relationships are intact than being direct or using argument to win their points.

Some Other Factors in the Communication Process

When we speak, how we view ourselves and our relationship to the person with whom we are speaking also shapes our interaction. We do not speak in the same way to a colleague as we do to our students; we change our stance and speech even more if we speak to the School Committee or the Chancellor.

Even as we make these changes in substance and style within the same macro-culture, such distinctions appear across cultures as well.

PRESENTATION OF SELF

Obviously, communication is more than just putting words or sentences together. The actual organization of our interactions or the assumptions regarding the interchange are also culturally shaped. "[T]he way ideas are put together into an argument, the way some ideas are selected for special emphasis, or the way emotional information about the ideas is presented . . . causes misunderstanding" (Scollon and Scollon 1981, 12). As one way to become aware of the variety of factors in communication, let's look at a section of a study done by linguists Ronald Scollon and Suzanne Scollon. Domains related to the presentation of self constituted one of the areas that yielded signal differences between Athabaskans and Anglos (both Canadian and American). Three aspects of how we perform in interactions proved to be different.

How Much We Talk. Scollon and Scollon point out that in general Anglos feel they must talk to get themselves known and to display their abilities; some of the most intimate details will be exchanged between strangers. Athabaskans, on the other hand, need to know people well before they open up; at that point, and only then, do they share of themselves. They avoid self-disclosure and persuasion because they feel strongly about personhood, theirs as well as another's. In other words, not only are they hesitant to display their own feelings and ideas, but also they take care not to dissuade others. In our application to the Anglo-American classroom, these hesitancies may hinder participation in classroom debates, in writing or speaking about personal feelings or events, or in making friendships.

Our Position in Power Situations. With Anglos, the person in the "higher" position is the spectator and the one in the "lower" position exhibits her skills, such as parents watching a child, or a teacher listening to students in the classroom. With the Athabaskans, the child does not show off for adults; the adults are expected to display abilities and qualities for the child to emulate. In our classrooms, the situation when an Anglo teacher sets students off on an independent project complicates this relationship. A child who has the sensitivities similar to those of the Athabaskan child possibly sees the teacher as incompetent because he is not displaying skills for the child to learn. At the point of presentation, the teacher sees the student as reserved or passive because the student, now in the superordinate position, becomes very uncomfortable as she sees herself as taking over the job of the teacher. These super- and subordinate positions are in all cultures; how they shape expression differs.

Culturally Sanctioned Behaviors. Anglos have a tendency to boast. How often will a child rush to tell others of a prize won; good résumés enumerate prizes and other accomplishments; applicants for jobs promote their credentials. In many situations we try to impress the other person with our achievements. Even if we are modest, the general aim is to put ourselves in as good a light as we can. Scollon and Scollon point out that Athabaskans are culturally restricted from putting their "best foot forward" because it is bad luck to display oneself in a good light. They do not feel they should anticipate good luck or predict what they will do in the future—even as far ahead as tomorrow (Scollon and Scollon 1981). In our classrooms, a student who comes from another culture where standing out is frowned upon or where plans must not be made far in advance may be reluctant to speak of herself or her plans for summer vacation. Culturally shaped behaviors have an impact on how the student presents himself in the classroom.

CONVERSATIONAL DISTRIBUTION

How to take turns speaking (either by interruption or by turn) is also culturally defined. The millisecond difference in the length of pauses trips us up in a different culture. I find that some immigrant or international students either make many thwarted attempts to enter a conversation or they give up and stay quiet. Of course, many come from cultures where their socialization prescribes that adults initiate the questions, where in a classroom situation they wait to be asked instead of volunteering answers. Others, coming from cultures where simultaneous conversations can be held at the same time (compared to the Anglo habit of one at a time), have no trouble simply starting one of their own, though that does not solve the problem of learning to enter the ongoing conversation. We will look at the value underlying that particular habit of simultaneous conversations in the chapter, interestingly, on non-verbal communication.

Specific Styles of Interaction

In addition to the amount of shared information surrounding talk (high and low context) and some of the other cultural aspects of speech (presentation of self, conversational distribution), verbal communication can be described in actual styles. Professors of communication William Gudykunst and Stella Ting-Toomey list four different styles of communication: *direct/indirect; elaborate/succinct; personal/contextual;* and *instrumental/affective* styles (Gudykunst and Ting-Toomey 1996). Roots of these styles can be seen in the fertile soil of individualism–collectivism, value orientations, as well as high- and low-context cultures.

DIRECT/INDIRECT STYLES

Direct and Indirect styles, the most widespread, reflect clearly high- and low-context messages. In the *direct style*, the message contains the person's true intentions, needs, and wishes. I asked my graduate students to list advice they would give to immigrants or international students in terms of getting along in the Anglo-American culture of the United States. Much of what they said was summed up in one terse expression, "Speak up for what you believe." The content as well as structure of the expression reflected the direct communication style of the speaker. The dominant culture values the use of forceful words of certitude (absolutely, definitely). Assertiveness and personal opinions rank high in communication, as does honesty. Direct, concise, clear speech is preferred. "So, what is your point?" is often heard in the classroom as well as the boardroom.

Verbal messages in the *indirect* style, on the other hand, are more oblique and hide the true intentions of the speaker. Many feel that these two styles are found in gender differences in the Anglo-American culture: The assertiveness and directness valued in the Anglo-American culture is more of a male trait; the intuitive and restrained, a female characteristic. In addition to these micro-cultural differences, style differences apply to macro-cultures as well. Those from high-context cultures and indirect styles (e.g., Japan) are more apt to use qualifiers (maybe, perhaps). They dislike brash pronouncements. Their cultural priority for harmony does not favor bold statements or personal wishes. The indirect style seems to be a more gentle manner of speaking, which, to unaccustomed ears, sounds hopelessly circuitous. A snippet of conversation from Japan: "'It isn't that we can't do it this way,' one Japanese will say. 'Of course,' replies his companion, 'We couldn't deny that it would be impossible to say that it couldn't be done.' 'But unless we can say that it can't be done,' his friend adds, 'it would be impossible not to admit that we couldn't avoid doing it'" (Clancy 1986, 214). To ears used to "This definitely cannot be done for the following reasons," this interchange seems wordy, confusing, and diffuse. However, to those accustomed to leaving possibilities open, the other, direct way seems extremely harsh.

ELABORATE/SUCCINCT STYLES

Elaborate and Succinct styles refer to the *amount* of speech that is valued in different cultures. The *elaborate style* prefers rich, expressive language in everyday conversation. For example, eloquence and emotion are valued in the Arab world. Emotion indicates sincerity, whether it be in an argument or in a compliment. Margaret Nydell, an Arabist who teaches and trains, comments that if a person speaks softly or does not repeat statements, Arabs may wonder about the veracity of the comments. Furthermore, the volume of speech with Arabs is not necessarily an indication of anger, as it might be in the Anglo-American culture of the United States; volume is for dramatic effect and used judiciously. In terms of eloquence, many adjectives, or metaphors or proverbs, garnish the feast of words. "[A] speaker's style of delivery and command of the language appeal to the listeners as much as does the message itself ... *In the Arab World, how you say something is as important as what you have to say* [italics hers]" (Nydell 1996, 117–119). Personal connections in speech are valued, whether it is a direct comment or a reference, by these people who treasure their place in the human web of relationships.

At the other end of the spectrum are those cultures that make use of silence and understatements in their speech, that is, who use the *succinct style*. The Japanese use silence as "a semicolon that reflects the inner pausing of the speaker's reflective state. Through *ma* [the Japanese concept of silence], interpersonal synchrony is made possible" (Gudykunst and Ting-Toomey 1988, 107). Silence speaks in positive ways. Most Anglo-Americans in the United States have a very difficult time with silence in a conversation; indeed from our own personal experiences we can see that often talk simply fills up the void, as opposed to saying anything substantial. International students in my classes have commented that sometimes it seems as though their Anglo-American classmates seem to enjoy hearing the sound of their voices instead of furthering the discussion at hand.

PERSONAL/CONTEXTUAL STYLES

The differences between the Personal and the Contextual styles reflect the individualistic–collectivistic continuum of Chapter Two. The messages and meanings of the *personal style* emphasize the individual person, informality, and equality. Communication in the *contextual style* emphasizes role relationships, formality, and hierarchy. Special vocabularies for age, status, and gender, or sentences that omit personal pronouns (particularly "I"), or the use of titles, or the level of formality, are just some of the ways in which a collectivistic background will surface in communication. Students from collectivistic backgrounds may use much more formal speech; student and teacher are not at the same level in the hierarchy and their communication honors that difference. The style differences may also result in the organization of a topic: In the personal style, the point is made first and supporting details are added later; in the contextual style, the context is set and the point is made at the end.

INSTRUMENTAL/AFFECTIVE STYLES

The dichotomy between Instrumental and Affective styles is similar to a product/process differentiation. The *instrumental* style aims to achieve a goal; the *affective* style pays attention to feelings in the verbal exchange. Here, again,

TRY THIS!

Take a moment to locate yourself in the interactional styles and then think about the students in your classroom, particularly about those with whom you may have some tension. Do they express themselves in different styles than you? Does that subconsciously bother you? Are you naturally more accessible to students who have interactional styles similar to your own?

one can see that these styles apply not just internationally, but across microcultures (e.g., gender) within our own society. We all have had times when we have spoken with another on a feeling level (process oriented), only to have the person answer with a "here's how to address the problem" (goal oriented) solution. People high in the "doing" end of Kluckhohn's human activity dimension (in Chapter Three on Values), who put a lot of emphasis on accomplishing goals, often have styles of conversation that will lead to that end. The responsibility of clearly communicating the message lies with the *sender* in this goal-oriented style. Hence, for example, teachers tend to ask, "Do you understand? Does that make sense?" In many collectivistic cultures, where intuition is paramount, the *receiver* of the message is expected to sensitively perceive the intended meaning before the sender has to actually verbalize it. The priority of connectedness within the network of human relationships means that such needs are known by virtue of being involved with each other. Somewhat similar to the cultures that are generally individualistic or collectivistic, the Anglo-American culture of the United States and some northern European cultures tend to be goal oriented, whereas Asian, Arab, and Latin-American cultures tend to be process oriented in their styles of speaking (Gudykunst and Ting-Toomey 1988).

VERBAL COMMUNICATION STYLES IN THE CLASSROOM

To be subtle and oblique in a culture where directness spells the norm does not leave a good impression. Nor does the reverse. Helping students learn about and possibly adopt some of the styles of the dominant culture is important anywhere in the world. However, in many cases, this adoption involves more than a surface behavior. The ability to switch back and forth between styles can be a boon as well as a bane. A Japanese friend, who had done undergraduate as well as graduate work in the United States, said that when she wanted to show anger, she had to do it in English, since her cultural background would not permit her to show emotion. In other words, changing one's communication pattern may require a change in one's identity. Learning a language is more than learning words; it is also learning the nuances, the subtle ways in which messages are expressed, and the cultural mindset, values, and thinking patterns that produce the messages.

In our classrooms, this cultural patterning happens throughout the day where cultural expectations are reinforced through such seemingly innocuous events as "Sharing Time," for example. In that event, the child is learning the culturally appropriate way of self-presentation. In addition, frequently we will coach a child in how to tell what the child wants to share: "What happened first, and then? . . ." In this way, with these prompts, the child is learning cultural as well as linguistic values. A study of a first-grade "Show and Tell" in the United States found that Anglo-American children used a tightly organized way of speaking and the theme was developed through linear, sequential cohesion. The African-American children, however, usually had a series of episodes that were implicitly connected, that required much inferencing, and that were not necessarily in sequence. The teacher, through her coaching, was preparing the children for the dominant-culture-valued accounting of an event (Michaels and Collins 1984).

When assigning oral or written reports, we often give a general outline that students should follow, an outline that reflects the styles of communication valued in the dominant culture. In our increasingly multicultural society, we, particularly those who take seriously Gardner's eight intelligences, more commonly permit students to give reports in a variety of ways, including multimedia presentations. Messages are conveyed to students by our allowing those options.

As another example, think of the way in which your daily schedule is exhibited in class. Does it reflect a direct, succinct, goal-oriented style? This is not to say that it shouldn't; it is to say that there are many ways in which the dominant culture creeps quietly into our class procedures. Another example might be hiding in our interactions with some students. Sometimes if a strategy for addressing an issue does not seem to bring results, we may want to look for a different melody, rather than continuing to play the same note. Professor Lisa Delpit comments: "In asserting personal authority, the key is not to look to change who you are. Instead, there are certain areas one can focus on to seek solutions when problems arise. For example, turning a directive into a question—'Would you like to sit down now?' or 'Isn't it time to put the scissors away?'—is a polite form of speech that is a mainstream, particularly female, structure. Many kids will not respond . . . because commands are not couched as questions in their home culture. Rather than asking questions, some teachers need to learn to say, 'Put the scissors away' and 'Sit down now'" (Delpit 1998, 17). This informative example indicates how different communication styles may be at work in the classroom and how creative changes can help.

Writing in the Classroom

How do the structures of oral language learned throughout childhood relate to the writing required in school? How is it that we start acquiring writing skills as soon as we are born? Scollon and Scollon state: "It is speaking that dictates the form of the written text" (Scollon and Scollon 1981, 47). How we speak is reflected in how we write: The forms, the cultural assumptions are all there. That was what had happened to me in the spring of my freshman year in college when my professor told me I could not write idiomatic English—the opening vignette of this book. I was transferring into English the discourse patterns of what had been my dominant language in childhood. Despite having been orally bilingual, despite two years in a dominant-culture high school in the United States, the patterns of the language I had used most of the day with my peers and teachers in Turkey still clung to my psyche. Back in the days of my childhood and even college, bilingualism was not common for Anglo-Americans and was still controversial. Indeed, research in those days suggested that it was perhaps detrimental to a child's development. Today, we know that not only is it *not* detrimental, but also it is beneficial. What we need these days is to be aware of the systemic impact of this gift, in order to help these fortunate students achieve their potential in both languages. The various characteristics of the Anglo-American style of expression are simply different from those of others in the world; they are not universal. No better, no worse, it is also normative in the mainstream schools in the United States.

Writing, then, as well as speaking, reflects culture. Students come to school with rich language experiences; they are familiar with the forms and functions of language of their cultural background. They may come with a different set of communication models. Children who are socialized to use fewer details when speaking (because the information was shared or obvious in some other way) or to be very factual will write very differently from children who have been socialized to be elaborate in their descriptions, or to be creative in retelling a story. A fascinating study compared the development of the expository paragraph in English with paragraph development in four other language groups. Expository paragraph development in English is often deductive, with a statement and supporting examples; it proceeds to the conclusion through reason; it does not digress into details that do not further the central idea. Professor Robert Kaplan's analysis contrasts the linear development of a paragraph in English with that in Semitic languages (e.g., Hebrew, Arabic), which tend to have series of parallel constructions; with Oriental languages (e.g., Chinese, Japanese, Korean), which are prone to circular constructions; with Romance languages (e.g., Spanish, French, Italian), which allow digressions; and with Russian, which is a combination of digressions, parallel constructions, and subordinate structures (Kaplan 1966). Author Anne Fadiman found that the Hmong feel it is important to put an event into context by showing how it relates to other things throughout *history*, that "you can miss a lot by sticking to the point" (Fadiman 1997, 13). If we can be aware that different ways of approaching paragraph development exist, not only can we use it in understanding our students' mistakes, but also we can point out these differences so that the students are then empowered to understand how they need to change when they write in standard English.

Reflections on Juan

In the opening vignette of this chapter, Juan was helped when Victoria pointed out to him, in simple ways, *why* she had made the corrections. Previously, she had tried examples ("This is the way the sentence/paragraph needs to read"); she had tried to have him speak the paragraph, suggesting alternatives to his expressions. Juan had not been able to internalize the differences between the two systems of writing to actually know what he was doing wrong. Now, in order to make sure that he was able to truly understand, Victoria also gave him scrambled paragraphs which he needed to put in order, as well as delete unnecessary sentences. She was careful not to denigrate his digressive or personalized way of writing, but simply showed him and practiced with him the more linear style that was expected in dominant-culture classrooms. She set up times during class when she would urge all her students to write in ways that felt comfortable and then at other times insisted that they write in the "classroom style." The students came to understand the difference; she felt she could support the cultural background of the student and also teach the necessary, dominant-culture style. Juan needed to keep his home-shaped rhetoric for communication within his home culture; he also needed to learn school rhetoric for his schoolwork and his future in the dominant Anglo-American culture of the United States.

English at Home

As a teacher of English Language Learners, I often heard both teachers and parents suggest that for the ELL to learn English quickly, the family should be speaking English at home. I have serious problems with this suggestion. Author Richard Rodriguez, in his haunting book *Hunger of Memory*, describes the change in his home when that very experience occurred in his life, when the nuns at his school asked his parents to speak English at home. While Rodriguez uses this experience against bringing the home language into school (i.e., against bilingual education), I see in it the importance of keeping the home language alive in the home. A certain warm intimacy of belonging, of affection, of acceptance suffuses the language used by loving parents in nurturing their children. Rodriguez describes how, shortly after his parents, siblings, and he started speaking English at home, life changed forever: "[T]he special feeling of closeness at home was diminished by then. Gone was the desperate, urgent, intense feeling of being at home; rare was the experience of feeling myself individualized by family intimates. . . . No longer so close; no longer bound tight by the pleasing and troubling knowledge of our public separateness" (Rodriguez 1982, 22–23). While Rodriguez does come, finally, to experience intimacy in English, a certain nostalgia emerges when he describes the feelings before and after the momentous event of bringing the public language into the private sphere. I believe maintaining the home language at home matters very significantly for the following reasons:

- Home needs to be a refuge. Learning a language is a very tiring job; being surrounded by a language and people you do not understand is exhausting, as anyone who has traveled extensively can attest. Learning a language can also be a frightening experience. Home needs to be a place where a student can relax and gather strength for the following day. Home needs to be a place where the student can express himself freely and fluently; where she can be reassured of her competence; where joy, frustration, and need can be easily verbalized and understood. Everyone needs a sense of belonging. Home needs to be a place where the aloneness of being in school can be assuaged by connection and acceptance.

- Home needs to be a place where the linguistic affiliation to the extended family can be maintained and the cultural bonds can be celebrated. Grandparents, extended family, and friends from the "old country" are still an important part of our lives, even after we have moved. Too many times I have heard that the relationship between grandparents and grandchildren who live on different continents has been broken simply due to the fact that the grandchildren cannot speak their home language. Culturally, students who have started making the transition from one culture to another and who are caught, momentarily, in between, need to have a grounding in their home culture, and need to have pride in their heritage. Strength proceeds from strength both in language acquisition and in adjustment.

- Home needs to nurture good attitudes toward the new language. Being forced to speak English at home, after a whole day of hearing nothing but that, may trigger more negative emotions than linguistic development. Learning English—or any new language—happens much more quickly when attitudes toward it are positive. Resistance, resulting from weariness or lack of motivation, for example, will retard learning. Negative attitudes toward the culture or toward the reason for being in the new country (e.g., for little children who are not part of the decision to move) or toward the language and what it symbolizes can retard grasping the language.

- Often, newcomer parents do not speak English well themselves. Asking parents to speak English at home puts them in an embarrassing position with their children. In addition to accent, the parents' structures of grammar may not be correct and that places the student in a difficult spot. Either she corrects and further embarrasses her parents, or she learns incorrect structures which she then must unlearn in school. That process, again, puts the student in a tense situation where she must admit that her parents are wrong (that comes soon enough in U.S. school systems).

- This is not to say that English must not be spoken at home. It is to say that the language at home should be whatever is most comfortable *for the student and family* at that time. Soon enough, the ELL will become much more comfortable and fluent in English and will want to bring it into the home. At that time, the family will need to make decisions as to how to proceed. It is the forcing of the issue that troubles me.

Uses of Language in the Classroom

Speaking the home language at home will not retard the student's acquisition of English. In fact, professor Shirley Brice Heath contends that academic success depends more on *how* children use their primary language rather than on which language they use and that the school's responsibility lies in using the greatest variety possible of both written and oral language (Heath 1986). In Heath's view, speaking English, in and of itself, will not ensure success in the classroom. What really matters is knowing, even in a different language, how to manipulate various aspects of language (e.g., being able to give running commentary on what is happening, or retelling an event, both of which are among language uses valued in the dominant-culture classroom). Heath points out that the single developmental style as reflected in the scope and sequence approach in classrooms assumes that one size fits all students. However, as we have seen in this and previous chapters, culture plays an important role in the acquisition of language skills; hence, language development is a varied experience. The key is how much the usage within the home language matches the genres of language used in the classroom. Knowing what is valued in mainstream classrooms is helpful so that we can recognize our own classroom expectations. Here, I would like to briefly mention the six types of language activities which Heath sees as most valued in the dominant-culture classrooms of the United States. They start in infancy.

- *Label quests:* These interactions answer "what" questions about naming objects or attributes For example, at home: "That's hot!" or at school: "What's the hero's name?" Usually they precede higher order questions of how and why.

- *Meaning quests:* These are used to determine meaning (at home with a toddler: "You want some milk?" or at school: "Tell me what the author meant").

- *Recounts:* The student is able to tell a story—or relate an event—that is known to both the speaker and the listener: "Tell Grandma where we went this morning." At school, written and oral summaries are in this category.

- *Accounts:* Only the speaker knows the information. At home, the parent asks about a child's afternoon activity. At school, this could be a "Sharing Time" description, or an interpretation of what a reading meant to a particular student.

- *Eventcasts:* This genre includes giving a commentary of what is happening, or giving directions, or planning for future events; for example, "We'll go to the store after we eat lunch." As teachers, we use this, for example, when telling students what to expect in the next hour or day or class.

- *Stories:* At home, these range from storytelling at bed- or other times, stories about a parent's youth; they are fictional as well as true. At school, expository prose and fictional accounts are examples of this genre.

While these types of language usage may seem quite usual to members of the dominant culture of the United States, not all cultures use language in these ways. Just an example or two will illustrate some of the differences. In the Mexican-American community of her study, Heath found that parents did not see a reason to ask a child information that was already shared (recounts), or to verbalize what they were doing even as they were doing it (Eventcasts). In Chinese-American homes, recounts were rare as well, though all the other activities seemed to be present (Heath 1986).

Again, we don't want to generalize all Mexican-American or Chinese-American students, but the study can serve as a reminder that there may be particular uses of language with which linguistic minority students may not be familiar.

Language, the vehicle of verbal communication for scientific discoveries and passionate feelings, for sweetest compliments and severest taunts, for joyous heights and aching depths, and for ordinary routines of our everyday living, is shaped by culture. Culture has molded the person to what is considered valued, hence what is given expression. Obviously, there is more to learning a language than just the grammar. One must also learn the ways of thinking to be truly a part of a community. But, the burden cannot rest only with the student; we teachers and our schools must be included as well. While this is difficult to say these days, given the proliferating responsibilities that we must assume, nonetheless, as our linguistic minority population grows, this issue cannot be avoided. We must understand that we need to teach more than the grammar of the language. ELLs must be exposed to not only correct syntax but also the underpinnings of the language. We need to realize (or question, as did Juan's teacher, Victoria) that there may be cultural reasons why students write as they do. Or they may not know just what is expected of a task. We need to remember, however, as we teach linguistic minority students the ways of the words, ideas, and thoughts of our language, just what it is that we are asking them to learn. From birth, they have been exposed to the patterns of their cultural interactions, which they have internalized and which have helped form their identity. By asking them to change their way of communication, which expresses their essence, we make no small request; we ask for no small task.

Chapter Six

"High Fives" and Raised Eyebrows: Nonverbal Communication

Actions speak louder than words.

—English proverb

My schedule for the day was worse than usual. I did not even have time for lunch. However, Mrs. Yousef was insistent that she had to see me about her son. So, I explained the predicament, arranged for her to come at 1:00, and told her that I had another appointment at 1:20. She arrived at 1:18 and was surprised and miffed that she had to make another appointment to see me. Frankly, I was surprised at her insensitivity and lack of apology for keeping me waiting. Fortunately I had all sorts of work to do so the time was not completely lost.

—(Roland, *a kindergarten teacher*)

Generally calm and collected, Roland was not happy as he spit out his troubles. According to Roland, Omar, the student, was doing fine; it was Omar's mother who needed some instruction in etiquette. This was not the first time Mrs.

Yousef had kept Roland waiting, but he wanted it to be the last. Fed up with her arrogance that never paid attention to anyone else's schedules, he wanted suggestions as to how to impress upon Mrs. Yousef that, in the United States, a busy teacher cannot be treated in such an offhand manner. The Yousefs had arrived from Egypt two months before—in fact, just two weeks before school began. There had been a flurry of arrangements to get Omar registered appropriately; Roland had noticed some late appointments at that time but assumed that the process of getting settled into the rental apartment, finding a car, and learning to navigate around town were the cause. Now in mid-November, Roland's schedule was increasingly busy and he felt that the Yousefs' schedule would be less so with regard to their only child.

Nonverbal Communication, in General

When I was a child, my mother used to caution me with the old adage, "Your actions speak louder than your words." I don't believe she knew just how true her words were. Estimates are that 60–90 percent of communication is nonverbal. When the term is mentioned, I think we usually think of some kind of gesture that has communicated a message that was unintended; our "body language" betrayed our true feelings. Or, it may have been a very intentional nonverbal interaction with others, such as a pat on the back or a glare, understood by the recipient who shared the same cultural assumptions. Or, our gesture conveyed a very different meaning to someone of a different culture. Actually, nonverbal communication encompasses far more than those actions. For example, colors have different meanings for people around the world: white is a color for mourning in China though Latin Americans choose violet; yellow, the color of foolishness or pity in Japan, signals envy in Saudi Arabia (Damen 1987). Above and beyond interactions, movements, or colors, some other areas of nonverbal communication are "clothing and hair styles . . . interpersonal distance . . . architecture and interior design . . . 'artifacts' and nonverbal symbols, such as lapel pins, walking sticks, jewelry . . . graphic symbols, such as pictures to indicate 'men's room' or 'handle with care' . . . art and rhetorical forms, including wedding dances and political parades . . . smell . . . synchronization of speech . . . cosmetics . . . drum signals, smoke signals, factory whistles, police sirens" (Condon and Yousef 1975, 123–124).

Nonverbal communication is very extensive and learned well before verbal communication. From infancy we start picking up the cues: We are

TRY THIS!

Using the previous list as a partial guide, discuss with students the way people "speak" without speaking. Together, make a list of categories (e.g., clothing, graphic symbols) and then add specifics in each category (graphically, i.e., nonverbally). Invite the students to add to the nonverbal chart for the duration of the project, as they see or experience new forms. Expand their understanding of the varieties of ways to communicate. In upper grades, discuss what they say to the world nonverbally by hairstyle and color, body piercing, and other "fashion statements." Help them see whether they communicate what they hope to.

held when we cry, we see frowns that convey displeasure, we come when beckoned, we learn with whom we can snuggle, what is pleasing to wear, and we have various reactions to odors (body, incense, food). As we mature, the list does not end with these individualized behaviors; it also includes, for example, the way we organize space and time, or the sounds we make that accompany language. In the classroom, we communicate nonverbally in numerous ways, ranging from how we dress, how the desks are arranged, where we stand or sit during class, or which gestures we use to signify "Come here," or "Good job!" for example.

The problem is that despite the fact that the larger percentage of our message is nonverbal, usually only the verbal part receives the speaker's attention. Surely you, too, have seen presenters at conferences or advertisers on television whose unconscious, repetitive hand motions detract from the speech or the ad. The famous glance at a watch during the Clinton/Bush presidential debates spoke volumes that President Bush and his advisors wished they could take back. Be it in public or private, people are apt not to think about their nonverbal messages.

When one does start to think about nonverbal communication, a dichotomy presents itself: On the one hand, some think that facial expressions and gestures are universal, since most are "natural" expressions. Crying, laughing, blushing, and smiling seem to be fairly global. Daily on television, we see horror or fear in the faces of those under attack. On the other hand, many people have compiled lists of "weird" or different gestures that are used in one culture and not in another and can tell anecdotes of funny or embarrassing situations due to misunderstandings regarding meaning. Is there any commonality across cultures? What is specific to a culture? In this chapter, after looking at what can be considered common across cultures, we'll take a look at what types of behaviors may be different. I have narrowed the field of the current discussion to just three areas: behaviors that are related to individual movements, to language, and to context. Also, listing all the non-verbal communication patterns of countless specific cultures would be an impossible and absurd task. My hope is that by exploring some areas of non-verbal communication, our own assumptions will become clear. That, in turn, will enable us to avoid the mistake of thinking that "A smile is the same in every language" and permit us to be open to new interpretations of habitual communication patterns.

Some Specifics of Nonverbal Communication

Darwin provided evidence of the innateness and universality of emotional expression. The feelings of anger, joy, and sadness seem to be expressed universally (Darwin 1872). What has been further researched, however, and found to vary by culture is the when, where, how, how much, and the why of that expression. In some cultures, you do not show anger in public, nor affection, though you may feel it; in some cultures, your smile may be a response to embarrassment; in some cultures, grief needs to be fully expressed, not limited to silent tears. That is, the circumstances which elicit the expression, the intensity of the expression, and the norms for displaying the expression are culturally specific. Let's look at those three areas of nonverbal communication, mentioned previously, related to the individual, to language, and to the context.

NONVERBAL COMMUNICATION RELATED TO THE INDIVIDUAL

Eye Contact. This behavior is very subtle and complex, with not only cultural differences but also gender, regional, and ethnic differences. It encompasses the sense of being stared at or being ignored, due to a gaze too long or too short or non-existent. This is perhaps one of the nonverbal behaviors that gives us the most concern: We are apt to feel insulted, or the student is not paying attention or telling the truth when the student does not look us in the eye. In the dominant culture of the United States, where the concept of equality is so strong, we expect to directly face those with whom we speak; we want to make sure we have the person's attention. Direct eye contact implies truth and honesty in the dominant Anglo-American culture. However, in cultures with more hierarchy in the family or society, students show respect by *not* looking an elder in the eye. To do so is to elevate oneself to the position of an equal and, in school, to challenge our authority. Of course exceptions exist, not only within cultures but also across seemingly similar cultures (one cannot say that all hierarchical cultures behave in the same way). So, if a student is not exhibiting the "proper" attitude of respect, before telling her to look at us as we speak to her and thus perhaps forcing her to be *dis*respectful, we need to consider the fact that she may have been socialized differently. At a later time, when the tension of a direct interaction has dissipated and we have ascertained that she had different socialization, we can have a generalized conversation with the whole class about some different nonverbal behavior patterns, making sure not to embarrass the particular student.

Touching. Another nonverbal behavior that confuses many of us, touching has many interpretations across cultures. For example, in many East Asian cultures, touching the top of the head of a child is an offensive gesture. But touching goes far beyond this one gesture. It covers the amount of contact in common, everyday conversations and situations, as well as a need to stand close to other people. Being packed *extremely* close in a bus in China is far more acceptable than it would be in the United States. As we will see later, Anglo-Americans have a very defined personal bubble that precludes a lot of touching of another person. We are seen as cold and reserved by people from many other cultures. For example, in the dominant culture of the United States, hand shaking as a greeting is not used as often as it is in Southern Europe, nor are two adults of the same gender seen walking down the street holding hands or with arms around each other. Arabs feel deprived and "alienated at the lack of close, intimate contact with North Americans, while North Americans find Arabs' need for close personal space anxiety-provoking and disturbing" (Gudykunst and Kim 1992, 278). However, to keep us from overgeneralizing about all Arabs, please note that, "in Saudi Arabia and the Arabian Peninsula countries, touching other people is not nearly so common and can even be offensive" (Nydell 1996, 52). The inter-relationship of touching and gender is an extremely important and defining factor in all cultures; not only whom we touch but also where such displays are acceptable vary by culture. For example, hugging a person in public is not acceptable in much of Japan. Many Japanese graduate students speak of how ambivalent they are as to whom, how much, and where to hug a person in the United States. On the other hand, Hispanic or some Arab cultures as well as some Mediterranean cultures enjoy a greater amount of public touching.

Posture. The universal aspect of this behavior indicates that we all sit, lie down, stand, and walk. But how we do these things varies across cultures. Tourists from the United States can often be identified from afar due to their usually bouncy, fast-paced gait when walking. "Come on, Laura, don't dawdle; we don't have all day," reflects the Anglo-American orientation to time as well as activity. Our walking depicts these values.

Sitting on the floor to eat occurs around the world, and having been socialized to sit on a chair at the table, I am in awe of people who can sit on the floor gracefully for long periods of time. I am also impressed with villagers in countless rural areas around the world who sit on their haunches for a very long time. Children in school may be accustomed to sitting cross-legged on the floor or a bench. When I was an elementary school student in Turkey in the late 1940s, at the beginning of every period or during class if our teacher thought we were getting sloppy, she would remind us that we were to sit properly. She would then walk around to inspect each child's attempt. That meant that erect in our seats (three to an elongated desk), we were to sit with both feet on the floor, arms stretched out straight in front of us and our clasped hands resting on the desk. We might be expected to sit this way for most of the period, if no writing were required. This posture was important not just to clear minds and unbuckle backs, but also to give appropriate respect to the education we were receiving. While intervening years have softened these behaviors, the example serves as an illustration of the differences in attitude toward education as expressed in posture. Contrast that to the "reading lounges" created in many elementary classrooms of dominant-culture classrooms in the United States, where the students are invited to "get comfortable" when reading a book, or to the myriad students sprawled all over the classroom or corridor floors, working studiously on a project. Cultural attitudes define different ways of behavior. Students coming from other cultures have a difficult time adjusting to the general informality of posture in the United States. When teachers sit on the floor to help students and people do not stand at strict attention during the national anthem, newcomers see in that behavior a casual attitude toward education and toward country.

Gestures. Gestures are probably what we think of first when nonverbal communication is mentioned. A few gestures may be universal but to assume such is dangerous. Nodding ("yes") and shaking the head ("no") might be considered a gesture known around the world. However, Turks are among those who informally say "no" with a quick raise of the eyebrows, a imperceptible upward nod of the head, and sometimes an audible "tsk"— a gesture incomprehensible in the United States. In India, wagging the head from side to side (slightly similar to but really quite different from the Anglo "no") shows understanding and agreement; the non-Indian takes a little while to catch on to its meaning. Obviously the same gesture does not always carry across cultures: "The same gesture (making a circle with thumb and forefinger) which means 'OK' to a North American can mean money to a Japanese, can signify extreme hostility to an Arab, and be obscene for an Italian" (Irujo 1988, 144). Gestures signifying "come" or "go" are also different across cultures: Some use the palm down to signal "come," and comment that the beckoning done with palm up and one finger by many Anglo-Americans in the United States is insulting in their view. While one can learn a few specifics that pertain to particular cultures, remembering all acceptable gestures in all cultures is impossible. However, one can be sensitive to the fact that gestures and postures do carry different meanings. If a student registers a look of confusion or alarm, it may not be the language that was misunderstood, but rather the nonverbal part of the communication.

Facial Expressions.   The propensity of Anglo-Americans to smile at strangers is confusing to many international students. An Arab student thought he must have dressed in a weird way; a Japanese man thought the women who smiled were showing romantic interest in him; a Korean commented that in his country, smiles were reserved for friends, not strangers; a Vietnamese felt that the perception of superficiality of Anglo-Americans was due to their excessive smiling (Barna 1988). For the Japanese, in addition to joy, a smile can also hide embarrassment, failure, dismay, grief, or even anger. Given the more narrow meaning of a smile for Anglo-Americans, it is difficult not to jump to conclusions of disrespect when a Japanese or other Asian student starts to smile when apologizing. That is the time to take a deep breath and wonder about what other cultural patterns might be at work.

NONVERBAL COMMUNICATION RELATED TO LANGUAGE

Have you ever listened to two or three people speaking in a different language and decided that they must be having a major argument? Or realized that despite the fact that someone has been in this country for a number of years and speaks English fluently, she still has a trace of an undefinable something that indicates that English was not her first language? Or shifted about with discomfort when lapses of silence seemed to fill the time with an immigrant adult? These indicate some of the different aspects of nonverbal

---

TRY THIS!

Have students list—from direct observation, if possible—the ways in which an infant or toddler who does not yet communicate verbally gets his meaning across. What language does she use? Talk about the expression of these early elemental needs and then how they grow into culturally shaped, individual nonverbal behaviors. Who shapes them? How?

communication related to language: vocal qualities, intonation, and the use of silence. They don't happen just with immigrants, either: "sighs too deep for words," or coughs or moans can convey a variety of expressions which family members (or same-culture persons) learn to recognize quickly; sometimes the lack of "uh-huh" as a response in a phone conversation makes us wonder if we are being heard or understood.

Since English is a non-tonal language (compared to, say, Chinese), we change word meanings with stress, for example, pre*sent* (verb) and *present* (noun). We can change meanings of sentences with intonation from a statement to a question or even an exclamation. "It's hot" changes with the addition of the invisible period, question mark or exclamation point as depicted in one's voice. These kinds of stress and intonation patterns vary across languages and sometimes convey unintended attributes to ears unaccustomed to them. We may think that someone sounds angry because his tone is louder and harsher than is customary to us. Intonation patterns learned from childhood are very difficult to overcome and often are the cause of much misunderstanding. Simple statements, such as "Oh, you mean next week," said with a non-English intonation pattern can seem inordinately aggressive or rude and cause defensiveness in the other person. If the non-English speaker uses her own intonation pattern, it may come across as "Why can't you explain yourself more clearly?" rather than the intended simple clarification.

Another aspect of nonverbal communication as related to language really has nothing to do with sounds: It is the use of silence. The presence of silence is universal; however, its meaning and use vary considerably from culture to culture. In the dominant Anglo-American culture of the United States, speech is valued over silence. In most scenarios silence often makes us uneasy. The Anglo-American low-context communication mode means words carry import; words persuade; words convey our unique ideas. Silence, then, is the opposite of that. In high-context communication that does not place emphasis on verbalization by the speaker, but rather intuition by the hearer, silence is seen more positively. Comfort with silence may be more prevalent also in cultures whose activity orientation is more "being" or "becoming" rather than "doing." For those from doing-oriented cultures, silence conveys a waste of time; being- and becoming-oriented people tend to see silence as a time for fulfillment. In cultures that are comfortable with it, silence has a variety of functions. In Japan, silence can convey dissension: "For example, when a person who is requested to do something wishes to refuse the request, he or she will pause and not respond within an appropriate time period. This sends a negative message to the person who made the request" (Nishida 1996, 115). Thereby, the hearer (or receiver of the message) knows by the length of the silence that the request has been refused; both sides avoid the embarrassment of a stark, uncomfortable response. Around the world, the meaning of silence is different: Some may use it as agreement; some, as privacy; some, as respect; some, as control. As people who are uncomfortable with lapses in conversation, Anglo-Americans need to be particularly mindful of the different meanings and values of silence.

NONVERBAL COMMUNICATION RELATED TO CONTEXT

Two aspects of nonverbal communication related to context are space and time. (Some others which we will not discuss are olfaction, clothing, personal appearance, and artifacts.) Space and time often do not even tickle the edges of our consciousness when considering ways in which we communicate. However, both these aspects can communicate so strongly that they cause misunderstandings or at least surprise among culturally different people.

Feelings About Space.   The use of space, both personal and social, varies across cultures. Our perception of space is such an unconscious assumption that when we are with people whose attitudes or boundaries differ, we may feel uncomfortable without knowing exactly why. Anthropologist Edward Hall, who has done a lot of work in this area, writes of three different kinds of space: fixed-feature, semi-fixed feature, and informal (personal) space (Hall 1969), all of which carry meaning for the mainstream teacher.

• *Fixed-Feature Space.*   Fixed-feature space encompasses the layouts of villages, towns, and cities, which are not really haphazard but generally follow a plan. For example, some cities are planned as radiating stars; some, as grids. Some cultures emphasize lines (streets) and name them; for others, intersections are more important. For example, in trying to locate an office in Macau (a Special Administrative Region of China), our daughter found that except for major thoroughfares, street names and building numbers are eminently unimportant; directions are given by using landmarks with which the inquiring individual is familiar (Clayton 2001, 344–346). In the United States, we are apt to apologize if we do not remember the street name and use landmarks to give directions, or we give them in addition to the street name. In western-style houses, each room has a specific function; in much of the rest of the world, one room serves many functions. From the beginning of life we become accustomed to particular amounts of space around us, whether it be in small apartments or in large mansions. Architects work hard to understand the attitudes of their clients in order to create the space within the building to fit not only their needs but also their culturally shaped psyches.

Fixed-feature space, familiar to most immigrant students, is a self-contained classroom with a few windows and four walls that meet the ceiling. "Open classrooms" or those with nooks and crannies or those with a bank of windows might add a little bit of unconscious adjustment. The students might feel, subconsciously, that the space seems too casual for rigorous work. On the other hand, students from warm climates may be accustomed to self-contained classrooms with half walls, surrounding an open courtyard in order to make the most of moving air in a hot climate. Even the fixed-feature space of a classroom or school may be an adjustment the ELL must make.

• *Semi-Fixed-Feature Space.* Semi-fixed-feature space refers to that which can—or may—be moved within a building or a room. In some societies, that can be not just furniture, but walls as well. In Japan, walls may be moved, depending on the current function of the room. Most people in the United States consider an armchair semi-fixed, but in both China and Germany, Hall found it a fixed feature during the time of his research: A person did not move the chair unless specifically suggested by the host (Hall 1969, 111; 1990, 40).

In the classroom, many immigrant students come from classrooms where desks have been in rows; desks in groupings or chairs in a semi-circle are unusual. Students may also not be sure of other semi-fixed features of the classroom: plants, classroom pets, paper stacks, communal versus personal magic markers, and so forth. The concept of activity centers in a classroom may be new to them as well.

• *Informal Space.* Informal space marks the space we maintain in our interactions with others. Hall has identified four zones, each with the understanding that our attitudes and feelings toward the other person determine the distance we unconsciously adopt. His sample came from the northeastern seaboard of the United States, and Hall readily admits that this is not representative of humankind. However, I believe that his research helps us understand the variety of personal and social space issues. While the zones are Hall's (1969), extensions to the classroom are mine.

Envision four concentric circles around you. The first circle, the *intimate* zone, extends from your body out to about eighteen inches and includes comforting, protecting, or any physical activity where there may be touching. In dominant-culture classrooms, we would be standing over a child in the classroom to correct work or speaking to a student about a personal or disciplinary matter that is not to be shared with the whole class.

The second circle, the *personal* zone, starts at eighteen inches and goes out to about four feet, the latter being the distance for most conversations in a moderate voice. Picture yourself in conversation with parents at a parent-teacher conference, or in the Teachers' Room for lunch. Except when lecturing, this describes the most commonly used distance in a dominant-culture classroom in the United States—at least on the northeastern seaboard.

The third circle, the *social* zone, starts at four feet and extends out to twelve feet. We cannot touch another person, but usually try to maintain eye contact for conversational purposes in the United States. In many classrooms, our desk will be in this zone, a place from which we can see the whole class and are accessible to everyone.

The final circle, the *public* zone, starts at twelve feet and extends to twenty-five feet or more. In governmental life, visits from heads of state are carefully choreographed so that breaches of conduct do not mar international relationships. My Chinese graduate students have told me that in China, people watch the placement of government officials at a conference dais to determine whether they are in favor or not. In schools in the United States, all-school gatherings fit into this zone; some speakers try to minimize the expected formality with informal stance or talk.

The limits of these zones are culturally shaped. Reading them, perhaps you have noted differences between the sample on which Hall based his observations and your own limits. Latin Americans and Arabs usually like to be much closer than Anglo-Americans feel is comfortable. Their conversational distance (personal zone) is often the Anglo-Americans' intimate zone. Sarah, one of the teachers in the vignette in Chapter Four, felt that Maria was "clingy," which may have been her way of saying that Maria seemed to stand too close to her. Maria intruded beyond Sarah's personal zone into her intimate zone. Maria, on the other hand, still felt within her traditional personal space.

Hall elaborates about the differences between Germans, English, French, Japanese, and Arabs in their concepts about space—both personal and social (Hall 1969). His primary assertion is that many misunderstandings occur due to these unconscious attitudes about space and its use. For example, northern Germans have such a sense of personal space that to look at others even at public distances is considered to be an intrusion. For Arabs, on the other hand, the person is deep inside the body, so they have no sense of a private zone outside the body. That enables them to be physically very close to others. Hall describes an Arab attitude: "To smell one's friend is not only nice but desirable, for to deny him your breath is to act ashamed" (Hall 1969, 160). You can imagine the misreading that might occur between two people—one who has been taught to shield one's breath from others and the other who has been socialized to envelop the hearer not only in words but in life-giving breath. We must use caution with this information since situational and relational features, gender, and social class also play a role in interactions. However, the concept is helpful in the event that a mysterious uneasiness or sudden inexplicable discomfort occurs in exchanges with students socialized to different expectations.

Attitudes Toward Time. Time stands as another component in nonverbal communication related to the context. The fixation on time in the Anglo-American culture of the United States, on appointments, on attitudes toward time, and on what time says within a culture led Hall to identify different cultural attitudes toward time. The Anglo-American emphasis on the future and getting there, our belief in shaping our fate, as well as the importance of the individual make us very time conscious. "Time is money." We consider time to be linear from the past to the future, which we use, waste, give, take, spend, or save. In many parts of the United States, if we do not know the guests very well, we might be considered rude to issue an invitation to dinner just one day in advance; appointments are made well in advance and quite strictly adhered to; we wonder how early or late we can call someone on the telephone; the passing of hours is marked by tolling from clocks. Indeed, this preoccupation with time expresses itself by watches on our person and clocks in our cars. Our lives are run by appointment calendars—which is not a universal pattern.

A different way of looking at time is one where life is not regulated by a clock or a calendar, but by "the fullness of time," that is, when it is appropriate for something to occur. Generally speaking, this attitude toward time occurs in cultures with more emphasis on a person's relationships than on an individual's schedule. Inanimate conventions of clocks or calendars do not carry the urgency of a present involvement with another individual.

This fundamental attitude toward time shapes life; the present is as important as, if not more important than, the future. People are relaxed about the timing of events; parties do not have a fixed beginning or end. The event will begin when everyone can get there, not when the clock says so. An illustration of this different attitude toward time was described by Linda Weltner. In an October 28, 1993, *Boston Globe* article entitled "Ever so humble: Freedom from the tyranny of time," she described a storytelling workshop she attended. A Masai warrior was describing the customs and traditions of his people to a fascinated audience when a workshop organizer told him that his time was up. He resisted and said: "'There is one lady in this room who says I must come to a stop . . . but I am asking you, do you not wish to hear more of my story?' We could have listened to him for the rest of the day, so he went on until the official came to the front of the room and ended the session. The words, 'Your time is up,' seemed to have no impact on him at all. He'd told us he'd never seen a watch or a clock before meeting Westerners.

Nor had his tribe invented a way of keeping time. 'We know dawn is near when the birds begin to sing. The sun tells us if it is morning or afternoon, and at night we look at the position of the stars,' he'd explained. The Masai neither know nor celebrate birthdays. They measure the length of life by the obvious. Is the person young or old, a child or an adult? 'What else,' Mpeti asked us, 'is it necessary to know?'" From another part of the world comes this vivid description of the difference between life in the United States and that in rural Italy: "At home in California, time often feels like a hula-hoop, a ceaseless whirl on a body fixed but rocking in place. I could kiss the ground here [Italy], not to feel myself in that tight space where the past gnaws the future but in the luxuriant freedom of a long day to walk out for a basket of plums under the great wheel of the Mediterranean sun" (Mayes 1999, 250).

In cultures where the present is valued over the future, delays are expected and actually are not considered to be delays, since that concept requires a sense of deadline and a sense of wasting time. Hall tells of a Sioux friend who had done well in the Anglo-American culture of the United States, graduated from an Ivy League college, and had gone back to help his people. He bemoaned the fact that the Sioux did not have any words for—or even the concept of—"waiting" or "late." He believed that one of his biggest challenges was to help the Sioux understand [not necessarily accept] the importance of time within the Anglo-American culture if they were going to be able to find work there (Hall 1973).

Definitions of "lateness" vary from culture to culture as well. Usually, in the dominant culture of the United States, we arrive at an appointment a few minutes early; we apologize if we keep a person (on either side of the desk) waiting five to ten minutes; a half-hour wait is almost inexcusable unless particular extenuating circumstances such as a blizzard, flood, or traffic tie-up are the cause. At that point, with many apologies, many will feel the need to make another appointment. To keep a person waiting more than a half-hour is considered inconceivable (except, it seems, in the medical profession). Equivalents of those definitions in other cultures may start at different points: that is, to keep a person waiting thirty to forty-five minutes is not necessarily rude, depending on their relative status. In some cultures, the determining factor is the relationship between the people involved. Friends will understand; officials or strangers may not be as accommodating. Most often, however, people are more important than schedules.

Hall (1990, 1973) sees people's attitudes toward time as two distinct camps: *monochronic* (one thing at a time) and *polychronic* (several things at a time). Generally in the dominant culture of the United States, people live and work with a basic preference for doing things "one at a time." In school, one of the first things we do is to teach children to get in lines, to learn to wait for their turn, and to appreciate the value of sequential, linear order. Interactions with people are generally one-on-one. In monochronic, Anglo-American culture, usually one person at a time speaks; in fact, there seem to be confusion and disorientation when more than one conversation occurs at the same time. We ask our students to give their attention to the one who is speaking. Often at dinner parties, dialogues will fade out and attention will focus on one speaker. During appointments, we expect to have calls held so that attention is undivided. If a call interrupts, apologies are made with the assurance that the call will be short and is extraordinarily significant. Slaves to calendars, the crux of the matter is what they represent. The dominant culture of the United States values being in control of external forces. At a European airport in 1978, the gates to a flight to Turkey were opened and the whole crowd surged forward, with no particular seat assignments or "orderliness" in getting on the plane. Our two very young children and we got jostled in the crowd. Passengers were not used to lining up; they came from polychronic cultures where several people could be accommodated at the same time. Even though I was familiar with polychronic practice, it gave my psyche a jolt because I had been away from it for a while. Our son had a similar experience in the late 1990s on a Korean airline. No one was being rude; they were simply exercising the behaviors to which they were socialized.

In *polychronic* cultures, because of the importance of involvement with the present and with people, several interactions can happen at the same time, without people feeling they are being ignored. In fact, to pay attention to only one person in those situations can be seen as overly arrogant. *Not* to acknowledge their presence or their requests would be considered ill-bred behavior. Visitors to polychronic cultures complain about clerks in stores waiting on numerous customers at one time, not in "their proper order." Polychronic people want to pack into the moment as much as they can, instead of segmenting time for each event individually and sequentially. Hall's description of the space of public places becomes a metaphor for time as well: "The Spanish plaza and the Italian piazza serve both involvement and polychronic functions, whereas the strung-out Main Street so characteristic of the United States reflects not only our structuring of time but our lack of involvement in others" (Hall 1969, 174).

Neither one of these orientations is the "right" one; both have their good points and their weaknesses. No doubt monochronic time with its emphasis on planning, schedules, and deadlines has enabled the industrial and technological advances of our modern world; however, often people and their needs are overlooked, or sacrificed to the schedule. Polychronic cultures have encouraged relationship building and the importance of the present but have relinquished the structure of getting things done in a timely fashion.

JOURNAL TIME

Think about your nonverbal communication in the classroom. What message does the arrangement of desks convey? What about the way in which you stand or sit? How about eye or physical contact between you and the students? Do you feel invigorated or drained by student intrusions into your personal zone? What kinds of questions or insights do you have as a result of this chapter?

Furthermore, cultures are not really totally one or the other, nor are individual people. Situations demand different approaches so that the same people will find that at some times they are being particularly monochronic, and at others, polychronic. Often contexts determine the approach, such as a monochronic orientation at work and polychronic at home, where parents must work with the innumerable demands of raising children. Despite the fact that we are increasingly multi-tasking in the United States, both at work and at home, I believe the difference between a monochronic and polychronic outlook is not in our activity level (one task or three), but in whether our orientation bends toward people, or toward the clock. When the fifteen minutes is up, are we set to stick to the schedule, regardless of whether the business at hand has been completed? The collision of monochronic and polychronic demands often results in gnawing frustration or fury. Different constituencies call for different strategies, but generally a culture has one which is dominant.

Reflections on Mrs. Yousef

In the vignette at the beginning of the chapter, tension arose over attitudes toward time. Many issues came into play: the general cultural attitude toward time, the increasing demands on teachers in the United States, the differing concepts about our day. Obviously, Roland was working out of a cultural background that emphasizes discrete bits of time, the importance of being punctual in keeping appointments, and the need to talk individually and sequentially with parents. In many cultures it is not unusual to expect to be seen the day that you call for an appointment. In the United States, we interpret a request for an "immediate" appointment as something of an urgency, which may not have been Mrs. Yousef's intention. Keeping the appointment was important to Mrs. Yousef; she was not intending to treat Roland "in such an offhand manner." Having been socialized to be more casual with reference to exact segments and passages of time, she may not have realized the importance of arriving at exactly 1 PM. She was "going with the flow" of the morning, and coming from a culture where the definition of "being late" was different from that in the United States, she probably did not realize that an apology was due.

Roland, no doubt, also felt the pressures of the increasing number of tasks and responsibilities that are being foisted upon teachers these days. In addition to the amount of required administrative paperwork, we are being asked to take on many responsibilities that used to be in the domain of parents. Squeezing all this into a standard workday leads to frustration. In many other cultures, teachers are available to parents later in the afternoons than is generally true in the United States. Hence there, the sense of urgency to fit everything into a shorter day disappears. While Mrs. Yousef needed to learn the general rules in the United States concerning making and keeping appointments, it helped Roland to understand the background out of which her actions arose, so that he was able to be more objective about it, to not take it so personally.

In the Classroom, Again

A range of classroom applications and practices apply to the area of non-verbal communication differences. Administratively, when asking parents or students to fill out forms, it might be wise to keep the following illustration in mind: "Foua is quite sure, however, that October is correct [for her birth-date] since she was told by her parents that she was born during the season in which the opium fields are weeded for the second time and the harvested rice stalks are stacked. She invented the precise day of the month, like the year, in order to satisfy the many Americans who have evinced an abhorrence of unfilled blanks on the innumerable forms the Lees have encountered since their admission to the United States in 1980. Most Hmong refugees are familiar with this American trait and have accommodated it in the same way. Nao Kao Lee has a first cousin who told the immigration officials that all nine of his children were born on July 15, in nine consecutive years, and this information was duly recorded on their resident alien documents" (Fadiman 1997, 7). Some immigrant parents and children may have a more cavalier attitude toward specific dates than we, whose lives are dominated by clock and calendar, are accustomed to. If a cultural-minority child does know his birthday, that might mean that birthdays are not celebrated in the same way, and with such emphasis as in the dominant culture. It usually helps parents immensely if we talk with them about some of the expected routines around birthdays and ascertain if any restrictions apply. In fact, a conversation regarding any of the holidays celebrated in class, such as Valentine's Day or Halloween, is most helpful to newcomer parents. The dialogue helps us understand how the parents feel about the child's participation and would help the parents know what the child will be experiencing in class and determine how they want to respond to those traditions.

Generally speaking, if we find some students who are highly distractible, who seem to not be able to stick to the task, who seem more sociable than we would like, or who seem to be interested in other people's lives, we need to stop for a minute to think about the socialization in polychronic cultures. The dominant monochronic culture of the United States reflected in the classroom suits the student who is task oriented, who customarily adheres to deadlines, and who usually leaves others alone. In the classroom, the loudness of a student's response may be a sign of sincerity; the belligerent-sounding comment may be awkward intonation; silence may signal self-restraint or respect for our authority; the quest for more personal interaction may indicate an unconscious need for closer contact with authority; the wince under our affectionate pat on the back may mean discomfort with physical touch; inflexible deadlines may be a new concept; many students crowding our desk or person at the same time may be a sign that a monochronic approach is an unknown perspective; an "inappropriate" smile may mask shame, embarrassment, or fear; a downward gaze may be deference to our position. We cannot possibly know all of the nonverbal languages of other cultures. What we can do is to be willing to lay aside our own cultural blinders, be sensitive to a variety of responses, be open to and affirming of different interpretations, and hopefully learn from our students even as we show them the ways of the dominant culture.

Chapter Seven

A Yeasty Mix: Acculturation

Little by little the cotton thread becomes a loincloth.
—Fon proverb (a language of Benin)

I am really concerned about Mikhail. It may be his personality, but I can't be sure. No matter what I do, I can't get an affective response from him, a smile, eye contact, greetings. He sits in class, hunched over, makes no initiatives to others, nor does he readily accept others' initiatives to him. I found out in our team meeting that he has made no connection with any student in other classes either. Since he studied English before his arrival, he can do a lot of the homework for my class; I don't have complaints in that area. He has been here for two long months—long for me and very long for him, I'm sure. I have never seen a lonelier guy; he is unlike any other immigrant student I've had.
—(Leslie, a seventh-grade math teacher)

Leslie felt that Mikhail had changed. He had been an eager, fairly enthusiastic student when he arrived, but had become taciturn after the first few weeks. He moved from class to class all by himself. Leslie's eyes would quickly search him out on her way to lunch and report him sitting alone. Her concern had even driven her to scout him out before school began, as students gathered in the cafeteria. There, she had seen him sitting at the far, tattered edges of different circles. She wondered whether adolescence took on a different cast in other cultures, since she had been with this age group long enough to understand the agonies that the majority of her students encountered. Or had something happened at home? What, she wanted to know, had gone wrong?

Immigration in Our Early History

Immigrants founded these United States. In 1607 and 1620 respectively, Powhatan Indians in Jamestown, VA, and Wampanoag Indians in Plymouth, MA, greeted the English settlers (the original "boat people"). Many other tribes met more newcomers pushing the western and southern frontiers of the fledgling country. Preceding the European influx by hundreds of centuries, Indian tribes were the established group as others encroached upon their territory. The contact between these various groups—native and immigrant—has a sadly checkered history and has left a painful legacy. The tendency of each wave to forget its own immigrant background continues to mar relations between ethnic, racial, and linguistic groups.

In the 1770s, Jean de Crèvecoeur, a Frenchman farming in New York, described his international but monochromatic milieu and the expected melding: "[The people] are a mixture of English, Scottish, Irish, French, Dutch, Germans, and Swedes. . . . I could point to you a family whose grandfather was an Englishman, whose wife was Dutch, whose son married a French woman, and whose present four sons have now four wives of different nations" (Crèvecoeur 1904, 54). Though part of the make-up of the country at the time, the American Indians, African slaves, and Mexicans did not merit mention. For many years, the vast majority of immigrants came from Western Europe and hence shared not only skin color but also many basic life orientations. While languages were different, they were not hugely so. In short, the people of whom Crèvecoeur wrote were not radically different from one another. Crèvecoeur assumed that connection to the homeland consisted primarily of the visible, and in his eyes, tenuous, bonds of language and people. He believed that the concept of a "new American" formed by a melding of all these backgrounds would be easy, desirable, and inevitable. He envisioned the original "melting pot" theory. Two decades later, however, President John Adams, in the midst of tense diplomatic negotiations with France, had to deal with the fears engendered by the twenty-five thousand French within our borders who had established an array of support institutions such as schools, bookstores, and newspapers (McCullough 2001). These French had wanted to retain their heritage through these institutions and had not "melted" as Crèvecoeur had envisioned.

As immigrants poured into the United States during the following century, the melting pot theory gained increasing prominence. It assumed that a distinctly "American" personality would be an amalgam of many different ethnic groups. Disparate sociocultural systems would fade in favor of an all-enveloping, superior one; socialization patterns for home and school would be monolithic. However, some argue that the melting pot existed only as a dream, since both immigrant groups and the dominant culture found it difficult to achieve (Glazer and Moynihan 1970). As shown by the French attempts to keep their heritage even in the early 1800s, immigrant groups pouring into the country did not immediately shed their traditions to become the new amalgamated "Americans." Additionally, the melting pot started to take on a different flavor. It became not a new mixture of many different groups, but one with strong Anglo cast. While never blatantly stated, attitudes of racial superiority implied that the characteristics of the "new American" would be those of the Anglo-American white majority. The dominant, established culture expected immigrants to assimilate into majority values. These attitudes toward conformity continued well into the twentieth century, strengthened by legislation constricting immigration especially of non-Western people, by efforts to break up enclaves of immigrant groups through making life so difficult in ghettos that people absorbed dominant culture values and moved into suburbs, and by efforts in school systems to homogenize the society by infusing Anglo-American assumptions. The concept of assimilation, rather than amalgamation, reigned.

A new era of greater diversity began in the second half of the twentieth century. The turbulent era of the 1960s and 1970s transformed cultural attitudes in all aspects of society. People came to value their ethnic roots. Professors of history Thomas Kessner and Betty Boyd Caroli point to a theory pioneered by immigration historian Marcus Hansen that "the third generation, confident of its American credentials, handles its past with greater ease, demanding the right as Americans to be proud both of its American nationality and of its ethnic heritage" (Kessner and Caroli 1981, 24). Cultural pluralism came into consciousness in the United States as a legitimate description of the society.

The A B C (and D)s of Cultural Pluralism

Four theories of groupings within society, as suggested by sociologist William Newman, speak to our past and our present. *Assimilation* is A+B+C=A. That is, the dominant group, A, replaces the traditions and culture of the other two groups, B and C. Society is homogenized, taking on the flavor of the dominant culture. *Amalgamation*, the second option, produces a different configuration: A+B+C=D. The many groups living together meld into a totally new dimension, new to all the groups. That reflects the original melting pot, as Crèvecoeur envisioned it. Newman contends that for amalgamation to occur, the groups need to be of equal status (not minority vs. majority) and they must want such an intermixing. These two very important criteria may have been true in Crèvecoeur's time for the Europeans in the eastern United States. However, when the melting pot idea became an expectation and was forced on to minority groups by the majority, both these criteria evaporated; assimilation replaced amalgamation. The third possibility of groups living together in a society Newman calls *classical cultural pluralism:* A+B+C=A+B+C. All groups maintain their own cultural identity over time; ethnic groupings do not fade into a general or overall culture. However, Newman feels that classical cultural pluralism does not allow for the dominant culture's influence in succeeding generations. For example, second-generation Swedes in the United States are not the same as the first-generation Swedes and far different from the Swedes in Sweden. Therefore he proposes the fourth theory, a *modified cultural pluralism:* $A+B+C=A_1+B_1+C_1$. The younger generations decreasingly maintain their ethnic identity and increasingly acquire the dominant culture, as signified by the subscript. Each ethnic group takes on different characteristics of the dominant culture to varying degrees (Newman 1973).

If the "melting pot" symbolizes amalgamation, the "salad bowl" reflects cultural pluralism. This food metaphor conveys the concept that from variety comes richer flavor; from differences come texture and zest. A cultural metaphor, the "mosaic," also reflects the colorful spectrum that now radiates through our country. Vivid proof of that fact is symbolized by an eight-page special section of the *Boston Globe* (29 November 1993) for new immigrants entitled "Boston Says Welcome." Written in English, Spanish, Chinese, Vietnamese, Haitian Creole, Cambodian, Russian, and Portuguese (a page for each language), it carried a brief history of immigration, useful information relevant to Boston, and a welcoming note from Martin Nolan, editor, "to all of you who have brought your dreams to this great country." While Boston enjoys many more language groups than those listed, this section celebrated diversity in a prominent and extravagant way. In the mosaic metaphor, an

JOURNAL TIME

Reflect on whether you agree with these theories of immigration and pluralism. Do they resonate with your own family's experience? What were the circumstances under which your family came to the United States? What were some of the decisions they made in terms of their response to the acculturation process? Were these decisions their choices, or were they imposed on them? Did they try to maintain part of their heritage or throw themselves totally into the dominant culture? How did they carry out their response? Do you agree with Kessner and Caroli's comment that later generations feel freer than the earlier ones to reestablish some of their ethnic ties? How does your family's story influence your attitude and expectations of immigrant students in your classes?

overall design holds the mosaic together; common goals of liberty, equality, and opportunity bind people together in this democracy. Issues constantly erupt; solutions vary due to differing perspectives, but when mutual respect and consideration prevail, the strength of diversity infuses all aspects of our life together.

Moving to a New Community

Migrations and subjugations occurred among Sumerians, Babylonians, and others in ancient times; Europeans began colonizing the world in medieval times, and immigrants and slaves have been coming to these shores since 1607. Cross-cultural living is not new. However, in recent years, increased technology and improved transportation have made worldwide interaction and migration commonplace, giving rise to fuller study of the process of adjustment to a different culture.

What changes occur when one moves to a new culture, whether across an ocean or across the state? *Physical* and *biological* changes are the most obvious: different surroundings, varied transportation systems, population density, foods, diseases, sanitation/pollution levels, and the like. But other, not so visible changes also occur. *Cultural* changes include not only how people "make sense of their lives" but also the political, economic, linguistic, and religious systems of the new location. *Social relationships* constitute another area of change: Friends and families have been left behind; forming or joining new in-groups and understanding various out-groups prove complex. Finally, changes in the area of *mental health* arise as new contexts and problems create different stresses (Berry, Kim, and Boski 1988). Often our usual ways of handling such difficulties may not be possible, which adds another stress. Some of these changes hit us immediately; we make our peace with them one way or another; others take much longer to handle or understand, especially if covert. No doubt newcomers to any part of the world echo thoughts attributed to T. E. Lawrence (Lawrence of Arabia): "How could I, as me, meet these new people? How would I have to change? What of me was superficial and might be sacrificed, and what need I keep to remain myself?"

The Process of Acculturation

Acculturation can be both a process and an end-state. Let's consider the process first. The traditional view of the process of acculturation is uni-dimensional, a one-way street: The majority culture has an impact on the newcomer in a linear process that proceeds through five or six identifiable stages to assimilation. In general and popular terms, the process resembles a *U* and is similar for a visitor of some duration or an immigrant. Refugees also go through similar stages, though they bring additional issues, as vividly described by psychologist Mary Pipher (2002). In the first stage of this linear process (from sometime before the move until a few weeks in the new culture) high anticipation usually mixes with a tinge of sadness (at the top of the *U*). Learning about the new location, packing up boxes or baggage, lining up a job or a place to live, and fantasizing a variety of situations in the new community all mingle with anxiety about leaving the familiar. The second stage encompasses efforts to become acquainted with the new community, similar to a spectator who does not fully participate, but takes notes. Where is the closest grocery store? How does the phone system work? What is the routine and the culture of public transportation? All these questions produce many feelings of excitement but a few of fear and discouragement. Increased participation in the third stage often brings feelings of a more despairing nature. Exactly how different (and hence highly deficient, it appears) things are than they were "at home" becomes increasingly clear. While some differences between the new country and the old might be welcome, other necessary adjustments add unexpected twists. So much seems to be awkward in the new community. This feeling leads to the fourth stage that can be quite negative, perhaps even questioning whether the move was a wise decision. Nothing seems to go right (the bottom of the *U*). Eventually, equanimity returns and a true negotiation with life in the new surroundings begins, which is the fifth stage (up the other side of the *U*). A return trip back "home" introduces reverse culture shock which is often more severe than the initial one. Whether the move is within the country or across the oceans, the traditional goal of acculturation is singular: assimilation. There may be variations in the amount of assimilation a person achieves, but giving up one's own and adopting the majority culture is the traditionally expected response.

As our culture has become more pluralistic and more research has been done on the topic, descriptions of a multidimensional process have emerged. *Adjustment, reaction,* and *withdrawal* are three different strategies which people employ when they arrive in a new culture (Berry, Kim, and Boski 1988). In using the strategy of *adjustment,* the newcomer will adapt her behavior to fit in with the surroundings: For example, the new English Language Learner participates in games on the playground even though she does not speak a word of English. *Reaction* strategies indicate anger or retaliation toward the environment, which may produce a change in the surroundings to provide a better fit: For example, the ELL is so disruptive in social studies that he gets reassigned to the ESOL room or gets a tutor for that period. Finally, *withdrawal* strategies involve blocking out the pressures that make life so difficult: Despite invitations to join them, the ELL shuns classmates and eats alone in the lunchroom. Whereas in the *reaction* strategy the context gets slightly changed to allow for some adaptation, in *withdrawal* neither the context nor the person makes an accommodation.

The End-States of Acculturation

Moving from a discussion of the *process* to the *end-state* of acculturation, research has also shown that in pluralistic cultures the end-state of acculturation does not necessarily result only in assimilation. Researchers Berry, Kim, and Boski (1988) suggest a paradigm in which a number of options exist, depending upon the person's response to two basic questions: (1) How important is it to me to maintain my own ethnic roots and distinctiveness? (2) How much contact do I want with other ethnic groups (including the dominant culture)? Figure 7–1 presents their chart.

In this chart, *integration,* a "yes" answer to both questions, means that the person hopes to keep both her ethnic heritage and the majority culture together in her life. Some compromises will be made, for example, in dress or in attitudes toward independent thinking or marriage customs, but she is able to operate in both contexts with ease and comfort. *Assimilation* signifies a "yes" answer to maintaining a positive identification with another group (in this case the dominant one) and a "no" answer to maintaining one's own ethnic roots. This person, consciously or not, decides that he wants to forget his ties to his heritage, and stops speaking the language or observing any of the holidays of his heritage. He becomes totally "Americanized." *Separation,* a "yes" answer to the first question and a "no" answer to the second, indicates

Figure 7–1

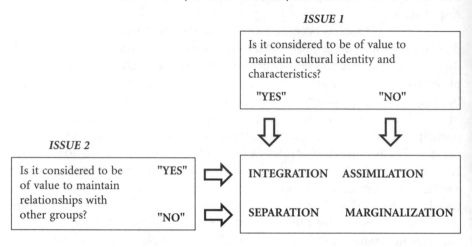

Four Modes of Acculturation (Berry/Kim/Boski)

a desire not only to keep one's ethnic identity intact but also to avoid relationships with other groups. The Amish are one example of that response, where contact with others in any meaningful way is kept to a bare minimum. Finally, *marginalization*, two "no" answers, is the sad state of a person who no longer has ties to her own ethnic origin, nor feels comfortable or welcome in the dominant (or any other) culture. She is caught between two worlds, unhappy in either one. In linguistics, this state is called semi-lingual, a person who has lost fluency in the home language but not yet acquired enough to be at ease in another, a person who is neither bilingual nor, any longer, a fluent monolingual. She might also be called semi-cultural.

Acculturation Issues for Children

While it would be presumptuous and impossible to list all of the issues that children will bring to acculturation, I would like to suggest a few that play key roles.

- Children usually have not had much input into the decision to immigrate to the United States. Often they have little time to psychologically prepare for the move. Young students have told me that they learned about the move when parents brought home the airplane tickets. In this day of jetliners, even the trip does not provide much time for any kind of preparation. For many children, the act of coming to the United States may be similar to the kind of uprooting

experienced by refugees. Far more than a physical relocation, it signifies a rupture that has given their lives meaning, a disruption somewhat similar to bereavement (Eisenbruch 1988). In my experience,
for most children this fear of the unknown and the sorrow in leaving
all that is familiar, especially extended family members and friends,
initially yield to the excitement of new beginnings.

• As parents must find ways to survive in the community, children must
do so in their context of school. While they may understand ration-
ally the reasons for the move to a totally different environment and
may enjoy some benefits not available in their homelands, emotionally and cognitively they must deal alone with the maze of unfamil-
iarities which confronts them daily at school. Parents can't help their
children figure out the system, since the parents aren't familiar with
it either. Not knowing the language of the classroom (to say nothing
of the culture) means that the students' search for friends, their search
to fill the very basic human need for connection, must be either dependent on non-verbal communication or temporarily suspended.

• For adults, a reference group of the same ethnic background provides
essential support for the acculturation process: It offers a place where
people share the same language, customs, and traditions, where they
can be themselves without explanation, where they can relax, where
compatriots can give tips on how to balance the sense of disequilibrium. These groups can form in a community center, in a church, in
an informal network among the particular ethnic group, or in an
English language class. They stand available and necessary even if
newcomers later decide to assimilate rather than integrate into the
new society. A reference group also plays a vital role for children,
whether in an ESOL (English to Speakers of Other Languages), bilingual, or mainstream class. If the reference group is very small, it can
be a little difficult since just being from the same background does
not necessarily mean that the students will get along. As teachers, we
need to make the cultural connection known, but not push it. Even
though children may not be from the same ethnic background, ELLs
receive psychological support when they get together in ESOL classes
and see that they are not the only ones who do not speak English.
One-on-one tutoring in the mainstream classroom does not accomplish this psychological support. In a similar vein, one teacher I knew
tried to be helpful by teaming up an East Asian kindergartner who
arrived mid-year with another who had been in class since September.
She wondered why the children had not sat or worked or played

together unless she arranged it—not realizing that since one student was from Japan and the other from Taiwan, they did not speak each other's language. No doubt both children were comforted not to be the only East Asian in the totally Anglo-American class, but for a while that was all they shared.

- To adults, the host culture's response matters. Newcomers continually assess the context and if, despite their good efforts, they experience rejection over and over again, that experience drives them deeper into their own community, into a response of separation. My research shows that the receiving culture of the school plays a role in determining how the student will respond. Students who perceive a warm and welcoming attitude will adjust easily; those who perceive a hostile environment will use strategies of withdrawal or reaction (Clayton 1996). In the imagery of the opening proverb, the host culture provides the warp and the students supply the weft to create the textured weave of acculturation.

Immigrant Students in School

How do these theories of acculturation relate to school? Even for older students who may have a life beyond the confines of school and family, the process of acculturation permeates all of life in some way. The student's personal qualities, the specific challenges of adjusting to a new school environment, and the culture of the school together shape the final outcome. The student's perception of his interactions, whether accurate or not, plays a major part: Negative interactions with the context produce a knotted, ragged cloth; a positive, warm welcome weaves a smoother fabric. Since the process is a dynamic one, change from one to another response is always possible. Let's look first at the characteristics of the students, then at some of the challenges facing the students, and finally at how the process and end-state of acculturation play out in school.

CHARACTERISTICS OF THE STUDENT

The Personal Stamp. "The thrust of the individual," as child psychologist Mary Ellen Goodman (1970) calls it, provides a very important factor in the adjustment. As expected, cross-cultural students who are gregarious have an easier time than those who are shy. In addition to a sociable nature, if the students are at all athletically inclined, the adjustment proceeds even more quickly, since the dominant school culture in the United States values the athlete. This gift enables the newcomers to show how they excel even though fluency in English still escapes them. Exposure to English in this more informal venue helps them along, as well. This entire setting means that some of their self-confidence is maintained.

Shy students, on the other hand, have a much tougher time: they struggle against their reserved nature as well as their inability to express themselves in a way valued by the dominant culture. Books and television provide a retreat from the pressures of adjustment, but preclude gaining confidence, making friends, or practicing English.

Differing socialization patterns can also play a role in the acculturation process in school. If young children come from hierarchical contexts, their initial instincts may be to relate to adults first, before forming peer relationships. On the other hand, if the context has been more horizontal (where peers have been more important than adults) the initial instinct may be to look for group acceptance (Willett 1987).

Self-Image. Many different markers make up our self-image. Often, for a student of any age, it will be related to performance in school. Immigrants who arrive with strong self-images as a result of their good academic records in their native countries throw themselves into the study of English. They also work hard in those classes where English facility is not crucial—for example, some aspects of math and science—from the very beginning. More than one parent I knew criticized the U.S. educational system for not giving enough homework. These parents believed that effort determined success, rejecting the argument that social development was as important as academic development. They felt that their children's enjoyment of school and participation in class was being hindered by not having more homework. Naturally, children who have been good students in their homelands expect to continue as such. In some ways, this strong self-image can become a negative force, since the children expect more of themselves and are shattered when they do not do well at first. Friends or activities can help replenish the unfulfilled goals; otherwise, the immigrant is left with an additional challenge of losing his self-confidence. Students who were not strong academically in their native countries present and face different challenges. Their journey of acculturation moves along the same road, but with more twists, turns, and digressions. With these students, we need to find areas in which the immigrant can excel to help maintain a positive self-image, through apprenticeships with local businesses, for example, or assistance in the office, or by tapping into categories of multiple intelligences more than we normally might.

Priorities. Obviously, the cross-cultural student's priorities will influence how she deals with the challenges of her adjustment. In my research, the need for social connection was an overwhelming priority, even with the academically gifted, who were continually haunted by the lack of friends. A scholarly attitude might initially insulate them from the need for friends, but will also make them seem aloof to dominant-culture peers. The sooner the newcomer can establish real friendship, the earlier she can pay attention to class work. With a particularly social girl I knew, the responsibility to accomplish homework became a major issue for her: She was unaccustomed to the freedoms she perceived in class and consequently took advantage of "not understanding" her homework completely. However, as she acclimated to the expectations of her teachers and the role of the student in the United States, she began to invest herself more.

Priorities are not always academic, as we all know. A particularly recalcitrant girl I met refused to speak the small amount of "survival English" she knew to express her needs in class; she insisted on speaking French to her teacher. Her teacher did not know French. It became clear she had adopted a reaction strategy (rather than an adjustment strategy) in response to her parents' decision to come to the United States. She was not happy with that decision and the difficulties it presented to her. Other newcomers have not had their minds on learning because they have more urgent issues confronting them or, because as sojourners, they look upon their stay as a vacation. In all these situations, conversations between the teacher and the family about the issue proved to be the key to an albeit slow recovery for the student. In some cases, further practical help was found for non-school issues the students were dealing with (e.g., clothing, furniture, transportation to work, etc.).

Family Support. The cross-cultural student's adjustment to the school parallels the family's adjustment process within the larger community. Parental involvement, which is considered foundational to a good academic career in the United States, will be discussed further in Chapter Eight. However, I have found that even though the ways in which families express support may differ from what we expect, they offer their children as much support as they can. Many immigrants come here so that their children will have a better future. Parents I have known have taken major steps to help their child despite their own issues of adjustment. They did not communicate extensively their negative adjustment experiences so that their child could concentrate on his own particular issues; they sacrificed their personal comfort and safety for the benefit of the child; they undertook tasks that were foreign to them in order to help him.

CHALLENGES THE STUDENTS FACE

In addition to the bundle of characteristics they bring with them, immigrant students face challenges in three different areas: *academic, social,* and *structural.* These provide the context for their acculturation.

The Academic Domain.

- *Learning the language* is, of course, the primary challenge for immigrant students. Their motivations, attitudes, natural inclinations, and degree of development of their linguistic intelligence (à la Gardner) in any language focus their language learning. The students are eager to become integrated into the classroom, as well as to make friends, and they need English for both purposes. A gregarious ELL commented to me that she really did not need English to *make* friends, but that when she knew some English, the relationships changed. She was sought out more when she knew the language better. The process of learning the language is fraught with emotion, as students who had been perfectly able to express themselves in one language suddenly find themselves barely able to get immediate needs understood by the majority surrounding them. They face great pressure, not only for their academic and social career in school, but possibly also as the family link to the broader community.

- The *role of the student* in the United States presents a challenge to many students, dominant culture and minority alike. When young children enter school, they embark on another phase of their socialization. As secondary socializers, schools help the students learn how to be good students, imbue them with values of the dominant culture (which may or may not be different from the home culture), as well as teach them how to be good citizens of the country. Even for students comfortable with the dominant culture, entering a new school or even a new grade involves a period of uncertainty and adjustment as they learn new roles and expectations (Staton 1990). Imagine then, how newcomers feel who cannot understand or speak the language or culture that surround them. I have known students who, for example, had a difficult time getting used to the variety of acceptable behaviors, especially for "good students." In their experience, "good students" did not wear jewelry to class, did not dress inappropriately, and did not question the teacher or even address the teacher. Immigrants were surprised by the amount of freedom and, of course, by the accompanying responsibility allowed the student. The student in the United States has more leeway to shape her own identity; she need not fit a template. Students here have more control over their image. Most cross-cultural students entering our systems come from cultures where the teacher was highly respected and the student was shaped by a rather rigid mold. Disruptive behavior by a cross-cultural student may be a response to the frustrations of the adjustment process or ignorance of expected behavior rather than outright disrespect.

- *Teacher expectations* constitute a third challenge within the academic arena. Naturally, we expect the newcomers to behave according to school and class rules, but just how much can we expect academically from a newcomer? Mainstream principals and teachers in my experience have run the gamut: a nine-year-old put into first grade because the work was easier than that in fourth grade; an implausible number of pictures to color for a fifth grader; full-blown essays expected from a student in the country only two months; nothing expected from a student in the country only two months. A tough situation exists for a mainstream teacher who has twenty or more other students in class expecting ongoing learning. We may make hasty judgments if we are not acquainted with the stages that ELLs experience in learning a language or with the affective responses to the pressure of being surrounded by unintelligible babble all day. For those of us who have ESOL specialists in our school systems, close connection and cooperation with them will help determine how best to help the student. These ESOL (sometimes known as ESL for English as a Second Language) teachers will be able to help with appropriate expectations and will have titles of recent, informative, readable books on the subject at their fingertips. Among other resources would be professors at a nearby School of Education or a favorite publisher of books for classroom teachers. In the TESOL (Teachers of English to Speakers of Other Languages) website (www.tesol.org), the *K-12 Corner* or *Case Studies* categories of their publications, for example, carry books to help mainstream teachers.

- A *different approach to education* forms the fourth academic challenge immigrant students face. Many learners come from cultures that use a didactic form of teaching, a direct transmission model. Adjusting to a discovery model presents a psychological impact. Students may not feel learning is occurring when they "play games." It may seem to them like a waste of time. They may not believe that this vaunted education is worth their parents' and their own sacrifices. In most elementary schools in the United States, textbooks are kept in school, whereas ELLs may be accustomed to taking them home to memorize a chapter at a time, to be ready for an oral recitation in class the following day. Often, they are accustomed to being told exactly what to do.

Also, expectations from home differ from the practices of school. Many times I have heard teachers complain that immigrant parents were expecting far too much academically from their child. While this attitude certainly may exist as a result of parental sacrifice, the disagreement with school personnel may be a result of different attitudes in socialization to individual or communal goals, or attitudes toward effort rather than intelligence being the marker of success.

The Social Domain. Immigrant learners are very keen to make friends, not only to be social but also to practice their English. However, for a number of reasons this process is often not easy or smooth. Of course, the immigrant's personality and history play a major role. Shy, gregarious, bright, ordinary, needy, carefree, over-zealous, unambitious: These are markers not only for newcomers but also for native-born learners. Picking a friend for someone else involves some anxiety. The same can be true for picking out a buddy for a newcomer. Buddies are a must at least for the first few weeks to show the newcomer the way to the bathrooms or the cafeteria or the locker rooms. We cannot assume that the cross-cultural student has had experience, for example, with lockers or locker rooms, or has had a cafeteria in his previous school. The best buddies are those who really *want* to do it, who have some sense of what may be needed, and who have a capacity to understand what the immigrant may be experiencing. One advantage of having an expected short duration is that if the buddy finds the responsibility a burden, no stigma is attached when the relationship peters out. If the two get along famously, how grateful both students will be. A group of students assuming such a role spreads the responsibility and the immigrant makes more than one friend. Obviously we must inform the immigrant of the selected buddy. Chapter Eight, "Classroom Culture," will include other aspects of the classroom to which the newcomer must acculturate.

The Structural Domain. This domain of the student's adjustment to school is the most concrete and most quickly achieved. These adjustments include the infinite variety of class schedules at all levels (for example, my Turkish elementary school had a ten-minute recess after each subject, and one and a half hours at lunchtime). Conventions such as snacktime in elementary schools, different titles for teachers (e.g., a name instead of the honorific title of "Teacher"), and ways to answer questions (e.g., not having to stand, or raising a hand instead of a finger) are some other simple differences cross-cultural students may face. Although the visible aspects of these conventions can be learned fairly quickly, underlying values will take longer: the openness that encourages students to share their own thoughts instead of parroting us, and the philosophy that allows students to question us, and the informality that allows rearranged desks.

TRY THIS!

In anticipation of or very soon after the newcomer's arrival, involve your whole class in thinking about ways they might welcome an immigrant student into their midst. If the student has already arrived, let the immigrant parents and student know that you will be doing this project and enlist their help. With examples of music or orthography or a taped story from the immigrants' homeland (if possible), set the scene for your class. Talk with your students about how they might feel if they were in a school where they did not know how to speak or read the language or how to go about doing things. What would they want or need to know right off at school? What would be important to know in a couple of weeks, a couple of months? Encourage them to imagine the feelings the non-English speaker might be experiencing in your class or school. Make a list of ways to help out, with volunteers named next to each suggestion.

ACCULTURATION IN THE SCHOOL CONTEXT

Using the attributes described earlier of the process and the end-state of acculturation, I would like to look at those distinct aspects as they apply to school.

The Application of the Process of Acculturation in School. Reflecting on the *process* of acculturation as described previously, I have found that students experience a combination of linear and multidimensional processes, a mixture of the *U* and the varied strategies. They arrive at school scared, but with high hopes and anticipation. For the first few days, that hope keeps them going, as they learn to negotiate survival in the school setting—that is, finding bathrooms, the cafeteria, or different classrooms. This naturally leads them into a period when they sit back to see how things work. Shortly thereafter, they *try* to participate in the on-going life of the classroom. But they may soon plunge into a dark mood because of their inability to communicate thoughts, the misperception that they are ignorant, and the enormity of the task ahead. Newcomers constantly compare the unfamiliar new with the comfortable old ways. During the constant barrage of newness, English, and confusion, students often need a rest, perhaps by gazing out the window. We must realize that when newcomers are not paying attention, they may be taking a break from the very hard work of learning a language and being surrounded all day by customs and a language they don't understand.

The second month is the worst, say parents, corroborating my experience as an ESOL teacher. When the newcomer feels the most dejected and doubtful, a positive response from the context (students and us) is crucial.

This is not to say that the context has not been important in the first month, but that at the point where the newcomer seems to be the most unreachable, the students and we need to reach out even more. Interestingly, this point is often when we may be at the lowest point in our assessment of the ELL's adjustment. I think that we ourselves experience the *U* with respect to the immigrant's progress. The same heady excitement mixed with anxiety starts the year, and as the ELL experiences a downturn, we, too, become discouraged by the apparent failure of our various attempts to include the newcomer. We, however, have the perspective and maturity to understand that strategic support can send the immigrant up the other side of the *U*, where both the newcomer and we can celebrate the accomplishment.

Usually ELLs will be able to work through the low point of the process and continue to a point where they are comfortable in their surroundings by using adjustment strategies. However, other responses during the particularly stressful second month can occur as well. Strategies of reaction or withdrawal can become set so that the acculturation process takes a stubbornly negative hue. The newcomer's seemingly hostile behavior in class may be an indication of his frustration with the whole process. We may feel that our steps to help the student have not met the student's perceived needs. Similar to marginal students, "[t]hese learners . . . have adopted from their environment a set of limiting self-views that prevent their full participation in school. By rejecting, resisting, avoiding, or passively enduring school, they are searching for accommodation in an institution where they have not been successful or accepted" (Sinclair and Ghory 1987, 181–182). Finding ways to make the student feel competent, of course, is the best. For example, we need to give plenty of think time to an ELL who has been brave enough to volunteer an answer. We can have her work in a limited leadership capacity within a responsive small group. In order to establish a real connection with him to learn his strengths, we can invite the newcomer and a mainstream student or two to have lunch with us now and then. We might change the environment that is causing a reaction strategy as much as possible. We must work with, rather than just speak to, individuals who harass the student.

Additionally, for our own mental health, we *must* accept and communicate to the rest of the class that "fair" does not always mean "equal." Newcomers may require more time at the beginning of the year so that in the long run they will be better adjusted students. For that matter, any student who needs extra help gets it, since students must understand to succeed.

The End-State of Acculturation in the School Context. Schools are the community to which cross-cultural students acculturate. In elementary schools, where strong pressure already exists not to be different, students are eager to melt into the crowd. Assimilation happens here so quickly that parents must make timely decisions about how much of the dominant culture will be acceptable in the home. As all students generally become more individualized in middle and high schools, the pressure for group membership becomes more particular. An interest in maintaining one's heritage resonates with many, though not all, newcomers.

Students work on the same questions in the school context that adults face in the larger community: How much do I want to maintain my own ethnic roots and how much contact do I want with other ethnic groups? Cross-cultural students will experience the four sections of acculturation modes shown in Figure 7-1. Some students, with or without their parents' blessing, may choose *assimilation*. Influenced by the freedoms and independence experienced at school and in the culture at large, they opt to absorb as much of the dominant culture as possible. This response may create great conflict at home, as the student's behavior changes and the compliant child becomes challenging. Parents find that the instructions or expectations that were once obeyed without question are now scrutinized. Assimilation may not be just the student's or family's preference. As teachers, we convey our underlying attitude by, for example, calling the student by an "Americanized" name without knowing if that is the student's preference. It may be our preference due to the more difficult-to-pronounce original name, but it does convey an assimilationist attitude on our part. If we attempted the student's given name, it would indicate an appreciation by us of the newcomer's heritage that might, in turn, encourage her to not reject it, and might contribute to a response of integration. On the other hand, the Americanized name may have a different meaning for the newcomer: a new beginning, or a life separate from home. I always try to ascertain, especially from the student, or from parents of very young newcomers, which name is preferred.

In a California study, anthropologist Margaret Gibson found that most immigrant parents felt that assimilation was easier for their children to resist if they did not socialize with peers of the dominant culture. These parents urged their children to adopt the more superficial but beneficial aspects of the majority culture, to abide by school rules, and to study hard. For example, the Punjabi way, she was told, was "dress to please the people, but eat to please yourself" (Gibson 1993, 123).

Students may continue to value their heritage and the dominant culture and bridge both by choosing *integration*. These students enjoy being bicultural, able to switch back and forth not only between two languages, but also, more difficult, between two cultures. The two capacities (linguistic and cultural) don't always coexist. A cultural blunder becomes more pronounced if the speaker is fluent in the language; once again, culture is assumed until it is absent. Bilingual, bicultural writer Marie Arana likens being bicultural to a bridge that "connects points that might never have touched" (Arana 2001, 301). Minority students who choose integration touch and connect many points in two different cultures every day as they crisscross between home and the outside world.

Cross-cultural students seeking or being relegated to *separatism* are described eloquently in *Made in America*, a book about a California high school. Despite the celebrations of multiculturalism, at Madison High [as in many schools], the hidden agenda of resistance to diversity and of a narrow understanding of what it meant to be an "American" divided and doomed attempts at inclusion (Olsen, 1997). There, as in some schools of my professional experience, the context forced some students to separate instead of integrate, since opportunities to meaningfully mix students of different ethnicities were scarce.

Marginalization, a very painful state of mind, makes the student uncomfortable in either skin. I think that this may be both a transitional state and a permanent one. Students may exist here for a period of time as they try to decide what their final response will be. But they may dislike so much of either culture and feel so insecure that they remain unable to commit themselves to any of the other responses, becoming permanently marginalized.

Real dialogue between linguistic, racial, and ethnic minorities and the dominant culture is imperative for a society that has become as multicultural as the United States. People do not need to shed themselves of language and heritage to be good "Americans." Language infuses identity, so the demand to do so becomes a very personal attack. Many different tribes of American Indians experienced a loss of identity when they were taken away from their families as children and not allowed to use their language. In order to prepare for meaningful interchanges, connections

---

JOURNAL TIME

Reflect on your feelings about the drive in school systems toward immersion of linguistic minorities into mainstream classrooms. Relate that drive and the one in communities toward *English Only* to the acculturation patterns just discussed. What is the responsibility of the school? Can you support linguistic diversity? If so, what are some ways to do that?

across differences need to occur from the earliest time on so that in each succeeding generation people will know from experience how valuable these connections can be.

THE TEACHER'S RESPONSE

Instead of standing by and seeing what acculturation response the newcomers will aspire to, I believe we need to be more proactive in helping them. We need to seriously consider the pain inflicted by *imposing* assimilation rather than their *choosing* it. Losing our ethnic identity can haunt us for years if we did not acquiesce to it. Examples abound these days of people who are retracing their roots. I believe we should actively help students move toward a stance of *integration*. Being bilingual and bicultural has been an incredible gift to me—and hopefully to others with whom I have shared my life. It does have its rough moments, when I have to decide which culture to abide by in a particular instance, which culture to be faithful to. However, those instances pale beside the deep satisfaction of a broader world view. Bridging two cultures not only expands my horizons but also lets me help others to do the same. All this happened due to the decision of my parents to put me in a school of the dominant Turkish culture while maintaining their own, primarily Anglo-American culture at home, *and* due to the Turkish teachers who honored my home culture by celebrating it at school.

Reflections on Mikhail

We may think that if a newcomer did well at the beginning of school (well, after the first three frightening days), he would be fine from then on. We heave a sigh of relief and begin to feel that our trepidation about having a non-English speaker was really unfounded. Our expectation of smooth sailing may be the result of our own short visits to other lands or a remnant of the traditional view that all of the work of acculturation depends on the newcomer. Vagaries of the adventure of acculturation often surprise us. Mikhail had hit the low point in the linear model of acculturation. He had arrived in class full of hope and eagerness, but had been beaten down by the disparity between his expectations and reality. Leslie's description showed Mikhail using adjustment strategies in the first few weeks but now starting to withdraw. Probably part of his feelings at this time arose from his shy nature; but even gregarious newcomers experience a low point. His shyness only emphasized what he was going through. Something in the environment made him feel unwelcome; it stole from him the courage to continue through this passing phase to a more balanced outlook. Without some intervention by the teachers, he could easily have withdrawn further into himself, resulting in either marginalization or separation. Because he had no other Russian students as a reference group, classmates and teachers needed to make extra, creative, continued efforts to ease the pain he was experiencing. (That would have been true even if there had been a reference group, but was more imperative in its absence.) Getting teachers and parents together seemed to be the first step, so that the teaching team could ascertain how much of this solitude was his preference and how much was context-induced. The team was going to elicit suggestions from the parents as to how the school could realistically help ease the transition. Additionally, Leslie was going to devise ways in her class where his mathematical skills could outshine his struggling English. With concerned teachers such as Mikhail had, his future looked promising.

Chapter Eight

Looking for Familiar Landmarks: Classroom Culture

It is better to have trouble at the beginning than at the end.

—Telegu proverb (*a language of India*)

I don't understand school in this country. I was a good student in Hungary; I studied hard and learned what the teacher presented. Here, class time is playtime, really. We play games in math and science; we have to work in groups. There is no recitation of the lessons; in fact, we don't even take books home to learn from them. It is a waste of time.

—(Janos, *an immigrant fifth grader*)

*J*anos could articulate his frustration. A very smart young fellow, he knew that his parents had made major sacrifices to emigrate from Hungary to the United States. Though his parents tried to minimize it, Janos, as their firstborn, felt a lot of pressure to do well. He needed to make his parents proud. He needed to make the move worth the gnawing feeling in the pit of his stomach when he thought about how much he missed his grandparents, cousins, aunts, and uncles back in the familiar lamplighted streets. And he needed to be a good model for his younger sister. He had been in the United States only a few weeks and in school less than that when we spoke. He had studied English before the move, so though learning academic English took some of his energies in school, much was left over for what he assumed to be the "real" learning: math, geography, and science. Bryan, Janos' teacher, had faced the teacher's typical September avalanche: establishing routines with the rest of the class, getting English language help for Janos, setting up schedules for other students who needed extra help, and the like. So, Bryan had not yet noticed Janos' building frustration and was surprised when I conveyed some of Janos' feelings. Being caught off-guard, Bryan was initially defensive, then perplexed, then curious about Janos' expectation of school.

Defining Classroom Culture

Classroom culture defines all of the verbal and non-verbal interactions, the atmosphere, and the hidden and explicit goals that pervade the classroom. In other words, it makes sense of life in the classroom, representing the underlying assumptions and the students' and teacher's unspoken emotional needs that permeate all aspects of classroom life. Certainly, classroom culture is idiosyncratic, reflecting our personality in the same way that the general culture is tweaked by an individual's or group's idiosyncrasies. However, many aspects of classroom culture are generally similar because classrooms reflect the larger society. Indeed, one of the responsibilities of school, as the secondary socializer, is to make good citizens of the students and to pass on cultural values to the next generation. Many school reformists do not accept this anthropological view of education, preferring instead the view that education should not lead learners to conform to the values of the dominant culture, but rather empower them to transform it for purposes of social justice.

In order to make the idea of the classroom culture clearer, let me use a description of a contrast culture. Gail Benjamin, an anthropologist, documented her two English-speaking children's year in a Japanese school, in first and fifth grades in 1989–90. She writes about the extensive use of groups in Japanese classrooms, a striking contrast to the United States. These groups are known as a whole, rather than by the individuals in them; they change only at the beginning of each term and members within the group do everything together, from classwork to lunch preparation. All students in the group contribute to the group goals; the students view the group as a fun and a natural way to work. The Japanese were surprised at Benjamin's question about students who might not do their share of the work. Reflecting

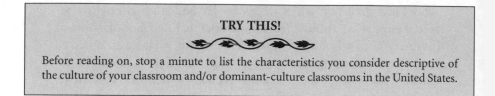

TRY THIS!

Before reading on, stop a minute to list the characteristics you consider descriptive of the culture of your classroom and/or dominant-culture classrooms in the United States.

on a possible difference in attitude between the United States and Japan about the idea of "freeloading," she observes that Japanese children naturally absorb the concept of working in a group because the culture of home and society so thoroughly regard it as being good, natural, and rewarding (Benjamin 1997).

The United States resembles Japan in terms of children learning what is valued in their context; however, what is valued differs. Parents and teachers convey in their everyday interactions what they consider to be important; they pass on the values that have been shaped by family, circumstance, and society.

Characteristics of Dominant Culture Classrooms in the United States

What are some of the dominant-culture values reflected in the classroom? Here is a constellation of characteristics I believe make our classrooms different from classrooms of other cultures.

THE IMPORTANCE OF THE INDIVIDUAL

Just as the Japanese school of Benjamin's experience assumed that the group was the way to accomplish all tasks, the emphasis in dominant-culture classrooms tends to be on the individual. We use group work, but generally not as the predominant approach. Of course all students are doing the same thing at some particular times, but our general underlying attitude emphasizes that students have individual needs and rights which need to be acknowledged. The potential of each individual student stands paramount. Consider how these practices emphasize the individual: a personal choice for silent reading, attending to personal needs as they arise such as looking up a word in the class dictionary, sharpening a pencil, or going to the bathroom. We honor individual differences by giving lists of activities to be completed at one's own pace, or even choices to suit different interests. We create individual educational plans for students who have particular difficulties in school. This attitude is different from what Benjamin reports about Japan: "Japanese . . . feel that education, *not unique inborn differences*, is the key to individual development. . . . [B]y having common experiences, they will all learn the same things and develop the same characteristics [italics mine]" (Benjamin 1997, 25). Developing similarly is an important goal in a culture dedicated to groups, where an individual should not stand out from that group. Increasing globalization may moderate emphases in both countries, but for now, the dominant culture prevails there, just as it does here.

Students from backgrounds where group work has been the norm will need help in adjusting to individualized work. If possible, assign a same-gender peer (or two) to work with the ELL, to complete a task *together*. The peer needs to understand the goal: to help the ELL learn how to accomplish certain tasks in class, not just to get correct answers. In this way, the ELL has someone who knows what is expected and who fills a social need. This person could be the same as the "buddy" assigned to the ELL, or different. A subsequent strategy would be to increase contact time with you (more than for mainstream students) when the ELL is working alone.

STUDENT-CENTERED LEARNING

This underlying emphasis on the individual in dominant-culture classrooms in the United States is buttressed by the philosophy of education popularized by John Dewey in the early twentieth century. Before (and I daresay past) the publication of his child-centered philosophy of education, traditional attitudes held that, in education, the child should listen passively. Dewey wanted to change the student's role. He wanted children actively involved, unmasking their distinctive personalities. Out of this philosophy grows the notion that method and curriculum cannot be uniform across the system— or the nation—because students have diverse capacities, abilities, and demands. As Dewey puts it, the focus changes from outside the child (the curriculum, the teacher, the book) to within the child (Dewey [1900]1990). Whether or not schools follow Dewey completely, dominant-culture schools in the United States generally focus on the student more than on the teacher. The student undertakes the responsibility to ferret out information; the student works, not to merely memorize what we say, but to discover more about the concept. The knowledge base includes the teacher's wisdom and the results of the student's hands-on experience and research. Learning is not a fixed, complete, massive block to be transmitted from teacher to student, but an ever-evolving, ever-expanding enterprise involving discovery, critical thinking skills, and experience.

Such a philosophy differs greatly from school experiences of many cross-cultural students. They may come from a background that reveres the past and the knowledge gained from the ages; they may come from a heritage that honors hierarchical relationships, where children are seen as repositories for the wisdom of the elders, descriptively called a "banking" style of education

(Freire [1970]1994). Many students and parents from other cultures are surprised at what we take for granted: the discovery form of education. Many of us do not think twice about this philosophy; we may have gone to school with it, we may have learned to teach with it, we may have assumed that it was the way of all schools across the world. It is not.

Of course, many from other backgrounds have expressed an appreciation of "Western education" with its emphasis on critical thinking, creativity, and freedom. However, newcomers will need time to get used to the different methodology, to the shift of focus away from us toward them. For them, that process becomes its own course of discovery. For example, immigrants may be used to being told exactly what they should describe in "free writing" time. Suggesting many different topics *and* helping zero in on one helps get the ELL over that initial hump of the first few months.

SELF-RELIANCE

Many recognize self-reliance as the core value of the Anglo-American culture. Growing beyond the individualism of England that gave it birth, self-reliance of the United States has spun into an all-encompassing obsession. The individualism of England was strictly for political equality. In the United States, that equality has become paramount and has spilled into other domains of life, such as the social and economic. Self-reliance has become inseparable from political, social, and economic equality (Hsu 1975). This characteristic is unique to Anglo-Americans. In China and Japan, for example, dependence is considered a virtue. Not to have connections to the extended family leaves one without identity. However, in the United States, from their early days, children are taught to make their own decisions and to take any consequences of their actions. In school, they are taught how to be confident in the decisions they make, and even to question authority. We often discourage dependence on peers; parents urge children to be on their own as soon as they are able. A fairly audible moan arose from many parents throughout the United States when, due to the job market, adult children started moving back in with parents after finishing college. Aging parents live in dread of becoming dependent on their children. Students are encouraged to stand up for their own ideas, which, parents and teachers both realize, sometimes backfires. I remember a conversation I overheard when in the stands watching our son's Little League game. A ten-year-old boy remonstrated with his mother about something she wanted him to do, outlining in great detail his reasons for not wanting to do the job. As he countered every point she made, she became angry and told him to stop. Then, realizing that he had provided a logical, clearly articulated argument, she acknowledged his feat and added, "But you use that tactic with your teacher, *not* your mother."

Students from predominantly collectivistic cultures have learned from childhood that being self-reliant does not win high praise. Friends and family bolster and nourish each other at all times. Once again, a group of "buddies" can support an ELL and show her the ropes for accomplishing many classroom expectations.

PATTERNS OF THINKING

A fourth assumption that pervades dominant-culture classrooms in the United States dates back to the analytic, linear, and logical world view of Greek and other European philosophers. The world view of many cultures in Asia differs. "The Eastern view places an emphasis on perceiving and knowing things and events holistically and synthetically, rather than analytically" (Kim 1988, 365). Intuition and contemplation are important. This "Eastern" approach leads inward, to a greater understanding of the self and the range of human experience. The "Western" approach has evolved into outward exploration, to numerous scientific discoveries and technological developments of the present. These two views are complementary, not competing, perspectives on the world. Each one has its advantages and detractions. Due to globalization and technology, many cultures these days incorporate both. However, part of our socialization involves absorbing the traditional patterns within our culture.

The Anglo-American culture of the United States champions objective thinking with measurable results. Fate, luck, or chance play a negligible role in the greater design of our lives. Contextual circumstances, personal intuitions, or emotion carry little weight in interactions. "In their suspicion of emotional statements, Americans differ from many others. Iranians, for example, have a tradition of eloquent, emotion-filled speech. . . . They seek to move their audiences to accept them and their viewpoints not because of the facts they have presented but because of the human feelings they share" (Althen 1988, 32). Another example: "Arabs respond much more readily to personalized arguments than to attempts to impose 'logical' conclusions" (Nydell 1996, 44). In the days when I was an ESOL teacher in elementary grades in the United States, I remember whole booklets written to help mainstream children learn the difference between a statement of fact and one of feeling. It was important not to confuse the two since one could be used for proof and the other could not; one was correct, the other was not.

Whether or not one agrees with the premise, in general, the classrooms of the United States reflect the notion that "facts are empirical, observable, and measurable . . . facts are reliable so that different observers will agree about them . . . facts are objective and therefore valid. In American thinking, facts exist in the external world and not inside the mind" (Stewart and Bennett 1991, 31–32). Since quantification validates facts, many people from the United States are preoccupied with numbers. Polls tell how candidates or ideas are received; advertisements gain credibility with the numbers of people who have tested, eaten, recommended, or sold a product; standings rank sports figures on dozens of criteria; bestseller lists indicate worthwhile books, movies, and music; temperatures and dewpoint readings quantify weather. Many researchers favor the numbers, amounts, figures, and statistics of quantitative research over qualitative studies.

Facts also lead people to think of a "right position" and a "wrong" one, leading to an adversarial view of the world. Unlike the yin and yang of Chinese culture which complement each other to make a whole, the two sides of thought in the dominant Anglo-American culture aim prove the validity of one side, or try to persuade the other. Professor of linguistics Deborah Tannen points out that many people in the dominant culture of the United States assume that "the best way to show you're really thinking is to criticize"(Tannen 1998, 4). Critical thinking is one of our responsibilities in dominant-culture classrooms. One of the aspects of U.S. education highly valued by other cultures, critical thinking is unfamiliar to many ELLs. In order to practice it, they must overcome their accustomed unwillingness to question a higher authority, whether it be a teacher or an idea in a book. Guided steps to understand *why* and how an idea should be critiqued may be necessary. Sometimes, students feel more comfortable writing their opinions, rather than speaking them. However, the reluctance to criticize or question still prevails.

COMPETITIVENESS

Our emphasis on independence and self-reliance leads to a competitive spirit in the classroom, created both by us and by the students. Many Anglo-American students have been socialized at home to compete. Thankfully, the practice of pitting boys against girls in the classroom is dying out. However, in some contests only one student wins in the classroom. Some of us feel that fanning those competitive desires enlivens students; others smother those sparks in search of a more harmonious atmosphere. The school culture feeds competitiveness: for example, the number of books read by children over vacation means corresponding glory (or funds) for the classroom. The ranking of school systems on statewide assessment tests brings distinction to the town and pressure to the classroom. Intramural as well as inter-mural sports used to be a popular venue for competition until fees for sports decimated or elitized many teams. Competitiveness shows its grip in the designer logos on clothing or sneakers or backpacks students bring to school.

Competition is not unique to the classrooms of the United States, but neither is it a universal trait. Some ELLs thrive in such circumstances and want to work on their own and strive to win; others are accustomed to a more cooperative atmosphere and wither under the pressure to compete. Just two examples will serve to describe the gamut, though they must not be taken as prescriptive for the whole culture: One is a Russian student who preferred to work alone. Highly competitive, accustomed to being the top student in his class before the family's emigration to the United States, he found group work to be an anchor holding him back. Initially, because he had difficulty expressing himself in English, he was doubly frustrated by his lack of English fluency as well as by his peers' low academic abilities. The other example is a group of first-generation Hispanic children in a pre-dominantly Mexican town in California. Researchers observed the children in school, at home, and at the community playground. The authors of the study found that practices at home and school differed sharply. When the children were asked to do something by their parents, they would find a friend to assist them. When they played games, victories would be shared by all; those who had more (cards, points, etc.) would give some to the others so the victory could be shared. However, at school, victory was limited to only one person or group. Only "the best" won. In school these children, too, wanted to win, but could not compete with those whose language and culture were a better match to the dominant-culture classroom (Delgado-Gaitan and Trueba 1991). These tendencies sometimes show up also across gender cultures in the United States, with competition considered more of a male trait; and harmony, a female trait.

The grasp of individualism can be exceedingly strong. Simply working in groups does not negate competition; groups compete to finish first or write the longer report or give the better presentation. Often even if the group works together efficiently and harmoniously, a sense of working independently within the group still prevails: Cooperative learning in our schools and cooperative projects in businesses still involve individual accountability. We do not have the outlook of the Japanese students described at the beginning of the chapter or of the Mexican-American students described previously; nor do they have ours. Cooperative learning helps fulfill social and cognitive needs of ELLs, aims to take advantage of the skills of all participants, and produces academic as well as affective benefits for all students. However, it stands as just one strategy among many.

TRY THIS!

Create a list with the class about all the ways in which competition occurs in a person's life. Use it as a springboard for a class discussion about how they feel toward rivalry. Do they think they do better with rivalry or are there some students who would prefer not to be so competitive? What do students who thrive on cooperation do with the "race track" style in the classroom?

HUMOR

Humor is another component of many classrooms in the United States, another indication of the informality that pervades the classroom. Seeking to avoid a hierarchical relationship, we use humor to create more of a sense of equality. Also, sharing a laugh together builds cohesion, breaks tension, succinctly makes a point, and feeds our inner need to be likeable. So humor has many uses. However, it comes as a surprise to many newcomers who come from cultures with hierarchical, formal relationships in the classroom. Additionally, humor is very cultural: What is humorous in the United States is not necessarily humorous in Egypt. Should we avoid humor? No, but we need to realize that cross-cultural students may have trouble understanding the words or sense of the joke, as well as the different relationship with the teacher that such a joke implies. Jokes make light of things—and many cross-cultural students feel that education is not to be taken lightly.

ENJOYMENT

Enjoyment also pervades many dominant-culture classrooms; we need and want to see happy children in order to sustain the thought that learning is fun. We choose activities not only for educational worth but also with an eye to the children's pleasure while participating. We search the classroom like a lighthouse beacon, looking for troubled faces.

However, the idea that learning should be fun is not universal; indeed many students as well as parents feel that such an attitude demeans the power of knowledge. Many cross-cultural students have had to memorize pages of books each night and have prepared to recite passages in class. So solemn faces should not put us off. (We might hope, indeed, that some dominant-culture students would absorb some serious-mindedness from immigrants who have sacrificed a lot to obtain an education.) However, as usual, we must try to be sensitive to whether the student is making a cultural adjustment or is really having a problem.

TRY THIS!

English is itself a symbol of the diversity within our borders. Start a discussion about the ways in which languages borrow from each other and ways in which language evolves over the years. Students who know other languages might be able to suggest English words in their language; older generations can help with new words they don't understand and old words no longer used. Have groups of students explore the origins of the following words and answer from what language and how they might have come into English: (1) brocade, (2) algebra, (3) chocolate, (4) tulip, (5) noodle, (6) piano, (7) mammoth, (8) satin. See footnote for answers. (Adapted from Jim Carnes 1994, pp. 56–63)*

---

*(1) Spanish, (2) Arabic, (3) Nahuatl (Native American), (4) Turkish, (5) German, (6) Italian, (7) Russian, (8) Chinese.

THE PHYSICAL ENVIRONMENT

The physical classroom environment also contributes to the culture within. The arrangement of desks and bulletin boards filled with student work reinforce the concept of a student-centered approach. Student projects displayed around rooms or hallways send messages of collaboration between teacher and students. Different linguistic and artistic interpretations of a common theme celebrate individuality. Posters can motivate students, remind students of expectations, expand the subject matter, or make a personal or political statement wherever in the world they are displayed. Even as structures, schools conform to their context or the latest educational research. In some areas of the world, classrooms are under trees; in others, they have roofs but no walls; they may be floating in a bay, or huddled around a fire in a yurt.

JOURNAL TIME

You have just heard that you have been selected from a number of other applicants to have a teacher intern from China with you for three months in your classroom. It has been made very clear that Mei Mei is an experienced teacher at home; she is a member of a group of teachers who are coming to get better acquainted with education in the United States. You are really excited about what this will mean for your students. You had to submit some general guidelines of what you wanted to accomplish, so the basic outline of the time is complete. You now realize that you should perhaps help your colleague understand your classroom. Write her a letter, introducing her to the culture of your specific classroom.

A Few More Tips for Mainstream Teachers

In addition to the tips provided throughout the book, let me mention just a few more.

- Do not worry too much if your ELL does not speak in class for the first three months. Remembering the process of acculturation, you will recall that those are the most difficult. The student is a sponge soaking up the sounds of the language and the cultural cues as to what to do. She may talk more in her ESOL class, but may not be ready to attempt much in the more intimidating milieu of the mainstream class. Furthermore, not all cultures value verbal communication as much as we do. We must not neglect the student during this time, however, and must make sure she is participating in other ways in the life of the class.

- Use as much "total communication" as possible when you have an ELL in the classroom. Visuals (outlines, pictures, math symbols, real articles) of any kind always help. For example, holding up the book of the chapter under discussion, as you tell the students to take the book out, helps focus his attention to that task. Putting up an outline of what you hope to accomplish or of your notes for the lecture contributes to better comprehension for the ELL. Some of the mainstream students may wonder at this new technique; others may be grateful.

- Try to use a natural tone and slightly slower rhythm in your own language when speaking with the ELL. Often when people do not understand us, we tend to speak louder or exaggerate our enunciation. Neither really helps. The student needs to hear language as normally spoken. Simplify your language, but do not use telegraphic English. That does not help the student learn good usage. ELLs need to hear words in context to learn how to use them correctly.

- ELLs also need a chance to participate in the regular classroom jobs along with all the other students. Most of the jobs do not require much language and the student will feel more a part of the whole scene. Integrating the ELL as much as possible will encourage language development as well as self-confidence.

The Role of Parents

While they don't contribute directly to the culture of the classroom as created by the teacher and students, parents are an integral part of a child's education, particularly in elementary and middle schools in the United States.

Before getting into the specifics of that involvement, let's first look very briefly at the different parental attitudes toward education between Japan and the United States. When I read Gail Benjamin's comment, "We . . . shared the feeling of many American parents that what our children would miss in a year away from American schooling wasn't too important, that it could easily be made up" (Benjamin 1997, 4), I recalled the urgency with which the parents of my elementary-aged Japanese students located the Japanese school in a nearby community and signed up their children for Saturday classes as soon as they arrived. The Japanese parents, like Benjamin, were confident that their children would learn a great deal from the experience of being in school in a very different culture, but they also knew that missing a grade of Japanese school would hamper their children's ability to compete in the Japanese educational system. The importance of school permeated Japanese conversation and life. Benjamin reports that school images dominate how children were referred to (e.g., "my son, a second grader," rather than by age), admonished ("that's not how a fourth grader would behave"), and introduced (again, by grade rather than by age). Children new to school received backpacks in a special ceremony. Clothing requirements and specific walking groups to school indicated that the child was entering an important occupation. And to assist in that important occupation, many mothers, with their own title of "education mom," totally dedicate themselves to their children's education. Acceding that this relatively new pursuit resulted from increased spare time, it symbolizes the importance of education and of a mother's efforts in helping her children achieve success (Benjamin 1997).

Many parents in the United States feel more ambivalent toward education than the typical Japanese mother. For many in the United States, education has not been a way out of economic hardships; great differences exist in educational opportunities between cities and suburbs; equity in education seems to be a distant dream. Parents are disillusioned with what education has not accomplished and with what they feel constitutes poor-quality education. More education has not necessarily meant a job or greater financial success.

ASSUMPTIONS OF THE ANGLO-AMERICAN CULTURE

Dominant-culture schools in the United States regard parental involvement vital to student achievement. However, not all parents are as involved as they or we would like. Disillusionment is not the only reason for parental absence. Other reasons may be time, inexperience, distress, timidity, or deference. From our standpoint, involvement means checking that homework is done (though not helping with it or doing it); making sure that the child is prepared for the day in mind, body, and timely arrival; showing up for a variety of school activities (e.g., bake sales and other fund raisers, student performances, parent-teacher meetings), and supporting us in our classroom endeavors. The parents and we work together for the benefit of the student. If parents of cross-cultural students do not fulfill these assumptions, many of us assume that the parents do not care about their children's education. Instead, however, the parents may view their role differently.

ASSUMPTIONS OF ELLs' PARENTS

My research has shown that parents of ELLs hold the teacher in very high regard. Most cultures view education as a powerful vehicle by which to escape generations of economic hardships. Generally, teachers are considered very influential. A Chinese teacher shared with me a common Chinese saying: "A teacher for one moment is a teacher for life." In other words, a teacher's positive influence lasts a lifetime (Clayton n.d.).

Psychologist Çiğdem Kağıtçıbaşı suggests an insight about parental roles across cultures. Some parents view their jobs as providing love and nurture; others see their roles as preparing their children for school and success. These assumptions play a part in how they view their involvement in school (Kağıtçıbaşı 1996). In addition to the differences in the perceptions of their roles as parents, these linguistic or ethnic minority parents may subscribe to different concepts of the division between home and school. In many cultures, the parents' responsibility is at home and the teachers' domain is in the school. These parents do not want to interfere in a domain in which they are not trained; their feeling is that the teacher knows best how to manage school issues just as the parent knows best how to handle the home. For such people, the whole concept of parental input into their child's education is new, even inappropriate.

Hence, linguistic and ethnic minority parents have different concepts about the meaning of parental support. Participating in bake sales or other fundraising activities does not spell "support" for them. Rather, support is helping out with homework when they can. Often, parents will know less English than their children, which means that they cannot help with that task. For others, support is making sure that the child gets to school, or understands the importance of school. For others, a child's education must be balanced with urgent family matters that may include looking for an apartment or getting a job. All in all, I have never met a parent of an ELL who did not value education, though I have met many who valued it differently than the Anglo-Americans.

BARRIERS FOR LINGUISTIC AND ETHNIC MINORITY PARENTS

Given the assumptions on both sides, are there other reasons that parents of ELLs do not get involved in school? Yes, many. First and foremost, many parents do not have the fluency in English to manage a meeting with us. They have not yet learned the cultural expectations of this country nor the language needed to face a person of our authority. If they think that school is not a place for parents to interfere, finding a friend to translate may not be urgent or practical. Furthermore, many come from cultures where they are used to going to the child's school only for bad news. They are not eager to add that to their already full plate of adjustment fare. They, similar to non-ELL parents, may have had bad experiences in their own schooling or even dropped out and hence lack confidence. They are reluctant to be told to do things that they know they will not be able to manage. Finally, many do not have the time or the resources to be able to take off from work or physically get to school. If public transportation does not go to near the school, the parent will need to either walk or take a taxi, which may not be in the budget. If they work at night, evening meetings are not possible; if they work during the day, getting to school at night may present other problems.

ENCOURAGING INVOLVEMENT

As can be seen, parents may hold different expectations of their relationship to their children's education. Thus, we need to be clear about our expectations of the parents, with an understanding and sensitivity to what they can afford both in time and money. These parents spend so much of their lives not knowing the expectations around them that they often appreciate help with specifics. Here are a few suggestions to help with those conversations:

Giving Suggestions. While identifying expectations is good, we must also be careful how we interfere in family life. Many parents have already experienced a disruption in the family culture and are living with shifting sands under their feet. Reading to or with children, particularly at bedtime, is not a universal custom. If they do not practice this habit, it need not imply disinterest or neglect; the custom points to a cultural practice energized by current research on literacy. Finding and expanding on an already familiar custom will help parents incorporate any "new" practice into their family life. If reading to their children is not already part of their established routine at home, it may become an extra task encumbered by negative feelings from both the overworked parents and the embarrassed student. Reading at bedtime is just one way in which literacy can be supported at home; others include observing and recording the world around them, telling stories, or using math in food preparation.

Family literacy programs may be needed to help parents with their own literacy in English. That, in turn, results in more interest in supporting their children's progress in literacy. The important issue is to find a way to incorporate practices so that they are a normal part of the day.

Eliciting Their Thoughts. Parents want to be *asked* for their input on issues affecting home life. Finders and Lewis quote a Latina mother: "Whenever I go to school, they want to tell me what to do at home. They want to tell me how to raise my kid. They never ask me what I think" (Finders and Lewis 1994, 53). Learning about the students' family life in a sincere, non-bureaucratic way is an enriching personal experience for us, a professional boon to learn how to best reach the child, and a welcoming act for the family. Some families may not wish to share much information, especially if they come from cultures where such information has been used against them. The father of one of my Russian students could not get over the amount of information that was available for the general public, the openness of the Anglo-American culture. The sensitive among us will understand when to stop asking and just listen.

Explaining Procedures and Practices. Just as we ask for information, we need to be forthcoming about some classroom practices: for example, silent reading and selection of books for that time or invented spelling. Coming from cultures where choices were non-existent and correctness was paramount, parents of some of my ELLs felt very uncomfortable with these two practices. Once they understood the underlying philosophy, though they did not feel such practices would work, at least they understood that I was not being lazy!

At certain times we must inform parents of school-, system-, or statewide regulations. For example, if we experience timeliness and attendance problems with the student, we need to ask the parents about the reasons, see how we might contribute to the solution, and possibly inform them of the laws that govern their children's education. Parents whose children are in systems that have some kind of orientation for newcomers are fortunate. In systems that don't have such a program, we take on that task throughout the year, since immigrant parents may experience an overload of information and may not recall all they hear on the first day.

Some Russian parents have told me that individual conferences are new; their school culture dictated that all parents sat in their child's classroom and listened as the teacher read aloud each student's grade for the previous term. Other parents may trust the teacher so completely that they may not understand why a parent-school partnership is needed. Most parents do want a connection with their children's education. Sending home communication on a regular basis helps build a bridge for the parent to cross, but translators must be found to establish such a welcome connection. By inquiring about the parents' mode of participation, we can devise creative strategies that will accomplish our goals as well as honor their dedication to their children's future.

Recognizing Their Needs. Linguistic minority parents may be looking for an unusual connection that we may not expect. For example, if parents come from collectivistic cultures where common values are shared across family and community institutions, they may assume that we will naturally be a part of forming the child's character, not just his mind. The parents may expect that just as we want the family to be supportive of school at home, so we will be supportive of the family at school. They may hope that we can urge the students to respect and cherish their heritage, which, given the emphasis on assimilation in the United States, is not often done at school.

Though visiting students' homes is a custom that is taking root very slowly in the United States, more and more of us are practicing it. Many immigrant parents in my experience were honored and delighted with such a request, but many will not realize that they need to answer with a "tear off and return to your teacher" form. Most teacher education programs unfortunately do not urge teachers to make the concrete connection to their students' lives outside of school in order to better understand their strengths and capitalize on them in the classroom. A student's personal story, her previous education, the family members, and their history constitute the prior knowledge base on which we can build effectively.

Providing Help. Ethnic and linguistic minority parents have suggested having a host family from the class guide them through their first year, using parent expertise in the classroom and bringing in guests (not necessarily parents) of different heritages into the classroom to share their experiences. Some advocated having a schoolwide meeting of the parents of ELLs to share questions and answers, which would assume either a level of English fluency or translators if it were a multilingual meeting. A systemwide meeting by language groups could accomplish the same goals of disseminating information and sharing concerns.

Achieving Success. The parents' reception at school plays a major role in how much they will become involved. In my experience, while many schools and teachers bend over backwards to be accessible and welcoming, sometimes just the hint of an accent will throw some school personnel into a tailspin. Body language speaks louder and clearer than we would wish, effectively negating our words and sending the wrong message. Parents already fear seeming foolish or misunderstood, so any efforts to make them feel comfortable are rewarded with collaboration for their child's success.

SOMETIMES WE SEE ETHNIC OR LINGUISTIC MINORITY PARENTS AS A drain or a problem. They do take more time than do Anglo-American parents who are familiar with cultural practices, the school system, and the expectations in class. However, any efforts to increase communication with newcomer parents not only honors them, their children, and their culture but also opens the door for us, the class, the school, and the system to enlarge the view of our shrinking world.

Reflections on Janos

School is school, in Janos' view. Whether here or in Hungary, the experience would no doubt be the same. We tend not to think that something so universal as "school" could, indeed, be that different from culture to culture. But research has shown it is. Even within the United States, different cultures such as Indian tribes on reservations or small towns in the Piedmont Carolinas put their own imprint on schools. Since schools are mirrors of the culture they are meant to pass on, and since we now can identify much of what comprises cultural values in the Anglo-American culture, we can understand that schools can be different inside and out.

Janos' early experience included memorization and recitation. The memorization was the learning part; the recitation was the evaluation. Recitation played a very major role in my own elementary schooling as well. While much of Turkish education has changed by this date, some teachers in my childhood would even stop a student in mid-sentence of the recitation and ask another to continue. The teacher presented the material: It comprised all of the important thoughts that needed to be known; it signified not just an appreciation, but a reverence for the past. Schoolbooks were very important, for it was from those that you memorized. Parents felt involved because they could look at the textbooks to see what their children were studying each night; a family member could refer to them in order to help with homework. Checked regularly by the teacher, subject notebooks (copybooks) held notes copied from the blackboard and our homework. Students were responsible for supplying their own notebooks; there was no stack of paper for general class use. To graduate from elementary school (fifth grade), one week was devoted to final exams, a subject a day. Each student appeared before a group of three teachers (of different grades) who could ask any question relating to the subject, studied over the course of our school life. Called in individually, we were grilled for about fifteen minutes (I suppose; it seemed like fifteen hours) and then dismissed. We solved math questions, the only written part, at the classroom blackboard, in full view of the three teachers. It was a terrifying experience for every student. Similar types of exams were held to graduate from middle and high schools as well.

So, if Janos' background resembled mine, we can see why he questioned the idea that playing educational games could be a tool of evaluation or learning. He was not prepared to think that learning should be light-hearted or that it would not include memorization and recitation. He did not understand how the curriculum could not include geography, a particular favorite. The flexibility of the room and the schedule also removed some of the fixed structure that created the framework of school for him. He was in a foreign land.

Imagine Janos' parents. They moved here for the sake of their children. They left their families, vocations, and beloved homeland so that their children might thrive in this new land. Now they had to sit by as they watched their child's frustration. Not understanding the culture of school, which they thought was universal, they did not know what to do. They felt helpless.

We educators often feel helpless too, as complications from various students' homes intrude on our days. In some situations we can help directly; with others, we exhaust all our energies seemingly for naught. With linguistic or ethnic minority students we can make a difference. Understanding that schools and classrooms around the world are filled with different assumptions, we can ease our students' adjustment by ensuring that our classroom culture respects their backgrounds, recognizes their courage, and explores ways to integrate both student and parents into an appreciation of their new life.

Chapter Nine

Imagining All the Possibilities: Multicultural Education

You should not hate everyone who has a different nose than you.

—German proverb

Frankly, I'm a little bruised right now. The conversation at noon in the Teachers' Room really did a job on me. Most of the teachers were complaining about the increase in the number of non-English-speaking students in our school this year. They feel that the students are a real burden in class. I sense a simmering xenophobia, a hunkering down, a "you-do-it-our-way-or-get-out" attitude which I have not felt before. I tried to talk about our need to provide ELLs with equitable opportunities for learning and how the whole class is strengthened by the presence of these students from other cultures, but was pelted in a barrage of anger that surprised me.

—(Lucinda, *a fourth-grade teacher*)

Usually chipper Lucinda sought me out as we passed in the corridor of her school. We had known each other for quite a few years since her principal had found her approach to English Language Learners appealing. She had a very calm way

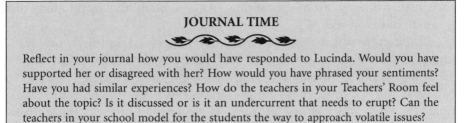

JOURNAL TIME

Reflect in your journal how you would have responded to Lucinda. Would you have supported her or disagreed with her? How would you have phrased your sentiments? Have you had similar experiences? How do the teachers in your Teachers' Room feel about the topic? Is it discussed or is it an undercurrent that needs to erupt? Can the teachers in your school model for the students the way to approach volatile issues?

with them; her interest and empathy conquered her fear of not being able to communicate. She found a variety of ways to integrate them into the classroom, in such a way that their classmates were open to these new and different friendships. She listened carefully to the tenor of the majority-culture students' comments about the ELLs to judge and either encourage or deflect early the developing themes. She knew she had to work a little harder to accommodate non- and limited-English speakers, but she also knew that she had a class full of eager helpers. She reveled in the many ways in which the ELLs expanded the horizons of her students in ways not included in her curriculum. This day, her distress seemed to weigh down not only her demeanor but also her very soul; she sounded more and more alone in her implementation of a multicultural perspective in her classroom.

Multiculturalism Rx: "Six Impossible Things Before Breakfast"

As the globe shrinks and travel is a "click of the mouse" away; as linguistic and ethnic minorities in nations all over the world begin to seek out rights for themselves within their own borders; as repressive regimes make life intolerable and citizens are willing to leave hard-earned professions to work as menial laborers in freedom-minded countries, the concept of multiculturalism takes on urgency around the world. Contact with people who have world views different from our own is no longer a rare occurrence. How we respond to this diversity and how we acknowledge its presence is a moral issue. Multiculturalism is an attitude toward all of life, not just education. Its goal is a mindset that respects differences and searches for similarities that can unite. This mindset accepts the inevitability of conflict between strongly held values among people and also envisions possibilities of positive growth through that conflict. This mindset seeks an understanding of others and their reality through an understanding of the self and the assumptions that generate our own reality.

Multiculturalism reaches across not just racial, cultural, or ethnic groups but also across gender, age, and disability. Multiculturalism means an awareness of all these various groups with their differing patterns of behavior, but it also reaches behind the *what* of those differences to investigate the *why*. Multiculturalism means being proud of the cultural diversity of this country. Multiculturalism means giving up melting pot or assimilationist theories whereby all minority groups lose their distinctiveness in favor of the majority culture. It means taking seriously the equality of all individuals as stated in our constitution and advocating for equity in opportunity and power. Multiculturalism means having our perspective transformed from the ethnocentric one we start with to one that encompasses a new world view. As discussed in Chapter One, multiculturalism is not static or instantaneous but grows gradually through stages of often-difficult transitions as our assumptions are challenged. Alice described the feelings many of us have:

> Alice laughed. "There's no use trying," she said: "one *can't* believe impossible things."
>
> "I daresay you haven't had much practice," said the Queen. "When I was your age, I always did it for half-an-hour a day. Why sometimes I've believed as many as six impossible things before breakfast." (Carroll 1897, 102–3)

Multiculturalism is a process similar to the one Alice lacked, that of imagining *all* the possibilities.

Multiculturalism in Education

The society of the United States is becoming more diverse and that change is very controversial. The challenge of the motto "E PLURIBUS UNUM" (from many, one) is interpreted in radically different ways. Some feel that the way to achieve that unity is through "English Only" legislation, English immersion campaigns, and a Euro-centric curriculum. These people see diversity as a threat to unity, a drag on resources, and a danger to the economy. Conversely, proponents of multiculturalism see strength in diversity, an expansion of economic possibilities, and a moral imperative in the modern world. The need of society in general and schools in particular to learn to live with diversity points to a curriculum that must try to teach not just tolerance, but rather affirmation and celebration of that diversity.

The classroom is a microcosm of the larger society. As we have seen over the course of this book, students bring with them a cornucopia of attitudes, skills, interests, identities, aptitudes, and accomplishments that have been shaped by their cultural socialization and individual talents and preferences. When students come from homes where orientations differ from the macro-culture (as represented by the school), they often find their self-esteem threatened, or their experiences devalued or dismissed. To teach effectively by making a connection with the student's prior knowledge, teachers must be aware of some of these differences and their possible impact on learning. While multicultural education cannot solve all the problems that schools experience today, it describes the only way *all* students can become empowered to learn, to treat others with respect, to respond when another's dignity is challenged, and to become familiar with the information and skills necessary for our shrinking globe.

Some people think that multicultural education attempts to denigrate Euro-centric education. This is unfortunate, since that is not the intention. The founders of this country were immersed in European philosophy, traditions, and thought. The roots of this culture are deep in Anglo soil. The intention of multicultural education is to bring the richness of non-Anglo cultures to the foreground along with those of Anglo traditions. *All* students need to understand the foundations of the dominant culture in order to succeed in this country just as *all* students also need to be prepared to work with the world at their fingertips.

A Definition of Multicultural Education

Multicultural education conjures up a variety of images in many people's minds: learning about the holidays of the cross-cultural students who are in class, discovering differences in cultural traditions, indulging in ethnic foods, participating in holiday activities, exploring the arts across cultures, or scanning the racial palette of inner-city schools. That is to say, multicultural education is often thought of as tangible *product*: usually, information about how other cultures are uniquely distinct; what their holidays, foods, heroes, and customs are.

Multicultural education should be much more than that. Primarily, multicultural education aims to promote equal educational opportunities for all students. As an approach to education, it offers *all* students, regardless of their backgrounds, an opportunity to achieve their fullest potential in their personal, intellectual, and social development. Shaped by an affirmation of cultural pluralism, it grows out of the values of a democratic tradition that seeks to promote an equitable and just society.

It aims to prepare students to gain the knowledge and skills required to participate fully in the global context. It ensures that each student has a full array of crayons to color her world, rather than just a few, broken, discarded, unwanted colors.

My understanding of this approach is anchored in *respect for human dignity*, an *appreciation of cultural diversity*, and in the *interdependence of our world*.

RESPECT FOR HUMAN DIGNITY

Even if our society doesn't always completely fulfill the ideals of its democratic foundations, people who come from around the world praise the ethos that honors justice, equality, and basic liberties. Forged from religious, philosophical, and political imperatives, this experiment in democracy offers the world a powerful alternative to other systems. Commitment to the ideals of democracy, not just a national language or a particular culture, holds us together. That ideal keeps the nation working toward the goal of recognizing and respecting the dignity of each individual regardless of age, gender, religion, socioeconomic level, disability, national, linguistic, racial, or ethnic origin.

RESPECT AND APPRECIATION FOR CULTURAL DIVERSITY

Cultural diversity enriches us because learning from other cultural patterns helps us become progressively effective in dealing with our problems. Appreciating different cultures—which should be seen as wells of collective experiences, knowledge, and wisdom—can make our own lives much richer. For example, many people have been struck by the warm hospitality they experience when visiting Turkey. When you ask for directions, very likely the person will leave his work and lead you all the way to your destination, no matter how far out of the way. Invitations for an afternoon visit to a home result in far more than a cup of tea and a plate of cookies. Seats are found on buses that previously were truly full. The list is endless. Turks' intense priority of relationships with others is an antidote to the loneliness we experience with our powerful emphasis on independence in the United States. But the learning goes both ways. My international graduate students in the United States, for example, struggle with and then come to appreciate a less hierarchical structure in class, more openness through class discussions, and more emphasis on independent thinking. No culture has found the universal way of responding to human need; cultures have found what best suits the needs of their people in their particular contexts. In looking at others' values and ways we are strengthened by having alternatives to choose or reject.

THE INTERDEPENDENCE OF OUR WORLD

The shrinking of our world is impossible to ignore, not only with increased travel, work, or educational opportunities but also with the explosion of technology providing immediate links to all parts of the world. What we do in our country has repercussions outside our borders; students must be prepared to interact with people whose thinking and behavior may be far different from theirs. Farmers in the heartland as well as business executives on the coasts need the knowledge and skills with which to communicate clearly with those who do not share our ways. We cannot assume an isolationist attitude; we have no choice but to respond to both the local and global community.

OUT OF THESE CORE VALUES GROW THE GOALS THAT WILL PROMOTE a multicultural perspective in the classroom. The educational intervention of the school deeply shapes the emerging identity of an individual. Whether members of the dominant or a minority culture, *all* students benefit from attempts to address the issues of educational equity.

Multicultural Education in the Classroom

What does multicultural education look like in a classroom? Multicultural education encompasses an ethos of respect and high standards which encourage achievement, curricula which reflect the diverse perspectives of the community and the world, and students who are encouraged to learn about their own and others' world views and take action to achieve justice. Below are six characteristics:

MULTICULTURAL EDUCATION SIGNIFIES A PROCESS

One of the main characteristics of multicultural education is that of an *approach*, a process, the practice of imagining possibilities. It uses the insight gained from the topics in this book when fashioning the ethos of the class. It means sensitivity in the relationships and interactions with students. It provides the high expectations that encourage students to work harder. It brings the whole world into discussions with questions and reflections that make the students think beyond their circumscribed world. It urges us to replace a biased curriculum. It encourages us to help colleagues remember the benefits of a multilingual classroom when they get lost in the tailspin of emotional reactions. It prods us to look at policies that might be disadvantageous to minority students. As a fluid, dynamic, and never-ending process, it cannot be contained. A separate subject encapsulated as "multicultural education" that can be taught or "done" (as in, "We did Multicultural Education last month, we're now on to Disabilities.") does not exist. Nor does having a Chinese teacher at the school fulfill the multicultural "obligation." As a process, it unsettles our thinking by introducing the reality and the validity of multiple ways of discerning or understanding or evaluating. It tries to provide the practice the Red Queen spoke of; that is, it seeks not only to shatter the "can't" of Alice's complaint but also to expand the horizons of "impossible things."

MULTICULTURAL EDUCATION PERVADES THE CLASSROOM

Multicultural education is pervasive in two ways: First, it is omnipresent. It can infuse all subjects. In math, counting systems from East Asian countries, different monetary systems, and percentages involving statistics from around the world are but a few examples of bringing the world into the classroom. These simple ways suggest to students how other cultures have solved some of the questions that confront us all. Suggestions for combining geometry and art (two-dimensional patterns and designs) from around the world can make the lesson even richer (Nelson, Joseph, and Williams 1993). Investigating social inequality and stereotyping based on biological determinism can be an example of a science class for high schoolers (Grant and Sleeter 1989). Students can practice critical thinking skills in deliberating whether the circumstances (or heroines or victims) in Disney movies, for example, describe everyone. Young children as well as older ones can review books (or even just pictures) to find bias—be it of gender, race, class, ethnicity, and/or physical ability. Many novels or short stories can be plumbed for similarities and differences to the students' own experiences, whether they were intended for the purpose of broadening global horizons or not. Science classes can expand research to include information about the discoverer and the context of the times in terms of the discovery; issues of acid rain or rain forests can be viewed from all sides, considering all effects. Grant and Sleeter (1989)[1] suggest including discussions about similarity and dissimilarity and issues of respect across various groups in a lesson with third and fourth graders studying the life cycle. Graphs in a high school class use census bureau statistics to talk about economic equity issues among minority groups in the United States (Bennett 1999).[2] Colonialism can be studied from different perspectives (Banks 1997).[3] "Current Events" can be transformed into a more substantial undertaking than

---

[1] This book shows how existing curricula can be transformed into one with a multicultural perspective.

[2] This book has a number of lesson plans as examples of lessons created with a multicultural perspective.

[3] This book looks at issues that have special resonance for particular ethnic groups at different grade levels and has annotated bibliographies in each chapter for teachers and students.

simply reporting the news (Davidman and Davidman 2001).[4] The sources of these strategies and many others show that almost any lesson can be transformed to lead students to a better understanding not only of the content matter but also of each other. They can show that there are many ways to interpret the world around us, that we must learn truths about each other rather than believe stereotypes and act on prejudice.

Second, multicultural education is also pervasive because it is for *all* classrooms, not just those with students from other cultures. Since many classrooms in the United States pursue an education that is strongly Eurocentric, bringing in other perspectives regularly is extremely important. If the students are of the dominant culture, they may be unaware of the power (or even existence) of their culture; ethnocentrism may induce them to think narrowly about the world. Shattering stereotypes fostered by the media becomes far more difficult in a monocultural class, but still imperative. *All* students, of dominant and non-dominant cultures, need to have their horizons expanded and that occurs best when all backgrounds are represented, acknowledged, and celebrated.

MULTICULTURAL EDUCATION FOSTERS INTERCULTURAL ADEPTNESS

When we learn a foreign language, the first steps usually include the alphabet, vocabulary, and grammatical constructions. However, all of that is not very effective if we do not know the social rules of how to use the language, or the nuances relative to how, when, and where to use certain forms. For example, one of my international graduate students used "wanna" (as in "want to") in a note to me asking me for a letter of recommendation. She had learned a new word but not yet the social rules that apply to its use. Vocabulary alone is not sufficient for effective communication. Similarly, knowledge of differences across cultures is not sufficient. Affective as well as curricular work helps intercultural adeptness. Knowledge is necessary, yes, and so is enabling students to be open to the validity of others' beliefs and experiences. Sensitivities awakened, perhaps they can become like Alice:

> "[W]e had *such* a thunder-storm last Tuesday—I mean one of the last set of Tuesdays, you know." [said the White Queen]

> Alice was puzzled. "In *our* country," she remarked, "there's only one day at a time."

---

[4]This is another book with both "before" and "after" multicultural changes. The authors have many examples of whole units that can be transformed into a multicultural approach.

The Red Queen said "That's a poor thin way of doing things. Now *here*, we mostly have days and nights two or three at a time, and sometimes in the winter we take as many as five nights together—for warmth, you know."

"Are five nights warmer than one night, then?" Alice ventured to ask.

"Five times as warm, of course."

Alice sighed . . . "It's exactly like a riddle with no answer!" she thought. (Carroll 1897, p. 185)

Still faced with unimaginable differences between herself and the magical land she had entered, Alice did not argue. She puzzled, she remarked, she ventured to ask, she sighed. She had finally come to accept the validity of the Queens' world. She did not accept it as hers, but she was ready to let them accept it as theirs. She was not defensive about the differences; she did not feel she had to argue or persuade. Curious, she asked questions, eager to know more, yet willing to let things go even if she did not fully understand. Such is the attitude of a multicultural approach.

Enabling our students to reach out in urban communities across neighborhood boundaries, or in rural farmlands across value-laden fences, or in factory lines across cultural barriers, or in hallways and playgrounds across dividing barricades, or in high-rise conference rooms across national borders constitutes as much a goal as the content of the textbooks. *Teaching Tolerance*, available at <*www.teachingtolerance.org*>, offers many excellent classroom suggestions from practicing teachers, a variety of resources for a variety of topics, and provocative articles about achieving peace across various boundaries. Seeds of positive attitudes toward those unlike ourselves, toward those "with a different nose" as suggested in the opening proverb, need to be sown early in a student's life and continually cultivated.

MULTICULTURAL EDUCATION REQUIRES UNDERSTANDING OUR OWN CULTURE

As mentioned earlier, multicultural education is often considered to be solely learning about another culture, hence the emphasis on the heroes or holidays or literature from outside our boundaries. We teach (and thereby learn) about people of China or Nigeria, hopefully by allowing them to speak for themselves. But that exercise does not always lead us to break out of our own ethnocentric view. Actually, some people can be world-travelers and still have a very monocultural perspective. Becoming a multicultural person is the result of a series of stages, as discussed in Chapter One. The process leads us to reflect on our own culture as we encounter others; for example, as we celebrate scientific discoveries that conquer illness, but realize that science has also paved over flowering meadows. We explore, as we have been doing throughout this book, where our particular values, orientations, and tendencies lie. We look more intensively at our classroom practices to check for stances or strategies that might be particular to us, as opposed to universal. Only as we know ourselves will we be able to better understand others. We need not abandon our own culturally tied practices, but if we are aware of them, we will be able to accommodate those who carry different culturally shaped needs and better evaluate our own.

MULTICULTURAL EDUCATION INSISTS ON MULTIPLE PERSPECTIVES

History is written from many different perspectives: The victor and the vanquished see the results quite differently. Disparate viewpoints apply to much more of life, not only in the history of the past but also in the present. A recent visit with some friends again crystallized this concept for my husband and me. As Anglo-American parents with a cultural emphasis on independence, we expect our sons and daughters to choose their own spouses. Young people know their own minds, they assume that this decision is their business alone, and they expect to make their own way in the world. Romantic love binds them together. Unfortunately, we have a fifty percent divorce rate. In many of the collectivistic cultures of the world, parents (or other caregivers) arrange marriages. Those of us from an individualistic culture cannot imagine such a decision being made for us or, alternatively, the responsibility for choosing a son- or daughter-in-law. Our friends are well-educated, middle-class professionals from a collectivistic culture who are in that very difficult process (their words) of choosing husbands for their two daughters. These young women have had a Western education; that is, they have been exposed to the individualistic values of the Western world. Nevertheless, they willingly assent to their cultural tradition of having their parents make the choices. In their culture, marriage is considered not just between two people, but between families of similar backgrounds, interests, and values. One grows into love, after years of life together working toward similar ideals. The divorce rate is non-existent in their homeland. These parents know their daughters well and have access to a large network of friends and relatives who will know of eligible men of the same culture, around the globe. A sign of these women's Western education is that both have insisted on two compromises. One allows the women veto power, which in turn implies that the couple will have the opportunity to meet and get to know each other. The other compromise insists that their parents end the interview of the prospective husband at the slightest mention of a dowry: The women assert they are not for sale. With these compromises, these women bridge both cultures. Listening to their mother explain this very different perspective made it more understandable. Neither our friends nor we wanted the other's position, but all of us were able to better understand how the customs fit in with the respective cultural foundations.

A monocultural curriculum represents the world in a flat, unidimensional manner, a rather self-defeating way to prepare students for the reality of societal complexities. The multicultural perspective acknowledges and explores the perspectives and the significant contributions of many backgrounds that inhabit our world.

MULTICULTURAL EDUCATION LEADS TO SOCIAL JUSTICE

"In the doing is the learning": Social action is an important element for a perspective that promotes respect for the individual. Multicultural education works in two ways toward this goal. First, it strives *against* stereotypes, prejudice, bias, discrimination, and racism, which have no place in a multicultural perspective. Multicultural education uses not only content to help achieve understanding but also strategies, because affective as well as cognitive understanding together overcome barriers and hostilities. Since we talk about what is important, we must talk about these issues to achieve a common peace. Rumored myths come tumbling down; stereotypes get exploded when people meet and work face to face. Discrimination and racism are harder to accept when students have listened intently to "the other side" and taken time to discover similarities across the divide. In addition to their own affirmation of all races in the classroom, teachers must make a conscious, determined effort to prepare students for the fight against racism. Racism stands as a major issue in our land and as such must be addressed in a coherent, well-designed curricular fashion so that the optimum place (school) for addressing and working through these issues can be optimally used. The school, to be a model for the community, must monitor and change its own culture.

I have found that helping the majority culture become aware of the unsuspected, pervasive extent of *white privilege* provides an eye-opening exercise (McIntosh 1988). Members of the dominant culture become acquainted with the many privileges they take for granted, which are faced daily by various minorities. International students extend this exercise to their own dominant-culture prerogatives. Additionally, class discussions about civil rights must include our responsibilities concurrent with those rights so that students discover actions they can take to address the many issues of discrimination—for example, poverty, housing, health care, national budget allocations—that have an impact on our multicultural society.

At one of the institutions where I worked, in the context of discussing social justice, the students decided that they wanted to discuss with the administration the lack of ethnic diversity in the faculty and the student body.

They asked my permission to invite the dean to come to one of our classes to speak with them about the issue. He wrote back that he would be happy to come and made it contingent on extra reading to be prepared by the students. Discouraged by the amount of additional preparation the discussion would need, the students did not pursue the issue. However, the students (mostly dominant culture) learned from that experience: They gave each other confidence to question practices; they discovered that they needed to be well prepared when addressing authority; they saw the subtle ways in which those in power can deal with those who question; they experienced the interaction with the dean as rejection, a feeling that many minority groups face regularly; they learned the depth of commitment required to stand up for their beliefs.

Social justice also includes striving *for* educational equity so that all students may have access to educational opportunities to develop their potential in the field of their choice. Lucinda, in the opening vignette, was engaged in such a battle in her school. She was trying to help the other teachers see that the ELLs had every right to education that was equitable. That does not always translate as "equal treatment"; obviously, those who need more help should receive it. But somewhere along the way, many ethnic and linguistic minorities are being shortchanged as evidenced by soaring dropout rates, by high representation in special education, and by poor facilities or faculties within some schools and systems. Part of the problem could be that the procedures of the school do not mesh with the backgrounds of the children it serves. Equity in education strives for recognizing and accommodating the variety of backgrounds which children bring to school. If we believe in developing the potential of each student, we must work for procedures, practices, and opportunities so that all students can find and polish their talents and thereby contribute to society.

Multicultural education provides a transformative approach to education that can be used at all ages and levels of education. We can transform any curriculum to confront racism, sexism, classism, ethnocentrism, disability, or xenophobia. Fairy tales, Disney movies, science discoveries, current events, and mathematical concepts can all expand global consciousness and generate discussions of unconscious stereotypes and prejudices. We can transform the curriculum to include perspectives of those on the fringes whose voices remain unheard by the dominant society. Social studies, history, and literature can incorporate questions about how others see issues. We can transform the curriculum to include action on issues relevant to students, all of them at all ages, so that they become empowered to address injustice when they see it. We can transform the ethos of the classroom by expanding and varying teaching strategies, by fostering assessment that provides a variety of evidence of mastery, by using

TRY THIS!

One way to better understand others is to know the faith that influenced them. Religious convictions lead people to war as well as to peace. Assuming that a variety of faiths will be represented, invite speakers to your classes—parents of your students if possible— to share significant parts of their faith. Help your students prepare questions ahead of time that will reflect a meaningful interaction. Encourage newcomers to share their faith beliefs with the rest of the class. Have your students investigate as best as they are able, the faiths not represented in the class. This project can work across many different grade levels.

peer groups judiciously, and by acknowledging whenever possible the skills that immigrants bring with them. We have the power to help all our students not only to envision but to reach their personal dreams.

An Image for Multicultural Education

When I was a child, I had long hair. I do not remember the hours or the loud objections my mother endured every morning when brushing out the snarls in order to braid my hair. I do remember that when I started second grade at the neighborhood Turkish elementary school, school rules stipulated that hair had to be either cut even with my earlobes or be braided. My hair was cut and so were the objections and time-on-task. My mother declared that I was allowed to grow it out only if I learned to braid it myself. In third grade, I had braids. I enjoyed the daily process of bringing together different strands to make an attractive whole; I enjoyed the variety of ways to wear my braids. However, in those days they were not for decoration; they were a necessity for those who wanted long hair.

I see the braid as an image for multicultural education, interweaving many strands that include tangible and intangible aspects. Multicultural education is not a decoration; our multicultural society and our interdependent world necessitate it. One strand of the braid might be the tangible art, literature, music, and other such items by which we start to become aware of another culture and through which our intercultural competency grows. However, one strand cannot exist without the others; it unravels and no longer serves a purpose. Stopping there, with only that one strand, can perpetuate stereotyping. People from a culture can become frozen, can be reduced to a flat, unidimensional image that was selected by others rather than by themselves. The word "China" will conjure up chopsticks more often than not, though that is not what most Chinese would choose as a symbol of themselves. As a child I used to hate it when, upon hearing that I was from the

United States, peers in Turkey would immediately quiz me about Hollywood. We often come to believe *our* creation of another culture, not *the people's* own experience of it. With just this strand, we come to know other cultures by their distinctiveness, but not their totality. Just one strand prevents teachers and students alike from a better understanding of the geographical, historical, and ecological heritages that shape a culture's response to the problems common to all societies.

Other strands of the braid will include the multiple perspectives, the social action, the cultural awareness, and the insight brought, as with Alice, by "imagining all the possibilities." Each or any one of these strands can be woven in so that, for example, Judaism is more than the dreidel at Hanukkah, African-American history is more than Rosa Parks and Martin Luther King, Jr., or Mexico's rich culture is more than Cinco de Mayo. Each of these strands makes the braid stronger and more beautiful; each binds with the others into a combined whole. Strands do not just stop; they run throughout the braid or become incorporated into other braids. They also need regular tending; they can take different forms each day. Delightfully, these days, unlike my childhood days, braids have expanded to include a number of different forms, for example, English, French, and African, creating distinct, colorful, beautiful patterns.

Beyond the Classroom

Using multicultural education within our own classroom empowers our students, but the effort cannot stop there. Making systemic changes in curricula that reflect the reality of society presents a fairly tangible goal; changing the perceptions and expectations of teachers and administration toward equitable education and high standards would introduce an ultimate though much more difficult goal.

THE ENVIRONMENT WITHIN THE SCHOOL

Another context that has an impact on multicultural education is the environment of the school. The total environment of the school is an important part of multicultural education. By the environment, I mean the total picture: attitudes and expectations of the teachers, staff, *and* administration; school policies; counseling and other (e.g., ESOL) programs; extracurricular activities; even the library. The way the school population in general and the class in particular receive the ethnic or linguistic minorities will affect the acculturation of those students. If school constituents see minority students as clogging the flow of information or hindering the accomplishment of business-as-usual, rather than adding personal contact with a life different from that of the dominant culture, newcomers will feel it and many will either withdraw or act out. In the opening vignette, Lucinda appealed for a change of attitude toward the ELLs. Teachers or staff who are continually frustrated by the presence of these students say a lot by their non-verbal (and unconscious) behavior, which all students are quick to read, with or without knowledge of English. ELLs do take more effort than students familiar with dominant-culture educational practices in the United States. However, small steps toward accommodation and celebration incrementally make a big difference in the total picture.

Personal contact, by student or teacher, welcomes newcomers in a major way. But the whole school can participate, as well. Minimally, posters and maps that depict life around the world displayed throughout the school, not just near the ESOL room, help the students see themselves recognized and validated in the school community. Highlighting homelands and some of the contributions of different cultures, creative ways of displaying foreign words or phrases spoken by ELLs not only will help the ELLs feel welcomed, but also expand the world view of the other students. However, we're not stopping just with these tangible expressions, right? A schoolwide committee, consisting of both students and teachers (not the "International Club," but a group that includes a few of the less inclined) can find specific ways in which to integrate both newcomers and oldtimers into activities of the school which may help prevent major conflicts. Negative attitudes in students—both dominant-culture as well as other immigrants—exacerbate the challenges for new ELLs. This necessitates a careful look at the ways in which school personnel and policies are working with the newcomers to see if real needs are being addressed appropriately. Allport suggests that barriers are apt to decrease when equals across racial [and other] lines join in a task to be completed, with enough time on task to get to know each other and with institutional support for the project (Allport 1954).

Often, linguistic or minority students become integrated into the school through extracurricular activities. However, two barriers hinder such an

TRY THIS!

Talk with your students about the social boundaries they experience in class and in school. Who creates those boundaries? Why? How do students feel about the boundaries? What happens if those boundaries are crossed—to both the perpetrator and the group? How do we differentiate between good, legitimate boundaries and those born of ignorance, stereotyping, and arrogance? How do we address issues of crossing boundaries inappropriately? How do we break down boundaries that are unjust or harmful?

attempt: for a number of students, this form of integration is beyond both financial reach and transportation logistics. The school administration must answer these policy questions of equal access.

SYSTEMIC POLICIES

While oases of multicultural education can exist within a school or a system, they are fed and watered by school policies that seep into the ground of the whole system. An educational philosophy toward diversity that works out of an assimilationist attitude will be reflected in, for example, whether the libraries portray the diversity of the campus. The weighting of standardized testing in a newcomer's profile highlights one rigid evaluation. The comparative importance in the school budget reflects attitudes toward ESOL and other programs (e.g., mental health, tutoring, career counseling) designed to help linguistic and ethnic minority students. In my experience, cross-cultural parents need an advocate who might inform and help them with some of their rights as far as the school system is concerned. As a group, they do not have much clout because they are not aware of what they can ask for and are not confident enough to be assertive about their children's needs. Surrounded by teachers or specialists who, in the parents' eyes, wield great authority and expertise, parents of ELLs often feel stymied by their own lack of English fluency, educational knowledge, or political rights. However, hearing their viewpoints enables an equitable solution.

Furthermore, ELLs, in my experience, often have to put up with circumstances that dominant-culture parents would not tolerate for their children. In my last year as an ESOL teacher in a wealthy school district, due to space constraints many specialists met their students in closets. The noise in my classroom, a closet off the school gym, created substantial problems for my students who *had* to learn to hear differences between vowels (e.g., sheet and sh-t). Understanding the problem, the principal changed the closet the following year.

School policies, in their support of diversity, will also ensure that all teachers have the assistance needed to be proactive in addressing the needs of their linguistic and ethnic minority students. The system should insist on continuing education courses or systemwide workshops as well as support for the teacher in class itself (e.g., mentors or translators). Linguistic and ethnic minority students are a gift to a system, if only the system can see them as such.

The Gift of Linguistic and Ethnic Minority Students

We have spent a lot of time talking about the issues that face the linguistic or ethnic minority student and the mainstream teacher in classroom interactions. These discussions are meant not to overburden or overwhelm, but to broaden the possibilities of what may be happening in the classroom. However, I do not want to leave with the thought that all the work has few rewards. When we change our approach to help a student attain a higher academic level, we achieve great personal satisfaction. When perplexing student behaviors become clearer, we gain huge rewards. When other students seek out and enjoy the ELLs due to their personalities rather than their quaintness, we can feel gratified. When these students and parents from around the world share their life stories and genuinely participate in the life of the classroom, growth occurs for everyone.

The gifts of diversity are richer still. When multicultural education becomes less ephemeral and more rooted in our daily plans and strategies, all students' learning multiplies exponentially. Dominant-culture students will experience the reality of our twentyfirst century where working cross-culturally will not be an option but a requirement. Students will be empowered to understand others' perspectives. In the cross-cultural interchange, friendships will blossom, and lines between "them" and "us" will get erased. Young people will become inspired to work alongside others "who have a different nose"; they will learn firsthand how to negotiate differences before they lead to turbulence. Cultural conflicts will not cease, but their resolution may be clearer and more feasible. The world will become less intimidating; global issues will become more personal and urgent. Both sides will become true global ambassadors.

To live by our democratic ideals and our belief in the equality of all, we must give ethnic or linguistic minority students full access to educational equity. It is not just that the United States will give something—an education—to these students. The people of the United States will receive a precious gift, the opportunity to truly understand "the other." The affirmation and partnership in that wonderful mix of humanity will be the force that moves the world away from ancient feuds and toward genuine community. Therein lies the true and ultimate aim of multicultural education

References

Ahmed, Leila. 2000. *A Border Passage: From Cairo to America—A Woman's Journey.* New York: Penguin Books.

Allende, Isabel. 1995. *Paula.* Translated by M. Peden. New York: HarperCollins.

Allport, Gordon W. 1954. *The Nature of Prejudice.* Cambridge, MA: Addison Wesley Publishing Company, Inc.

Althen, Gary. 1988. *American Ways.* Yarmouth, ME: Intercultural Press.

Arana, Marie. 2001. *American Chica.* New York: Dell Publishing.

Armstrong, Thomas. 2000. *Multiple Intelligences in the Classroom.* Alexandria, VA: Association for Supervision and Curriculum Development.

Banks, James A. 1997. *Teaching Strategies for Ethnic Studies.* Needham Heights, MA: Allyn and Bacon.

Barna, L. A. 1988. "Stumbling Blocks in Intercultural Communication." In *Intercultural Communication: A Reader (5th ed.),* edited by L. Samovar and R. E. Porter, 322–330. Belmont, CA: Wadsworth Publishing Co.

Belenky, M. F., et al. 1986. *Women's Ways of Knowing.* New York: Basic Books.

Benjamin, Gail. 1997. *Japanese Lessons.* New York: New York University Press.

Bennett, Christine. 1999. *Comprehensive Multicultural Education.* Boston: Allyn and Bacon.

Berry, John W., Uichol Kim, and Pawel Boski. 1988. "Psychological Acculturation of Immigrants." In *Cross-Cultural Adaptation: Current Approaches,* edited by Young Yun Kim and William B. Gudykunst, 62–89. Newbury Park: Sage.

Camarota, Steven A. 1999. "Immigrants in the United States."*www.cis.org/articles/.*

Carnes, Jim. Spring 1994 "An Uncommon Language." *Teaching Tolerance* 3, (1): 56–63.

Carroll, Lewis. 1897. *Through the Looking Glass and What Alice Found There.* Philadephia: Henry Altemus Company.

Carroll, Raymonde. 1988. *Cultural Misunderstandings: The French-American Experience.* Chicago: The University of Chicago Press.

Castañeda, Alfredo, and Tracy Gray. December 1974 "Bicognitive Processes in Multicultural Education." *Educational Leadership* 32 (3): 203–207.

Clancy, Patricia. 1986. "Acquiring Communicative Style in Japanese." In *Language Socialization Across Cultures,* edited by Bambi Schieffelin and Elinor Ochs, 213–250. New York: Cambridge University Press.

Clayton, Cathryn. 2001. "If We Are not Different, We Will Cease to Exist." (Ph.D. diss., Anthropology, UC Santa Cruz).

Clayton, Jacklyn Blake. n.d. Engineers of the Soul.

———. 1996. *Your Land, My Land.* Portsmouth, NH: Heinemann.

Condon, John C., and Fathi Yousef. 1975. *An Introduction to Intercultural Communication.* Indianapolis: Bobbs-Merril Educational Publishing.

Crèvecoeur, J. Hector St. John. 1904. *Letters from an American Farmer.* New York: Fox, Duffield & Company.

Damen, Louise. 1987. *Culture Learning: The Fifth Dimension in the Language Classroom.* Reading, MA: Addison-Wesley Publishing Co.

Darwin, Charles. [1872] 1965. *The Expression of the Emotions in Man and Animals.* London/Chicago: John Murray/University of Chicago Press.

Dasen, P., and A. Heron. 1980. "Cross-Cultural Tests of Piaget's Theory." In *Handbook of Cross-Cultural Psychology: Developmental Psychology, Vol. 4,* edited by Henry C. Triandis and A. Heron, 295–341. Boston: Allyn and Bacon.

Davidman, Leonard. March 1995, 7. "Issue." *Education Update*–(ASCD, Alexandria, VA). This is Co newsletter. ASCD is a Publisher, Assoe, for Supervision and Curriculum Development.

Davidman, Leonard, and Patricia T. Davidman. 2001. *Teaching with a Multicultural Perspective: A Practical Guide, 3rd Edition*. New York: Longman.

Delgado-Gaitan, Concha, and Henry Trueba. 1991. *Crossing Cultural Borders*. New York: The Falmer Press.

Delpit, Lisa. Fall 1998. "Lessons from Home." *Teaching Tolerance* 14:15–19.

Dershowitz, Alan. 30 January 2001. "A Savior not Shared by All." *Cape Cod Times* (Hyannis, MA), A9.

Dewey, John. [1900] 1990. *The School and Society and The Child and the Curriculum*. Chicago: The University of Chicago Press.

Dunn, Rita Stafford, and Shirley. A. Griggs. 1995. *Multiculturalism and Learning Style: Teaching and Counseling Adolescents*. Westport, CT: Praeger.

Eisenbruch, M. Summer 1988. "The Mental Health of Refugee Children and Their Cultural Development." *International Migration Review*: 282–300.

Fadiman, Anne. 1997. *The Spirit Catches You and You Fall Down*. New York: Farrar, Straus and Giroux.

Farman Farmaian, Sattareh. 1992. *Daughter of Persia*. New York: Anchor Books, Doubleday.

Feiler, Bruce S. 1991. *Learning to Bow: Inside the Heart of Japan*. New York: Ticknor and Fields.

Finders, Margaret, and Cynthia Lewis. May 1994. "Why Some Parents Don't Come to School." *Educational Leadership*. 51, no. 8 50–54.

Florio, Susan. 1978. "Learning How to Go to School: An Ethnography of Interaction in a Kindergarten/First grade Classroom." Ph.D. diss., Harvard University.

Freire, Paulo. [1970] 1994. *The Pedagogy of the Oppressed, 20th Anniversary Edition*. New York: The Continuum Publishing Company.

Gallimore, Ronald, Joan Whitehorn Boggs, and Cathie Jordan. 1974. *Culture, Behavior, and Education*. Beverly Hills: Sage Publications.

Gardner, Howard. 1989. *To Open Minds*. New York: Basic Books.

Geertz, Clifford. 1973. *The Interpretation of Cultures*. New York: Basic Books.

Gibson, Margaret. 1993. "School Performance of Immigrant Minorities." In *Minority Education: Anthropological Perspectives*, edited by Evelyn Jacobs and Cathie Jordan, 113–128. Norwood, NJ: Ablex Publishing Corporation.

Glazer, Nathan, and Daniel Patrick Moynihan. 1970. *Beyond the Melting Pot*. Cambridge, MA: MIT Press.

Goodman, Mary Ellen. 1970. *The Culture of Childhood*. New York: Teachers College Press.

Grant, Carl, and Christine E. Sleeter. 1989. *Turning on Learning: Five Approaches for Multicultural Teaching Plans for Race, Class, Gender, and Disability*. New York: Macmillan Publishing Company.

Griggs, Shirley. December 31 1991. "Learning Styles Counseling, ERIC Digest." In ERIC Digests. *www.ed.gov/databases/ERIC_Digests/ed341890.html*.

Gudykunst, William B., and Stella Ting-Toomey. 1988. *Culture and Interpersonal Communication*. Newbury Park, CA: Sage Publications.

Gudykunst, William B., and Young Yun Kim. 1992. *Readings on Communicating with Strangers*. New York: McGraw-Hill, Inc.

Gumpert, Peter, and Charles Harrington. 1972. "Intellect and Cultural Deprivation." *Teachers College Record* 74.

Hall, Edward T. 1977. *Beyond Culture*. Garden City, NY: Anchor Books.

———. 1984. *The Dance of Life*. Garden City, NY: Anchor Press/Doubleday.

———. 1969. *The Hidden Dimension*. Garden City, NY: Anchor Books.

———. 1973. *The Silent Language*. Garden City, NY: Anchor Books.

———. 1990. *Understanding Cultural Differences*. Yarmouth, ME: Intercultural Press, Inc.

Heath, Shirley Brice. 1986. "Sociocultural Contexts of Language Development." In *Beyond Language: Social and Cultural Factors in Schooling Language Minority Students*, edited by California State Department of Education Bilingual Education Office, 143–86. Sacramento, CA: Evaluation, Dissemination and Assessment Center, California State University, Los Angeles, CA.

———. 1983. *Ways with Words: Language, Life, and Work in Communities and Classrooms.* Cambridge: Cambridge University Press.

———. April 1982. "What No Bedtime Story Means: Narrative Skills at Home and School." *Language in Society* 11, (1): 49–76.

Hsu, Francis L. K. 1975. "American Core Value and National Character." In *The Nacirema: Readings in American Culture.*, 378–394. Boston: Little, Brown and Company.

Irujo, S. 1988. "An Introduction to Intercultural Differences and Similarities in Nonverbal Communication." In *Toward Multiculturalism*, edited by J. S. Wurzel, 142–150. Yarmouth, ME: Intercultural Press.

Ishii, Satoshi, and Tom Bruneau. 1988. "Silence and Silences in Cross-Cultural Perspective: Japan and the United States." In *Intercultural Communication: A Reader 5th Edition*, edited by Larry A. Samovar and Richard E. Porter, 310–318. Belmont, CA: Wadsworth Publishing Company.

Kağıtçıbaşı, Çiğdem. 1996. *Family and Human Development Across Cultures: A View from the Other Side.* Mahwah, NJ: Lawrence Erlbaum Associates.

Kaplan, Robert B. 1966. "Cultural Thought Patterns in Inter-Cultural Education." *Language Learning* 16, (1): 1–20.

Kessner, Thomas, and Betty Boyd Caroli. 1981. *Today's Immigrants: Their Stories.* New York: Oxford University Press.

Kim, Young Y. 1988. "Intercultural Personhood: An Integration of Eastern and Western Perspectives." In *Intercultural Communication: A Reader*, edited by Larry Samovar and Richard Porter, 363–373. Belmont, CA: Wadsworth Publishing Co.

Kluckhohn, Florence, and Fred F. Strodtbeck. 1961. *Variations in Value Orientations.* Evanston: Row, Peterson and Co.

Kohls, L. Robert. 2000. "Comparing and Contrasting Cultures." In *Finding the Middle Ground*, edited by Kurt W. Russo, 119–124. Yarmouth, ME: Intercultural Press, Inc.

Locke, Michelle. 18 January 2001. "Academics Wear Their Blue Collars." *The Boston Globe* (Boston, MA), A: 4.

Longstreet, Wilma. 1978. *Aspects of Ethnicity.* New York: Teachers College Press.

Mayes, Frances. 1999. *Bella Tuscany.* New York: Broadway Books.

McCullough, David. 2001. *John Adams.* New York: Simon and Schuster.

McIntosh, Peggy. 1988. *White Privilege and Male Privilege.* Wellesley, MA: Center for Research on Women, Wellesley College, 189.

McQuarrie, B. 15 February 1998. "Values 101." *The Boston Globe* (Boston, MA), E: 5–6.

Michaels, S., and J. Collins. 1984. "Oral Discourse Styles: Classroom Interactions and the Acquisition of Literacy." In *Coherence in Spoken and Written Discourse*, edited by Deborah Tannen, 219–241. Norwood, NJ: Ablex.

Nelson, David, George Gheverghese Joseph, and Julian Williams. 1993. *Multicultural Mathematics: Teaching Mathematics from a Global Perspective.* New York: Oxford University Press.

Newman, William. 1973. *A Study of Minority Groups and Social Theory.* New York: Harper and Row.

Nieto, Sonia. 1996. *Affirming Diversity, 2nd Edition.* White Plains, NY: Longman.

———. 1999. *The Light in Their Eyes: Creating Multicultural Learning Communities.* New York: Teachers College Press.

Nishida, Tsukasa. 1996. "Communication in Personal Relationships in Japan." In *Communication in Personal Relationships Across Cultures*, edited by William B.

Gudykunst, Stella Ting-Toomey, and Tsukasa Nishida. 102–121. Thousand Oaks, CA: Sage Publications.

Nolan, Martin F. 29 November 1993. "Boston Says Welcome." *Boston Globe* (Boston), 45–52.

Nydell, Margaret K. 1996. *Understanding Arabs*. Yarmouth, ME: Intercultural Press, Inc.

Olsen, Laurie. 1997. *Made in America: Immigrant Students in Our Public Schools*. New York: The New Press.

Peters Projection. 1983. *The World Map in Equal Area Presentation: The English Version*. Oxford, UK: Oxford Cartographers, Ltd.

Pipher, Mary. 2002. *The Middle of Everywhere: The World's Refugees Come to Our Town*. New York: Harcourt, Inc.

Ramirez, Manuel, and Alfredo Castañeda. 1974. *Cultural Democracy, Bicognitive Development and Education*. New York: Academic Press.

Rodriguez, Richard. 1982. *Hunger of Memory: The Education of Richard Rodriguez*. New York: Bantam Books.

Rosaldo, Renato. 1993. *Culture and Truth*. Boston: Beacon Press.

Schieffelin, Bambi, and Elinor Ochs, Eds. 1986. *Language Socialization Across Cultures*. New York: Cambridge University Press.

Scollon, Ron, and Suzanne B. K. Scollon. 1981. *Narrative, Literacy and Face in Interethnic Communication*. Norwood, NJ: Ablex.

Sinclair, Robert L., and Ward J. Ghory. 1987. "Becoming Marginal." In *Success or Failure*, edited by Henry T. Trueba, 169–185. Cambridge: Newbury House Publishers.

Spindler, George D., and Louise S. Spindler. 1990. *The American Cultural Dialogue and Its Transmission*. New York: The Falmer Press.

Staton, Ann Q. 1990. *Communication and Student Socialization*. Norwood, NJ: Ablex Publishing Corporation.

Stewart, Edward C., and Milton Bennett. 1991. *American Cultural Patterns: A Cross-Cultural Perspective*. Revised Ed. Yarmouth, ME: Intercultural Press.

Tan, Amy. 1991. *The Kitchen God's Wife*. New York: Ballantine Books.

Tannen, Deborah. 1998. *The Argument Culture: Stopping America's War of Words*. New York: Ballantine.

Tatum, Beverly Daniel. 1997. *"Why Are All the Black Kids Sitting Together in the Cafeteria?"* New York: Basic Books.

Triandis, Henry C. 1995. *Individualism and Collectivism*. Boulder, CO: Westview Press.

U.S. Census Bureau. January 2001. "Region of Birth of the Foreign-Born Population." In U.S. Census Bureau, Population Division. *www.census.gov/population/www/documenation/twps0029/tab02.html*.

Weltner, Linda. 28 October 1993. "Ever So Humble: Freedom from the Tyranny of Time." *The Boston Globe* (Boston, MA), A: 3.

Willett, Jerri. 1987. "Contrasting Acculturation Patterns of Two Non-English Speaking Preschoolers." In *Success or Failure*, edited by Henry T. Trueba, 69–84. Cambridge: Newbury House Publishers.

Wurzel, Jaime S. 1990. Family Orientation and Child Rearing Values. Boston University School of Education. Duplicated.

———. 1988. "Multiculturalism and Multicultural Education." In *Toward Multiculturalism: A Reader in Multicultural Education*, edited by Jaime S. Wurzel, 1–13. Yarmouth, ME: Intercultural Press, Inc.

———. nd. Value Orientations: A Didactic Continuum.

Zanger, Virginia Vogel. 1985. *Face to Face: The Cross-Cultural Workbook*. Cambridge: Newbury House Publishers.